THE
yes
BOOK

THE
YES
BOOK

THE ART OF BETTER NEGOTIATION

CLIVE RICH

2 4 6 8 10 9 7 5 3 1

First published in the United Kingdom in 2013 by Virgin Books,
an imprint of Ebury Publishing

A Random House Group Company

Copyright © Clive Rich 2013

Illustrations © Kathryn Lamb 2013

www.randomhouse.co.uk

Addresses for companies within The Random House Group Limited
can be found at www.randomhouse.co.uk/offices.htm

The Random House Group Limited Reg. No. 954009

A CIP catalogue record for this book is available from the British Library

The Random House Group Limited supports The Forest Stewardship
Council® (FSC®), the leading international forest certification
organisation. Our books carrying the FSC label are printed on FSC®
certified paper. FSC is the only forest certification scheme endorsed by
the leading environmental organisations, including Greenpeace. Our
paper procurement policy can be found at www.randomhouse.co.uk/
environment

Printed and bound in Great Britain by Clays Ltd, St Ives PLC

ISBN: 9780753541098

To buy books by your favourite authors and register for offers,
visit www.randomhouse.co.uk

CONTENTS

To my wife Joanna for her unstinting love and support. And also to my children Tabitha, Felix and Hugo, and my stepdaughter Emily, for regularly proving that children are the world's most natural negotiators.

INTRODUCTION

Negotiation is something that we have to engage in every single day of our lives. However, negotiation has changed. We have been brought up to believe that negotiation is a competitive, confrontational business; a game in which there are winners and losers. The measure of success is whether you can 'kick ass' and get what you want. The louder, bolder and brasher you can be the better. Characters who adopt this approach have been celebrated in the media and on TV. So what if the other side loses? Losing is for wimps.

That kind of attitude is no longer sustainable. A number of social and economic factors have combined to create an interdependent world where collaboration *not* competition is the name of the negotiation game. This book is intended to provide you with a practical framework to help you negotiate the modern way.

So, why is this book called *The Yes Book*? 'Yes' is the word we all want to hear from all parties at the end of any negotiation. However, 'yes' is a less common word than you might think. In fact, according to World-english.org, of the words commonly used in written English it only just creeps into the top 500 at number 486 (unlike 'no', which is in the top 100). By the time you finish this book you should have a framework which helps you to get other people to say 'yes' more often when you are negotiating. However, that is not all you will be able to do. You will also be better able to say 'yes' to the following questions:

- 'Do I have the most effective negotiating attitude I can bring to the negotiation?'
- 'Do I understand the sources of bargaining power in a negotiation?'
- 'Can I manage the stages of a negotiation?'
- 'Do I know how to prepare properly?'
- 'Can I get more of what I want from a negotiation?'
- 'Do I know how to close deals?'
- 'Do I know how to stand up to tough guys?'
- 'Do I know how to negotiate when I am in a different country?'

The subtitle of this book is 'The Art of Better Negotiation'. The book does not guarantee that you will turn into the world's perfect negotiator, but it will help you to be better at all of these facets of negotiation

Why is that valuable? Good deals don't happen by chance. Effective negotiators have a conscious blueprint for success. This book will provide you with a framework for generating that success. It is based on skills I have acquired from all the different facets of my career as a negotiator over the last thirty years working with major media and technology companies, and multinational brands as well as hundreds of smaller companies from sole traders to those with a couple of hundred employees – 'small and medium-sized enterprises' (SMEs).

Applying these insights will enable you to improve as a negotiator so that you consistently get more of what you want from your deal making. Such insights will stand you in good stead whether you are negotiating a business deal, a salary raise, buying a house or selling a car. They are insights that are valid whether you are negotiating at home or overseas, and whether you are an individual, a small business, a big corporation or even working for a government.

Before We Start

Here are a few markers about the way this book has been written:

1. The framework set out here recognises that you always have a choice. There are some very good negotiation textbooks available, including a few which argue, correctly, that you need to focus on the other negotiator in order to get what you need in return. However, they generally have a prescriptive approach to the theory of negotiation – 'Do it like this and you will be okay'. The world is an increasingly complicated place full of billions of people with their individual personalities and quirks, and millions of different negotiating scenarios, all at different stages at any one time. There is not 'one way' to negotiate these many different deals. You have a choice as a negotiator – a choice as to the attitude you bring to the table, the attitude or state of mind you create in others, the way you handle the process and which behaviours to use. There is no 'right' and 'wrong' about how to do it, but there may be a most effective choice you can make in the circumstances – a better choice. The insights in this book will help you evaluate each situation and make better choices more often. That is the secret of effective negotiation.

2. This is intended to be a practical book. A number of its insights are supported by research conducted by academics, and where applicable you will see allusions to that research as we go along. However, academic research can sometimes be impenetrable and forbidding to the uninitiated, and negotiating is a very practical activity. When you are stuck facing a 'tough guy' in a negotiation, or you have run out of options on a deal you need to close, or you feel that the other side holds all the bargaining aces then you need a practical response and academic literature, however well researched,

may not be the first thing you reach for. You might say this book takes something of a 'pracademic' approach – trying to extract useful insights for everyday use and unpack academic jargon, without losing touch with the patient and meticulous independent research where it supports those practical guidelines.

3. You will also find plenty of negotiating stories here – some of my own but also many from people I know who have very kindly contributed their own stories. We all love stories when we are children and most of us love stories when we are older as well. When I coach negotiation or lecture on the subject I find that stories are a great way to bring negotiating insights to life. In addition, when people are trying to remember a key message about better negotiating they often remember the story first and then the message. Stories are a very good way of cementing our learning.

4. Everybody has a different natural style as a negotiator. In order to make the right choices as to how you negotiate you need to have a clear picture as to the natural kind of negotiator you are. Having that picture in your head will also enable you to read this book with your attributes and habits as a negotiator in mind, which means that your experience of reading it will, by definition, be an individual one. In order to do that you can visit the website for my negotiating app at www.closemydeal.co.uk where you will find a questionnaire you can fill in about each of the three sections of the framework (Attitude, Process and Behaviour). These questionnaires will show you how often you display certain negotiating attitudes; how frequently you display the mindset required to engage in different stages of the negotiating process; and how often you display certain

negotiating behaviours. They are like your personal horoscope as a negotiator – your own individual chart revealing your negotiation energies and your preferences. The reason they are on the website rather than in the book is because the app website has some software which can calibrate your answers automatically and help create a personal profile chart for you. By dint of buying this book you have a special code which enables you to have special access to that section of my website. Use that to access the questionnaires and fill them in.

1

THE KEY COMPONENTS OF NEGOTIATION

We engage in negotiations on a routine basis, but how many of us can honestly say that we know the fundamental ingredients of a negotiation? For a negotiation to take place the following elements must be present:

- There must be two or more parties.
- They must at least be prepared to reach agreement.
- They must have some interests in common and some conflicting interests to resolve.
- Those involved must have the freedom to meet each other's needs.
- Those involved must be willing to be explicit to some degree about their wants and needs.
- Those involved must be prepared to compromise to some degree.

It's worth dwelling on this list for a moment because a lot of people spend time involved in what they think is a negotiation when in fact they are not, because one or more of these elements is missing. For example, if one party is not prepared to reach agreement then there can be no negotiation. Various iterations of formal Israeli/Palestinian

6

'negotiations' have drifted on for decades and, unfortunately, may drift on for decades more, because arguably we have still to arrive at a moment when key decision makers on both sides want to reach agreement at the same time. Sadly, no enthusiastically engineered 'peace process' or 'road map' can overcome this essential problem.

Equally, those involved must have the freedom to negotiate. If they have no freedom because, for example, they are acting under the strict orders of someone else, then the negotiation cannot get started. You may have a very constructive and enjoyable discussion with them, but you may ultimately find that it was not a negotiation.

If there are no conflicting interests then it may still be that you are trying to influence someone but you are not negotiating. If my wife and I are driving home together from a night out at the cinema and we disagree about the route, we may each try to persuade the other that we know the best way home, but that is not really a negotiation since we both have exactly the same interest in taking the most efficient route, so there is little at stake other than pride in being right.

For there to be a negotiation it is also essential that the parties must be prepared to compromise to at least some degree. I am a qualified mediator and a big supporter of mediation as a better mechanism for resolving disputes than litigation through the courts. Mediation between the parties is normally much quicker, cheaper and also has the advantage of being confidential. However, I know as a mediator that the process can only work if both parties come to the mediation prepared to compromise in some way. If they are just paying lip service to the idea of a mediation, and in reality they do not want to compromise because they are happier continuing their legal fight, then mediation cannot work.

The Negotiating Framework

The negotiating framework we are going to explore has three elements which connect together like one of those Venn diagrams you used to draw at school. Research shows that effective negotiators are able to handle effectively the following three areas:

- **Attitude:** they can manage their own and others' negotiation attitudes.
- **Process:** they are able to manage the stages – the overall structure – of the negotiation.
- **Behaviour:** they understand and manage their own and others' negotiation behaviour.

Negotiating attitude influences negotiating behaviour and both negotiating attitude and negotiating behaviour influence your success in handling the negotiating process. So, the three ingredients fit together like links in a chain:

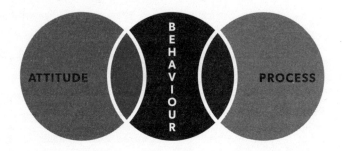

Master these three ingredients to the point where you are able to exercise these skills systematically and consciously and you will be able to make deals happen on a routine basis. It is important to note that all of these three ingredients are far more important than the 'content' of the negotiation – e.g. who wants which price and which delivery date – even though it is the content which is normally the only thing people talk about when they make deals. If you bring the right attitude to the table, manage the process effectively and can manage the behaviour of the participants (including yourself) then the content will take care of itself. Really? Yes, really.

So, with these markers in place we are now ready to start. However, before we set about providing you with a practical framework of 'how to do it', it's worth spending some time exploring the way that negotiation has changed and why there is now an imperative to negotiate 'we' deals rather than 'me' deals. A practical book on negotiating has its roots in an understanding of the social context in which negotiation now takes place.

2

THE NEW DEAL ECONOMY

The required shift in perceptions about negotiation from 'competitive' to 'collaborative' has not previously been highlighted, perhaps because negotiation itself is a subject which is not frequently discussed or analysed on a day-to-day basis. However, even a brief look at some of the economic and cultural trends underpinning our modern world supports the view that the requirements of negotiation are changing, from a battle of wills into a quest for mutual advancement.

So what are the changes which have accounted for this required shift in perception?

The World is More Competitive Now

There are more people, companies and firms out there who will simply steal your business if you don't look after your commercial relationships. That militates towards cooperation rather than conflict in deal making. If you don't maintain and develop your commercial relationships you will be more isolated than your competitors. The trend towards greater competition affects big companies, small enterprises and individuals competing for jobs. I keep up-to-date research on this topic available on the blog page of the website for my negotiation services, www.cliverich.com. You can see there stats on, for example, the increasing competition in sectors like the mobile phone industry, where, in the space of the twelve months (up to the last quarter of 2012), Samsung more than doubled its share of the market in two years while Nokia lost two-thirds of its market share. You can also see stats on the growing number of small businesses in the economy – currently increasing at a rate of 15,000 new businesses per month in the UK. In addition you can see how competition is increasing in individual job sector markets such as the market for lawyers and other professionals. I maintain this data because it's a constant reminder of our need to be able to negotiate more collaboratively and creatively in the face of growing competition. If you think you are operating in a world of your own, then that's where you will end up.

The Constant Threat of Recession

The ongoing prospect of recession makes us all vulnerable – especially in developed markets like the UK, Europe and the US where the future long-term prognosis for growth is poor, irrespective of the end date of the deep recession which began in 2007. Think that in this climate the best strategy is to try to exploit your deal partners? Think again. I also keep statistics on actual or threatened slowdowns in economic growth on my website, and their corollaries such as spiralling national debts and currency vulnerabilities – not because I am addicted to bad news, but because it's a good reminder that in times of economic uncertainty we all need deal partners. We need to be able to negotiate collaboratively and constructively in order to create partnerships which enable us to stand stronger and withstand the destructive buffeting of the economic headwinds. We certainly cannot afford to rip off and take advantage of existing partners – that is a sure way to end up isolated and alone. We either learn to sink our differences, or we sink. Moreover, economic growth is the best way to conquer the effects of the recession – and growth requires deal making – whether between sole traders, SMEs, or big companies.

The Rapid Development of New Technology

This has made a massive difference to our world. New technology has made the world go faster. In order to be able to access burgeoning audiences for products, services and attention, we need to be able to execute strategies with deal partners at pace – not waste time in attritional negotiations with them. Take too long to set up your partnership strategy and your opportunity may have passed as technology rushes off in a different direction.

In 2001 there were 'only' a billion handset owners worldwide. According to the International Telecommunications Union there are now almost as many mobile subscribers as there are people in the world, so the growth has been astonishing. In a growing number of countries the mobile phone penetration rate is more than 100 per cent (according to *Business Week*), indicating that many people have multiple subscriptions. An amusing article sponsored by *Go Mobile* author Jamie Turner, with input from blogger Nicole Hall, debates whether now there really are more mobile phones in the world than there are toothbrushes – Hall concludes, with the help of data from greenlivingideas.com, that this is not an urban myth, it is the truth.

More than a billion people use social network sites, according to TechCrunch, of which 90 per cent use Facebook and 200 million people use Twitter. YouTube streams four billion videos per day.

As part of my initiative to keep abreast of how social changes are impacting our approach to negotiating, I keep www.cliverich. com updated with these kinds of statistics and others – growth in internet penetration, growth in tablet sales, as well as illustrating how technology growth means that major services such as MySpace can both grow and then decline in rapid time. The explosive growth of devices, internet access and usage, and the rapidly shifting terrain that characterises technology success (and failure), has created its own lightbulb moment for negotiating. It means that we need more partners, to do things more quickly, to access and influence users of devices, tablets and social networks, to take advantage of the opportunities which disrupted markets represent and to protect ourselves from the threats they convey. None of this can be achieved by working on our own or having a 'screw you' attitude to deal partners.

New Technology has also Contributed to Making the World Smaller

As the 2008 banking crisis indicates, what happens in one country can have a huge impact overseas. Think of all that trading connectivity which simply didn't exist twenty years ago. This is both a threat and an opportunity for businesses. To make the most of that opportunity we have to recruit, motivate and retain local deal partners. Globalisation means there are now opportunities to access international markets in a way that didn't exist previously, but we need to be cooperative negotiators to do it. Equally, to deal with the threat from economic globalisation, so that our domestic markets are not undermined, we have to negotiate either with potential overseas partners or domestic allies effectively.

Consider this extract from a recent 'Department of Business Innovation and Skills' report on manufacturing in the UK, showing the impact on the UK of globalisation.

A key feature of the latest phase of globalisation has been the globalisation of the manufacturing value chain. As a result of ...

advancements in information and communication technologies
… manufacturers are now able to separate the different parts of
the manufacturing value chain and carry out particular economic
activities in different geographical locations around the world.

As the rate of globalisation has accelerated, competition in
domestic and international markets for manufactured goods has
intensified [and] the proportion of firms which are exporting is
increasing in many manufacturing industries. Engaging in other
markets can prove highly beneficial for UK manufacturers [too].

What is required in order to create greater exports that the BIS aspires to? Better and more effective negotiating skills.

Technology is Causing Convergence

This is potentially enabling different industries to move into each other's space. The media sector is a good example. In the physical world it was easy to see boundaries between manufacturers of hardware, software, broadcasters of content, distributors and advertisers. Now, those lines are all blurred, so those affected need alliances to help them defend their own patch and diversify into other related sectors.

Here are some examples of convergence from the media sector. It's just one sector but the story is equally true of many other sectors.

- Advertisers such as Peugeot, Audi and Bacardi are becoming content owners creating advertising that is desirable to watch in its own right and taking that to consumers through digital channels.

- Mobile operators such as Virgin have moved into broadband supply.
- Virtually all mobile operators, and some handset manufacturers, have attempted to become suppliers of content such as music, films, games and TV programmes in order to build audiences and reduce regular customer loss or 'churn'.
- Internet service providers such as BT and AOL have become distributors of content such as music and Premier League football matches.
- Online content distributors such as Hulu, Netflix and Amazon are creating their own content.
- Broadcasters such as ITV are becoming digital advertising hubs.
- Hardware manufacturers such as Apple have become highly successful distribution channels for content.
- Providers of hardware set-top boxes like Samsung are becoming a focal point for TV broadcasting and internet distribution.

Again, I keep www.cliverich.com fresh with details of these kinds of examples.

What does convergence do to negotiation? It creates a need for partnerships. When people find themselves thrown together in the same boat, they have to learn to row together in the same direction. Just look at the deals that need to be done in order to take advantage of convergence. Content owners with ISPs, aggregators with content owners, brands with content creators, ISPs with sports rights' owners, broadband operators with music services, broadcasters with advertisers around their social media presence, hardware owners and mobile operators with content owners … and so on.

Powerful Shifts in the Global Economy are Taking Place

Think of the shift in influence from the developed nations to the emerging nations, or the tilt from West to East. The IMF's list of the twenty largest economies shows that between 2007 and 2011 China accounted for almost a quarter of world economic growth all by itself. The Brazilian economy grew even faster, with an annual GDP growth rate of 20.7 per cent. India's GDP growth rate was 15 per cent a year, while Russia's was 11.3 per cent. In the same period the annual GDP growth rate in the US and the European Union struggled above 1 per cent.

The fast-growing economies of Brazil, Russia, India, China and South Africa have become known by the acronym 'BRICS'. As the five largest emerging economies in the world, BRICS account for about 45 per cent of current growth.

By 2020, there will be further major shifts in the world economic order in which emerging economies will become more important. China will overtake the USA to become the largest world economy by 2017. India will overtake Japan, Russia will overtake Germany and Mexico will enter the top ten at the expense of Italy.

If we look further ahead, to 2050, the change is even greater, with Turkey, South Korea, the Philippines, Indonesia, Argentina and Egypt all predicted by HSBC to be in the top twenty economic nations.

A hundred years ago we might have responded to these kinds of power shifts with military and economic aggression. Now we know that will no longer work. Apart from anything else there are signs that the emerging economies are beginning to organise themselves to act collectively. Despite their individual differences, all five

BRICS feel that the West has virtually monopolised international diplomacy. The BRICS countries are seeking to strengthen their joint negotiating positions, at a time when a future world system is being created.

The growth rates in these countries represent an enormous opportunity for business. However, if emerging countries are getting stronger and potentially more united we have to negotiate more smartly – working with deal partners in these countries, not against them.

Social Media Trends Indicate a Levelling Out of the Playing Field

Even governments and big brands can be laid low if they don't treat people in a socially responsible, ethical and equitable way. The same applies to smaller companies with a reputation to protect and individuals such as celebrities. Increasingly their ongoing quest for support and engagement with constituents, customers and fans alike will resemble the negotiation of a partnership, rather than a one-way communication channel fuelled by spin.

We have all witnessed the power of social media and its effects on society. From the Arab Spring to the global Occupy movement, citizens of all nations are more empowered than ever. Connected individuals have generated crowds around a cause, created enormous audiences, organised riots and caused the overthrow of political regimes by communicating their message through social networks.

We've also seen the impact of the social revolution on business. Negotiations for the goodwill of customers are different now. Burberry's CEO, Angela Ahrendts, recently remarked: 'You have to be totally connected to anyone who touches your brand. If you don't do that, I don't know what your business model is in five years.'

Just as positive behaviour to customers can make a difference for brands because of its amplification through social media, negative behaviour can be amplified as well. Consider these examples.

- When United Airlines broke David Carroll's guitar he felt they made no real effort to compensate him. He made a music video about it which went viral. Four days after the video release, *The Times* newspaper reported that United Airlines' stock price had dropped 10 per cent, costing shareholders over US$180 million. So far the video has had over ten million views
- When Netflix announced it was changing its pricing structure, its customers revolted, posting 45,000 negative comments across its blogs and on Facebook and Twitter. Within months the company lost 800,000 customers and two-thirds of its market value.
- A Twitter campaign by Qantas, aimed at channelling positive brand feedback, was instead hijacked by angry customers complaining about poor service resulting from an ongoing industrial relations dispute which had caused cancelled flights and the earlier grounding of the entire fleet because of technical defects. The Qantas campaign – dangerously hash-tagged 'Qantasluxury' – invited customers to fantasise about 'their dream holiday' but instead provoked an avalanche of angry tweets and became a top trending topic. One tweet referred to it as 'the Hindenburg of social media strategies'.

The development of social media means that those who 'negotiate' for our attention and goodwill – whether they are governments, celebrities or consumer-facing businesses and brands – need to become much more genuinely focused on our interests in the way that they negotiate with us. If they try to take advantage of us, treat us like small fry, or brush us off with poor service, they will be found out and users will tell them very vocally that 'the deal's off'. Old-style negotiating, ignoring other people's interests, will not work in this new environment. At www.cliverich.com you can see detailed examples of how social media continues to change the rules of negotiating.

Governments and Companies Can No Longer Support Us

We live in an age in which all of the trends and uncertainties identified in this chapter combine to make it harder for traditional sources of support to operate. We can no longer rely on governments to support us – they have run out of money and seem increasingly powerless to defend us against complex international developments and uncertainties, as citizens of debt-stricken countries like Greece and Spain will attest. Even a reformer like President Barack Obama is regarded with scepticism. When pollsters for the *Washington Post* and ABC News asked a representative sampling of Americans how much they felt Obama had achieved in the first three years of his presidency, more than half said the President had accomplished 'not very much' or 'little or nothing'. Only ١٢ per cent of the poll's respondents answered that Obama had accomplished 'a great deal'.

We can no longer rely on big companies to support us either. Their margins are increasingly under pressure as a result of a combination of the trends identified in this chapter, and their strategies are constantly being altered. The net result of this is that restructuring and the shedding of jobs has become routine. Jobs for life are a thing of the past. The traditional fabric of support for communities is coming apart at the seams. What does this mean for negotiating?

It means we are increasingly operating on our own. And if we are on our own we had better know how to negotiate effective alliances and partnerships with others, as we are much stronger standing together than by ourselves. It's for this reason that I keep track, through my blog, of the struggles of governments to influence our lives positively, and announcements of job cuts made by big companies such as Hewlett Packard, J. C. Penney, Best Buy, Nokia, Pepsi and Yahoo. They are a reminder that all of us increasingly need to be resourceful negotiators, able to work with others in order to look after ourselves.

Global Resource Shortages and Climate Change Require a Collaborative Approach

The imperative for partnership will only intensify as increasing resource shortages become a global reality. How will we resolve future potential conflicts over food, water, oil and gas? How will we address the impact of climate change on resources? Negotiations will be required in which we work together or face the consequences. In my website blog I frequently consider statistics on global warming, and predicted shortages of global resources such as water. I also monitor the behaviour of nations as they respond to these developments. There is a stark choice – do nations negotiate cooperatively or do they behave selfishly? I note plenty of evidence of the latter from the stockpiling of certain scarce resources by countries such as Japan and China, through to the tough guy tactics adopted by Russia in its gas disputes with Ukraine, and the selfish short-termism evident in successive climate change negotiations from Bali, to Copenhagen, to Cancún, to Durban.

How will these kinds of problem be dealt with in future? By wars, perhaps? It doesn't bear thinking about. By strong-arm tactics? Maybe, but how effective is that likely to be in the long term? Only well-informed, constructive negotiating which takes account of all the stakeholders' interests can offer hope that today's sense of crisis over economic issues will not be replaced by a similar sense of crisis concerning the resources of the planet we all share and upon which we all depend.

For Britain and many other countries, the kind of macro-economic and social developments discussed in this chapter mean that we now live in a 'New Deal Economy' where negotiation is about cooperation, not confrontation. It is only the most sophisticated deal makers who will prosper. We all need to make the most of what we've got.

3

MIND THE GAP

Despite all the trends outlined in Chapter 2, negotiation skills are rarely taught or practised: the penny has yet to drop. There is a negotiation skills gap. People pick up negotiation informally from their bosses or their peers or from watching or reading about business celebrities such as Donald Trump. Most people negotiate by instinct. So when it works they don't know why it works, and when it doesn't work they don't know why that is either.

Research commissioned for this book supports the same conclusion. Deal making has never been more important and yet businesses and individuals do not list negotiation as one of their top priorities, do not focus on negotiation skills training and never consider the premium they could derive from more effective negotiation. I know you are keen to get on to the negotiating framework which forms the heart of this book, but this contradiction between what we do and what we need is worth dwelling on for a moment.

Initial negotiating research for this book was commissioned from YouGov, one of the leading research agencies in Great Britain which specialises in providing robust objective research for businesses and governments. YouGov collected data from 1,000 respondents, comprising small and large businesses in the UK, about their negotiations with customers and suppliers. They also took soundings from some public-sector companies as well as private enterprises, and a representative sample of companies from across eleven different regions throughout the UK and from fifteen different business sectors, so that a very wide area of UK business was covered. Questions were put to a mix of company owners, partners, directors, senior and middle managers – again this was done so as to give a representative response across UK businesses. Strategy on deal making may be led by directors and senior managers, but much negotiation on a day-to-day basis is carried out by middle managers.

Once the data had been collected it was analysed by an economic research agency, the Centre for Economics and Business Research (CEBR). CEBR are one of the UK's leading agencies in this area, and you will frequently hear their name associated with independent economic analysis prepared for the government, FTSE companies, and leading business organisations. The results of the research were fairly startling and showed that very little priority is given to negotiation by UK businesses even though good negotiation skills are becoming more and more important, for all the reasons outlined in the previous chapter. The CEBR analysis of the quantifiable impact on UK Plc from not negotiating better was startling as well.

Here are some of the qualitative responses to the YouGov research:

- When respondents were asked to list the three most important ways of improving profitability, better negotiation was not mentioned. Cutting costs, product development and developing new markets were all considered more important (between 50 and 100 per cent more important than better negotiation). Better negotiation skills came sixth on the list.
- Fewer than 50 per cent of respondents said that, when preparing for a deal, they always (or nearly always) consider key aspects of negotiation such as what key concessions are available to the other party; what their

worst alternative is if the deal doesn't go through; who is on the other negotiating team and what roles they play; what kind of behaviour the other negotiators are likely to display; how the negotiation agenda should be created; where the negotiation will take place and over what period of time; who is going to be on their own team; and who is authorised to make concessions for their team.

- Almost half of respondents (49 per cent) said that they always (or largely) act on impulse when negotiating rather than thinking about the deal in advance.

- Almost half of respondents (48 per cent) said that either they always (or mostly) use the same style and strategy when they negotiate; or that they don't use any strategy or style; or that they don't know whether they use any strategy or style. By contrast, as we shall see, tailoring your approach to the specific person or situation you are dealing with is normally the essence of successful negotiation.

- Respondents were asked whether they use a range of tough-guy and unproductive tactics in negotiation, such as: setting false deadlines; presenting take it or leave it ultimatums; falsely claiming that company policy 'won't allow them to agree'; making threats or lying. Perhaps not surprisingly, respondents were reluctant to acknowledge that they employ these tactics very often themselves – the top scorer was using 'take it or leave it' ultimatums which 22 per cent of respondents admitted to. However, when asked whether they felt that other people displayed any of these tactics their use seemed to be much more prevalent – often the same tactic was considered twice as likely or more to be displayed by a third party rather than the respondent themselves. This may suggest that people in fact use selfish and manipulative tactics – which are noticed by their deal partners – more frequently than they care to acknowledge.

- This may be supported by a finding which shows that only 22 per cent of respondents disagree with the statement 'people I negotiate with never seem to put themselves in my shoes'. It may be easier to attribute poor negotiating approaches to the other side than it is to acknowledge that we may be guilty of such approaches ourselves.

The general picture arising from the YouGov research is of a nation that does not particularly understand, value, prioritise or exercise good negotiation skills.

CEBR took these findings and worked out their financial impact. Respondents had been asked to say how often poor tactics impacted on their negotiations. They were also asked by what percentage the deal would have been improved if these factors had not been displayed. Overlaying these results on data showing how often each company negotiates with customers and suppliers, and what their annual turnover is, CEBR quantified the lost financial benefit to each company and then to UK Plc as a whole from not negotiating effectively. The loss figures included an element of loss covering the fall-out from the other side using antiquated tough-guy tactics, and also an element to cover the lost productivity from having to manage other negotiation failings which respondents had observed such as poor preparation, rigid behaviour and inadequate bidding and bargaining skills.

Among CEBR's conclusions was that:

- The UK is losing £17 billion a year through ineffective negotiation. This amounts to almost £9 million per working hour, £70 million per working day and £350 million per working week.

- Across the duration of the current recession UK turnover could have increased by almost £90 billion through more effective negotiation.
- The average UK company could increase its profitability by 7 per cent a year through more effective negotiation.
- Almost one working week every year is wasted by every UK company through having to deal with the consequences and delays caused by ineffective negotiation tactics.

These are striking statistics. To put it in context £17 billion equals almost seven times Google's estimated UK turnover for 2011 and 100 times Facebook's estimated UK turnover for the same period (according to the *Sunday Times*). It is more than half the total amount spent on advertising and marketing by UK companies annually – with an extra £17 billion, every company in the UK could run advertising and marketing campaigns for an extra 200 days per year. Alternatively, £17 billion represents the lost opportunity of 650,000 extra jobs based on UK average gross salary. What does your share of that figure mean for your business? Furthermore, bear in mind that the raw data was provided by the respondents themselves. It may be that many were reluctant to reveal how much they actually think was lost through poor negotiating, even in an anonymous survey. It may also be that others genuinely don't realise how much better they could negotiate or what benefits more effective negotiation could bring them. That would certainly coincide with my anecdotal experience as a negotiation coach. So the actual financial impact from poor negotiating technique may be far higher than that projected by respondents to the survey; this may just be the tip of the iceberg.

This survey was only conducted in the UK, but one can speculate intelligently on what the impact would have been if the UK results had been replicated globally. The UK accounts for 3.4 per cent of the world's GDP. Grossing up the results of the UK survey would suggest that the world economy could be losing £500 billion a year in turnover from poor negotiating. Across the five years of the current recession that amounts to £2.5 trillion. Large numbers indeed.

There is some evidence in the survey that respondents are beginning to understand that good negotiating is a priority, with 29 per cent of surveyed respondents in the UK agreeing that negotiating is becoming more important to their business. But that is not the same as being prepared to do something about it – 53 per cent of respondents did not disagree with the proposition that 'I see no real benefit in negotiation training'.

Some readers will object that, just because one party reports that it could improve its position through better negotiation, this does not mean the economy overall would benefit if that improvement was realised, since any improvement in deal terms obtained by one party must be at the expense of the other. However, this is to treat negotiation in the old-fashioned way, as a zero sum in which any gain for me must equate to a loss for you. This book is predicated on the basis that modern, collaborative negotiation can benefit all parties to a deal. By focusing on the needs of the other team each party can get more of what they want and so there is no 'fixed pie' to fight over; there is simply a potentially bigger pie to create for everybody. The negotiating framework we are about to discuss will show you how to do this. So it is perfectly possible that the projected improvements arising from better negotiation and reported by respondents to this survey could be secured without the other side being worse off.

All this data is regularly kept up to date at my website, www. cliverich.com so you can go there if you want to see the latest negotiating research. In the meantime, there could not be a more dramatic juxtaposition between:

(i.) the social trends outlined in Chapter 2 which militate towards an urgent requirement for better, more co-operative negotiating skills

(ii.) the results of the independent YouGov research indicating at best a very patchy understanding and application of basic negotiating skills, and a general indifference to improving those skills within UK business, and

(iii.) the economic research carried out by CEBR indicating the dramatic lost financial benefit from a failure to negotiate more effectively.

We can all agree that at a time when the UK, in common with many other countries, is struggling with the ravages of seemingly unending economic uncertainty, none of us can afford to ignore this kind of research and the opportunity represented by negotiating more productively. It's time to look in detail at the framework which can bring that about – 'the Negotiation Chain'.

THE
NEGOTIATION
CHAIN

PART ONE

NEGOTIATING ATTITUDE

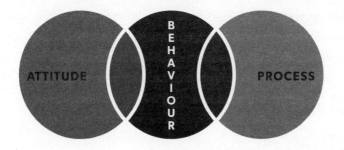

4

THE WINDMILLS OF YOUR MIND

Having the right negotiating attitude is one of the three key elements of negotiating success. Before we go on to discuss this attribute of successful negotiators I want to ask you to go to the website for my negotiating app. Go to www.closemydeal.co.uk/upgrade and fill in the details, including the voucher code: THEYESBOOK01. Then follow the on-screen instructions and fill in the first part of the questionnaire we discussed in the Introduction. The first section is all about 'Attitude'. It will help show you how often you display certain negotiating attitudes. It is not a measure of right and wrong; it is just a measure of frequency. It's best for you to fill this in now, before you are influenced by some of the aspects of negotiating attitude which we will now go on to discuss.

Forming Attitudes

Have you ever had a tough negotiation when you felt down-trodden and pushed around by the other side, and then found yourself re-running the episode in your mind, over and over again; feeling cross, thinking about what went wrong, and then thinking about other instances where negotiations have gone badly in the past? Maybe you then go on to behave in a way that corresponds to your mood the next time you negotiate – feeling apprehensive and nervous, expecting the worst, looking out for signs that the other side is going to take advantage. Or maybe you resolve to get your shot in first next time, and act more aggressively than normal. These are examples of how our experiences affect our state of mind.

Why do we develop these attitudes? Psychologists have filled volumes considering this issue. *Cognitive psychologists* believe that if we want to know what makes people tick we need to understand the internal processes of their minds. Cognition literally means 'knowing', so cognitive psychologists study the mental act or process by which knowledge is acquired.

Cognitive psychologists focus on the way we treat information that comes in, and how this treatment leads to internal responses. They study internal processes including perception, attention, language, memory and thinking. In the situation in which we believe we have been unfairly treated in a negotiation, cognitive psychologists might attribute our resulting attitude – our sense of foreboding and injustice – to the way we habitually process information about situations such as this. That way of processing might be enough to establish a pattern of thinking which is repeated when the same situation presents itself, regardless of whether our attitude or belief is, in fact, well founded. Maybe your pattern of thinking when deal-making is 'People always take advantage of me in negotiations', and this accounts for the way you are thinking about the incident.

Cognitive behaviourists believe that people often experience thoughts or feelings that reinforce faulty beliefs, and which result in damaging behaviour. So they focus on both the thinking *and* the activity which result from that thinking. Such beliefs can result in problematic behaviours that can, in turn, affect numerous aspects of daily life, including family, romantic relationships and work. For example, a person with low self-esteem might have negative thoughts about their own abilities or appearance. As a result of this, the individual might start to avoid social or work situations which trigger these negative patterns of thinking. This reinforces those unhelpful thought patterns. In order to address these destructive thoughts and behaviours, a cognitive behaviour therapist begins by helping the individual to identify the problematic ways of thinking, and then focus on the resulting behaviours that are compounding the problem. The individual begins to develop new approaches to thinking and behaviour, which are more productive and can help them cope better.

Neuro-linguistic programming refers to the theory that there are systematic, patterned connections between neurological processes ('neuro'), language ('linguistic') and learned behavioural strategies ('programming'). NLP has been described as the next generation of psychology, although it is not formally recognised in the UK by the British Psychological Society. NLP is not a form of therapy, but shares elements with cognitive behaviourism in that it began as a means of studying how people process information and construct meaning schemes (cognition), and then perform skills to achieve results (behaviour).

NLP works on the premise that by recoding the way you process such information you can change your pattern of thinking in order to implement more effective behaviours – particularly in relation to communication skills. Its core belief is that our experience of the world is not 'true'; rather, it is based on a series of filters through which we perceive the world. These perceptions are our map of reality and are stored as 'patterns' which influence the way we think and behave. These patterns will affect our state of mind at any time – how we feel on the inside and how we appear on the outside – but the patterns can be changed. So, in the example of being taken advantage of in a negotiation, an NLP practitioner might say that it is our perception of the situation which triggers a response such as anxiety or anger, and those perceptions will be based on viewing the event through the filters of our own experiences, even though there may be many different interpretations of the sequence.

For our purposes we don't need to decide whether cognitive psychologists, cognitive behaviourists or NLP practitioners are 'right' about the way that attitudes are formed. *But we can agree that we code our experience of life to create our attitudes and states of mind.* If you have this 'pattern' that says negotiations always go wrong, you will be on the lookout for experiences or stimuli that corroborate that pattern, and you will respond accordingly, so that whenever you are deal-making you will expect the worst.

This attitude or belief may, in objective terms, be mistaken, so the attitude and your resultant behaviour may not be at all helpful. Maybe you have exaggerated how badly the last negotiation went. Maybe you have obtained more concessions than you realise. Perhaps you just had a 'bad day at the office', because you were not prepared for this particular negotiation or were preoccupied with other worries. Maybe the other negotiator was only pushing you hard because they had been told that their job was on the line – or they were applying exactly the same standard as they apply to every other negotiation, they weren't singling you out for rough treatment.

These attitudes can bring about self-fulfilling outcomes. If you bring negative or anxious states of mind to the negotiating table that will have an impact on the outcome. If you feel negative or anxious you are likely to be unambitious in your expectations from the negotiation and bid low. You may appear hesitant or lacking in confidence, stumble or stammer. The other negotiator will pick up on these negative signals, either consciously or subconsciously, and will inevitably start to push you harder than they might otherwise have done. Now you are well on the way to making your anxieties self-fulfilling. *A negative attitude fuels a negative outcome.*

The opposite is equally true. If you feel positive and optimistic about the outcome, that feeds into your behaviour. You bid more ambitiously, you appear relaxed and confident. The other party picks this up and starts to feel that they must accommodate your requirements, because you are generating an expectation that they will be fulfilled.

So what are the typical negotiation attitudes which people exhibit and which one should you strive to adopt?

The Four Typical Negotiating Attitudes

From a practical point of view, there are four broad categories of attitude or state of mind which can be relevant in negotiating – 'fusing', 'using', 'losing' and 'confusing'. There are many other states of mind which can prevail as well – people can be happy, sad, depressed, bored, irritated, optimistic, hopeful, puzzled, inspired, cautious, but fusing, using, losing and confusing are particularly relevant states of mind with regard to negotiation. Let's look at each of these in turn.

Fusing

The most effective negotiation attitude to have is that of a 'fuser' – wanting to 'fuse' the agendas of both sides in order to create common currency for each participant. This is a modern 'state of mind' for negotiating which recognises the interdependent world in which we now live. For all the reasons we looked at in Chapter 2 collaboration is generally better than confrontation; partnerships are more important than punishments; 'pair-shaped deals' are better than 'pear-shaped deals'; incentives are better than insults.

'Fusers' bring a positive, confident and optimistic attitude to the negotiation table without being intent on putting one over on the other side. Their positivity brings about self-fulfilling positive outcomes. They may have an outlook, which can be summed up as:

- **'My needs and the other team's needs are both important.'**
- **'They may have ideas and views that can benefit all of us and so do I.'**
- **'Negotiation can satisfy both parties.'**
- **'Negotiation can strengthen our relationship.'**
- **'Negotiation can be really enjoyable.'**
- **'Both of us could end up with more than we expected.'**

'Fusers' are not just focused on the other deal-maker, so this is not necessarily an altruistic proposition. Fusers want both parties to benefit, including themselves. They believe that instead of fighting hand to hand, negotiators should work hand in hand. Academics have noted the benefits of this 'dual concern' approach[1] and report that the most successful problem-solving stance in negotiation consists of a 'firm but concerned and flexible stance'. Firmness is still required from fusers because they need to make sure that their own goals are represented in the solution to the problem which is reached. In addition to being firm though, it's also important to be concerned about the other negotiator's welfare and flexible enough that their concerns can be included in the negotiating outcome. 'Problem solving' or 'high joint benefit solutions' is the predicted outcome of negotiations where both parties have strong other-concern.[2][3] What researchers call 'integrative agreements' providing joint benefit (and resulting from what we are calling a 'fusing' approach) have been shown to have other benefits, too. They are more popular with both parties, more likely to be complied with, more beneficial to the relationship and may enhance organisational effectiveness (where the participants are part of the same organisation).[4] Such agreements are also reported as often being the only way agreement can be reached if the parties both have ambitious aspirations.[5][6]

Here's a practical example of the positive effect of a 'fusing' attitude from Will, author, on the process of having his book published:

I didn't realise until after signing a deal for my book, on how bands could cope with the digital age, just how much power and sway publishers have over their authors. I was lucky with my publishers because they were open and honest and collaborative from the very start. Their problem was that I felt a mistaken sense of entitlement. I thought I knew what I was doing, but I was really just jumping without looking where I was going to land.

After negotiating the contract, the first main stage in the book publishing process was the cover artwork.

I already knew what I wanted the artwork to be so I was slightly surprised to see the book's proposed artwork drop into my inbox from the publisher. It sucked. Really sucked. Shockingly so. What were they thinking? I was writing a cutting-edge music industry book that was going to set the world alight, and they send me a book cover with a person on the front playing a fucking clarinet? I was almost outraged. I knew the idea I had for the artwork was genius. I instantly replied stating that I rejected their cover idea outright and that I would be sending my version to them in a day or so. It just so happened that my artwork was indeed on its way to me. Timing was everything.

In place of a clarinet was an illustration of a Jesus/Moses-like figure set against a blazing wall of fire holding the ten Rock and Roll Commandments. It was so epic it was fucking biblical. I loved it and that was that.

I did explain, though, that the target audience for the book was the worldwide rock and roll fraternity who would have a lot more in common with a blazing Jesus-type figure than a clarinet. If they thought my idea was too edgy then they had to at least come up with something a bit more dangerous than a clarinet. I was lucky. They took a collaborative view, even though the choice of artwork was up to them, and they pretty much let me have my way. All they asked was that I tone down the usage of the British flag which I kind of agreed didn't have much to do with my biblical figure on the front. It wasn't until much later that I found out that they simply didn't have to accept my idea at all; they could have gone with the clarinet but they knew they would get a better book by working with me rather than against me.

NB I have tried to make sure that I don't use so many stories to illustrate each insight that the point gets lost, but you can see plenty more stories about fusing at www.cliverich.com, including a classic one featuring the Bacardi drinks brand and the band Groove Armada. I want to build a repository of negotiating stories that everyone can share to gain more from their negotiating – so feel free to submit your own negotiating story at the website.

Now let's look at the three other types of negotiating attitude – all of which are to be avoided. It's always better to be a 'Fuser'.

'HAVE YOU THOUGHT ABOUT COLLABORATIVE NEGOTIATING AS AN ALTERNATIVE TO HUFFING AND PUFFING ?'

Using

Users have a more old-fashioned view. They take advantage of the other side. They may bring confidence and self-belief to the negotiation but at the expense of the state of mind of the 'other side'. They may be assertive and un-cooperative, focusing on their own needs and not caring about the other side. Typical states of mind which they might display are:

- **'Who cares about what you want as long as I'm okay.'**
- **'This is a contest I must win.'**
- **'There isn't any positive outcome for you that could also be a positive outcome for me.'**

Sometimes these are just 'casual users' who are simply indifferent to how you feel about the deal as long as they are happy. Sometimes they are 'abusers' who actually want you to feel bad. Sadly, there are a few inadequate people who derive some strange pleasure in their dealings from trying to make other people feel small. I can think of two people like that with whom I have dealt with in my career – I'm sure you have come across this type as well. Such 'users' are bad news. They believe in negotiating by cudgel and stick, not carrot and stick. They do not have your interests at heart, and they are often only interested in the exercise of power in their negotiations.

Much academic research has been devoted to the pitfalls of negotiating with a contentious 'using' kind of attitude. Firstly, users may create short-term advantage for themselves by adopting this approach, but they stoke up lasting resentment on the other side. It's not enough to bring positive intent to your own side of the deal if the consequence is that the other side leaves the negotiating table in bits. If they leave the negotiation feeling resentful or crushed, there will be consequences later. If they have to do a deal with you they will do so grudgingly or un-cooperatively.[7][8] They may then covertly work to undermine that deal or at least be unenthusiastic about its success, or they may decide to bide their time and wait for the moment when they deal with you again and can get their own back. This will apply whether you take advantage of them at the beginning, middle or end of the deal process.

We all tend to carry negotiating defeats with us for a long time. They rankle and annoy us: even if we tell ourselves that we have moved on, the after-taste of a bitter pill lingers. Think of an occasion in the past when you felt you had no choice and were made to agree or participate in a deal which made you feel angry or resentful. I bet you felt angry or resentful all over again just thinking about it. That's how easy it is for our state of mind to be influenced! Equally, academics report that overuse of a contentious attitude can lead to low-benefit outcomes because options for greater joint benefit are ignored.[9] [10] In addition, a contentious approach can fix participants to a rigid way of thinking that is incompatible with creative problem solving.[11] [12] A contentious approach also frequently prompts retaliation by the intended target. A number of studies have shown that such imitation of a contentious attitude is associated with failures to reach agreement in negotiation, poor ongoing relationships and escalating spirals or mutinies which create greater distance between the parties rather than moving them together.[13] Playing 'my way or the highway' has damaging consequences.

Apart from all of these disadvantages, those with a 'using' attitude tend to be shunned in the end. Here's a cautionary tale from the mobile phone ringtone business about a negotiation with customers that ended badly:

Jamba was the ringtone company that could do no wrong. It was a leading player in the new craze and even spawned hits out of its ringtone content, including the massively irritating

'Crazy Frog' single. It had good relations with all the content owners from whom it might need licences. The company was bought by VeriSign for US$270 million. However, as we observed in Chapter 2, brands are increasingly involved in an ongoing negotiation with their customers for their continued engagement and goodwill. In 2005, it became apparent that the company was allegedly luring unsuspecting consumers into subscriptions for its content, when customers thought they were just buying a one-off ringtone. The company was also accused of making it very difficult to unsubscribe. Worse still, a large number of those consumers were children, attracted by the craze for ringtones. There was a public outcry. The *Daily Mail* highlighted the case of one girl who had inadvertently run up a bill of £70 for purchasing ringtones and wallpaper. Almost overnight the company seemed to have lost its reputation for probity and gained an unwanted reputation as a 'user' – only interested in its own ends and not concerned about its consumers. Consumers and content owners lost confidence in the company. Its deal-flow reduced. It had been generating revenues of US$600 million, so should have been worth at least that amount of money, but that value plummeted – almost halving from this peak. What is worse, when you lose your reputation for honesty it's very difficult to recover. It's seven years since these events took place, and yet if you ask people about Jamba their memories will not be of a clever and pioneering technology company, but of the company that allegedly ripped consumers off, and so never moved beyond ringtones (and of course delivered that infernal 'Crazy Frog' hit). The company has virtually disappeared, having passed through the hands of News Corp to 'Jesta Digital', which vaporised in early 2012 ...

This example from TV executive, John, also illustrates the importance of not succumbing to the temptation to be a 'user':

I worked for a man who believed that in a world where you couldn't trust anybody you had to start off by establishing the attitude of the other side. Whenever he engaged with you he would deliberately start from a ridiculously weak position, but critically he would only start small. This allowed whoever he was working with to take advantage of him if they so desired. At this early low-cost low-risk stage he was more than happy to lose. If you took advantage of him more fool you. You had played your hand, and you had won very little.

He would never work with you again. This strategy was totally convincing, he always appeared naïve and charming, yet in fact he was sizing up how you would treat him if he did business with you. He was always happy to pick up every bill, every expense, and seemingly without ego he invited you to take advantage of him as a form of temptation.

Fantastically disarming and yet cunningly strategic, he was able to select or reject his suppliers and partners on the basis of whether they would take advantage or whether he could trust them.

Game theory and the futility of 'using'

Academic focus on 'game theory' of negotiation also tends to demonstrate that collectively the parties are better off if they work in partnership rather than 'using'. A 'game' in this context refers to a situation in which the following applies:

- There is a limited set of negotiating options available to the participants.
- There are rules for making decisions on these options and different values for outcomes associated with those decisions.

The term 'game theory' comes from a branch of mathematics which measures the values to each party from an analysis of all the various possible combinations of decisions they can make. In some respects negotiation can be modelled to reflect a game of this kind, because the parties have decisions about which moves to make and the impact of different decisions can be modelled on the prescribed set of rules imposed on the game. There are limitations on this approach, since it assumes that each party behaves rationally and in accordance with the rules at all times. Common sense tells us that in real life negotiations this is frequently not the case. Game theory analysis of negotiation is also associated with the use of complex mathematical formulae which are beyond this book and difficult for non-mathematicians to understand, let alone apply in practice. However, what is interesting about game theory is that the parties are also usually instructed to operate exclusively in accordance with their own self-interest (e.g. to apply a 'using' attitude). Despite this, and at the risk of taking a simple approach to a complex and vast body of work, various game theory scenarios seem to militate towards an attitude of mutual cooperation as one which provides the greatest utility to both players. So, it is worth pausing for a moment to cover this.

There are three typical 'game' scenarios which are commonly utilised in this kind of research. The first is 'the prisoner's dilemma'. In this game, typically two parties are given two options in a given scenario, one of which is cooperative and the other non-cooperative. For example, let's assume two students are playing a negotiation game where, between them, they have all the textbooks required for a course but they are divided equally between each student. They have to decide simultaneously whether or not to lend each other their own set of books. They would rather keep their set for themselves so that they can use them whenever they want and so that their own books don't get lost or damaged, but they need both sets of books to be able to complete the course.

There are four possible pairs of outcome choices. Either A can make a 'contending' exploitative choice (e.g. not to lend his books) and B can cooperate (by lending his books); or the reverse can apply and B can make an exploitative choice and A can make a cooperative choice; or A and B can both try to make exploitative choices (they both choose not to lend); or they can both cooperate (both agreeing to lend). Non-cooperation in theory provides an individual with the best possible outcome, (because they are best off if the other party chooses to lend and they choose not to). However, the dilemma for each party is that, if *neither* of them cooperates, they will both be worse off than if they cooperate (in this case mutual non-cooperation means they would only have half the books they need to complete the course). An approach which is rational for each party separately is irrational for the parties collectively – they are better off 'fusing' and engaging in problem solving.

The game of 'chicken', which is also used by researchers, is similar. This gets its name from the dangerous car game where two drivers hurtle towards each other at great speed and the first one to swerve off the road is regarded as the 'loser'. As with the prisoner's dilemma, this is a mixed 'motive game' since, if I decide I won't swerve (adopting a purely selfish stance), I will win as long as you *do* swerve. However, if neither of us swerves we will both crash with potentially fatal consequences – so mutual cooperation (we adopt a 'fusing' attitude and both swerve) is not just a way to avoid defeat, it is potentially a winning strategy, with a better outcome for me than 'using'.

'Resource dilemmas' is a third type of game used to model negotiation. Resource dilemmas often involve a resource which must be renewed – e.g. subscription fees for a club. As with the other types of game the rules are set up so that each party has the temptation to adopt a selfish attitude. I could be a 'user' and make a decision not to pay my subscription to the club on the basis that, as long as everybody else pays their subscription, I am better off, because I get access to the club's resources without paying for them. However, if everybody does that the club will collapse and we will all be worse off. So, although my individual interests would in theory be best served by taking advantage of everybody else, the best collective outcome arises as a result of a 'fusing' attitude where everybody cooperates.

Dealing with Users

Despite all the arguments against 'using', for the moment, 'users' are still out there in large numbers and you will have to deal with them. 'Casual users' are especially common. Often at negotiation coaching seminars, when I talk about the importance of 'fusing' in negotiations people will nod in agreement, yet in practice when they role-play during negotiating scenarios there is a marked tendency to focus only on their own interests and not on those of the other dealmaker at all. It is as though 'using' is a default approach, an unthinking attitude that comes naturally to many people, not because they dislike the other negotiator but simply because it is how many people are used to viewing negotiations. The traditional lexicon of negotiating supports this: we talk about 'winning' and 'losing', having 'negotiating opponents', and 'outsmarting the other side'. Negotiating research backs up this old-fashioned view of negotiation as a game of hardball. Struggle often comes before cooperation in negotiations. Companies, individuals, nations or unions strike a position first, or make and implement threats (e.g. strike action) and then go on to have a meaningful negotiation. A coercive approach may seem the way to go at the beginning, especially if one party believes it has more power over the other or has 'right on its side'.

It's only later that the problems with this approach develop, as the parties realise that it is costly or damaging to their own interests or a relationship, or upsetting, or the other party cannot be pressured into giving in. The parties then go into a phase called a 'hurting stalemate'[14] [15] before a serious negotiation commences.

However, although a 'user'-based attitude may be common and customary, it doesn't really work in practice. Its benefits are not supported by academic research – even simple and limited negotiation experiments based on 'game theory' support a collaborative approach. Most importantly, this is an approach that is becoming outmoded by the kind of social trends towards cooperative negotiation which we have already observed.

So, don't be a user yourself, and if you encounter users, the best way to deal with these people is to avoid them if you can. If you can't avoid 'users', try to tip them into a more constructive frame of mind early on. A good question to ask is: 'Are we agreed that the outcome of this deal should benefit both of us?' That's a difficult question to say 'no' to. If they say 'yes', they have set a standard for the negotiation - hold them to that standard throughout the deal. If they say 'no', you know you are in for a difficult negotiation. Marshal your bargaining power, be prepared to stand up to them and look after your side of the deal as assiduously as they look after theirs. Users are not normally difficult to spot ...

YOU SCRATCH MY
BACK AND I'LL STAB YOURS

Losing

Those with a 'losing' attitude come to the negotiation with a defeatist attitude. Unassertive and cooperative, they neglect their own concerns. Often this is to satisfy the concerns of others.

The typical 'losing' mentality might be displayed as:

- **'My needs aren't very important.'**
- **'Negotiation is a contest I am bound to lose.'**
- **'Getting the other person's approval and goodwill is more important than winning.'**
- **'The other side has the power to make me lose.'**
- **'I always make a mess of this kind of thing – they must think I'm really stupid.'**
- **'I can afford to lose this time as long as it doesn't set a precedent'** (yes, that is actually a losing attitude).

'Losers' tend to produce self-fulfilling losing outcomes. Anxious to avoid upsetting the other negotiator, they are more likely to avoid contests of will, change their position easily and yield to pressure. This applies even in negotiation settings where there is what academics call 'integrative potential', meaning that both parties could achieve their desired outcome. Research shows that soft negotiators who give up easily are not likely to explore the integrative potential of their deals and hence not likely to achieve beneficial outcomes.[16] [17] Sometimes 'losers' make such low initial demands and concede so quickly that they make it harder to reach agreement, and finding a solution takes longer than if they had been more ambitious. This is because fast concessions signal extreme weakness, leading the other deal partner to stop conceding altogether.

Here's a good example from digital strategist and product expert, Dominic Pride:

Picture this. In the boardroom of one of the world's largest telecommunications companies, the very shortlist of finalists for an important piece of business were pitching to a hardened team of business development executives. We were at the end of two gruelling days of grilling the potential suppliers. As 'good cop', I'd written the spec, the tendering templates and sourced the suppliers we knew could come up with the goods to pitch for the business. Now the bad cops were having their day.

The two suppliers had presented very different models. One had a sliding scale which incentivised the buyer to drive the service, with a better rev share the more units sold. Let's call them 'Slider' for the purpose of the story. The other had a flat fee per unit sold, which already made it less attractive for the big telco buyer – the 'Flatliner'.

On our side, the chief negotiator wanted to find out who really wanted the business and how far they would go. We'd already done the estimate of the cost base and wanted to find out how close to zero margin they would go to secure the deal.

Bang! In went the demand to both for the price which virtually eliminated any margin for the supplier in the deal. Flatliner conceded, Slider kept to their original pricing. We sent them out to their separate rooms while we deliberated.

'So that's it then,' said our chief negotiator. 'We know who we want.'

'Yes,' I said. 'We can't get a better deal than Flatliner. We've got what we wanted.'

'No,' said the chief. 'If they go to that price, they obviously need the business so much they'll do it for nothing. That's not the supplier we want.'

So one supplier stopped and drew the line where they knew they had to stop. One went further and showed they needed rather than wanted the business, and in one stroke weakened their bargaining power which proved difficult to regain.

Losing both ways

Sometimes 'losers' who ignore their own outcome try to make sure that the other negotiator loses, too, as that is the best they feel they can hope for or want from the negotiation. This is a very destructive attitude to bring to the negotiation. This kind of attitude displays as:

- **'They wouldn't negotiate even if I tried.'**
- **'If I look like losing I will make sure the other guy loses, too.'**
- **'There is no chance of securing my bottom line so I might as well wreck the negotiation.'**
- **'It's more important that the other team doesn't win, than that I win.'**

Here's a good example of mutually destructive 'losing both ways' from leading media lawyer Paul:

I was working as the lawyer for a well-known rock band who were having difficulties with their record company and also difficulties getting along with each other. Like many rock bands, this band had signed to the record company when they were unknown and, as time went by, their deal became more and more inappropriate, but the record company were not keen to make any concessions.

Ultimately, I attended a meeting with the senior executives

of the record company and told them that if I left the meeting without any concession of any kind, then, in my view, the band would split up and record no more together. It was my genuine belief. The record company were completely intransigent and refused to make a single concession. When I reported this back to the band, they did indeed split up and recorded nothing more together. Clearly the record company had thought that I was bluffing. As it turned out, making a concession would have been a less expensive option for the record company. Once the band had split up nobody was able to make any money. Taking a position that is too hard and inflexible can be self-defeating.

'Losing both ways' is a highly damaging attitude which normally benefits nobody. This kind of attitude often prevails in bitter industrial disputes. I blog regularly on industrial disputes which get out of hand, are marked by mutual recriminations and where a negotiated settlement seems elusive. In such a case this kind of self-destructive mutually-losing attitude is never far away. You can read on the website my accounts of attitudinal failures within major industrial disputes such as the miners' strike in Britain in 1984 as well as more recent strike action at British Airways and within the UK public sector.

Confusing

Confusers are people who labour under mistaken assumptions, misapprehensions or prejudices which may cause them to be 'losers' or 'users'. These mistaken assumptions would be readily recognised by cognitive psychologists. They would also be recognised by NLP practitioners, who would characterise this phenomenon as being caused by 'distortions', 'generalisations' and 'deletions' about reality. Such misapprehensions prevent the negotiation of what researchers call 'Pareto optimal' outcomes (as you will see there is plenty of jargon to digest in this area!).[18] [19] These are outcomes where neither party can do better in an alternative agreement without the other side doing worse – so each party has achieved the maximum gain possible.

Researchers argue that it is cognitive failures – limitations on our own powers of reasoning and processing – which can bring about these 'Pareto inferior' outcomes. We simply have a limited capacity for processing, retrieval and storage of information from our memories. This makes us 'cognitive misers'[20] [21] [22] who rely on 'damaging' mental shortcuts and simplifying assumptions to manage information (called 'heuristics' by researchers). We also use cognitive 'schemas' which are presumptions about certain situations and people. These are based on faulty prior observation, which misleads our attention and memory, so that some events and aspects are noticed and remembered while others are ignored or forgotten. These assumptions tend to be self-perpetuating, since we often notice and remember things which support our preconceptions. Put simply, we frequently (incorrectly) judge a book by its cover. Here are some examples of attitudinal 'blockers' which can arise from our own limited powers of cognition. Many of these distorting tendencies are described in Pruitt and Rubin's excellent *Managing Social Conflict* (1986). These distortions are responsible for the mistaken assumptions made in our hypothetical example at the beginning of this chapter about someone feeling taken advantage of in a negotiation. The theme has been taken up by Daniel Kahneman in his tremendous book *Thinking, Fast and Slow*[23]. Kahneman defines two notional systems of human thinking: 'System 1', which is very impulsive and makes snap judgements based on incomplete information, and 'System 2', which is much more considered and methodical in its judgements but also a bit lazy or often busy. As a result 'System 2' tends to leave many judgements to 'System 1' which operates at a superficial level and is therefore highly likely to make perceptual mistakes. Do any of the following distortions – many of them described by Pruitt and Rubin, and Kahneman – ever apply to you and result in you getting the wrong end of the stick and bringing a 'confusing' attitude to the negotiation?

1. The fixed pie assumption

This presupposes that the two parties' interests are directly opposed, and so your win must be my loss. This fixed pie assumption makes problem solving seem unworkable or pointless and so it encourages contending or 'using' behaviour.[24] [25] The fixed pie assumption originates from a concept called 'false consensus' where we believe that others must have similar priorities to ours – for example that 'price' is the only variable in the negotiation.[26] [27] A number of researchers[28] [29] have found that when negotiators have this view they will either not reach agreement or simply reach 'split it down the middle', compromises which miss the potential for fused outcomes. Once we adopt this attitude it tends to persist from negotiation to negotiation – we find it difficult to change our tune.[30] [31]

2. Imaginary conflict

This is the opposite and arises when neither party realises that both of them want the same thing, because we make an assumption that the other party opposes what we want without actually checking that the assumption is true.[32] [33] By leaping to this conclusion we may end up contending (or using) needlessly.

3. Reactive devaluation

This is a complicated phrase for a simple proposition.[34] [35] Research has found that proposals made by the other negotiator tend to be devalued in negotiation simply on the basis that the other side has offered them. Negotiators tend to discount concessions offered by 'the other side' on the basis that 'even if it looks like a concession, if it comes from them it must be bad for me'. This attitude may create a missed opportunity for fusing.

4. Negotiation attributions

These can involve judgements we make about the other deal partner's expected behaviours and attitudes which we believe should follow a certain script corresponding to the way negotiations 'should go' (e.g. if I disclose my hand so should you). When people deviate from these perceived standards we make negative assumptions about why they are doing that (e.g. they are being dishonest) and that can cause us to assume a more confrontational (perhaps a 'using') attitude. It's equally easy to wrongly infer the motivations of the other deal partner from our own anxieties about the negotiation. If we fear that they might take a certain approach we are too eager to look for confirmation that we are right, and so we don't judge their actual motivations properly but through the one-eyed filter of our own fears about them.

5. Overconfidence

Some negotiators carry an assumption that the other deal maker will always make greater concessions than they actually will. This was demonstrated in an experiment to measure how well negotiators thought they would do in a forthcoming arbitration.[36] [37] Each side estimated its chances at over 50 per cent – they can't all have been right. Similar over-optimism was reported in a study to establish whether disputants were overly optimistic about the use of threats in negotiations.[38] [39] Kahneman speaks of a general tendency towards over-optimism in undertaking projects and enterprises – often caused by 'System 1' underweighting things that could go wrong (in this case, how robustly the other team might negotiate). If we feel overconfident about the other negotiator's likelihood of capitulation then this reduces concession making and encourages the adoption of 'using' attitudes.

6. Availability

Events and experiences which are recent and therefore fresh in our memory or are more intense or more concrete (even if short-lived) tend to be easier to access. They loom large and therefore we can rely too much on them in forming our current judgements.[40] [41]

Kahneman shows how recent media coverage of a topic affects our judgements in this way. This could affect our negotiating attitude either way. For example, if we have recently been humbled by a tough guy (or the experience was particularly intense) it may make us inclined to carry more of a 'losing' attitude next time round than if any such memory was distant, and so we do not attach much importance to that memory.

7. Representativeness

We make judgements based on the most obvious characteristics of a situation and ignore all the other background which would have enabled us to make a more balanced judgement.[42] [43] So, for example, if we see that someone with whom we are negotiating seems to have a very successful product or service we assume they must have lots of bargaining power, even if deeper analysis might indicate that they have commercial problems, too, or we have lots of bargaining power as well if we stopped and thought about it. Kahneman describes this tendency as WYSIATI ('What you see is all there is'). In this particular instance it could set up a 'losing' mentality, but it could equally be the case that we selectively interpret the most obvious data about a negotiation at face value, jump to conclusions and come up with a 'using' mentality instead.

8. Framing

Negotiating attitudes can be affected by how we 'frame' or describe issues to ourselves. For example, there is some evidence that the prospect of losses on us has greater impact than the prospect of gains. This is called 'loss aversion'.[44] [45] Building on this, researchers have shown that when a negotiating task was framed as a potential loss, the participants were less likely to reach agreement than when it was framed as a potential gain.[46] [47] The attitudes of the participants facing what they framed as a loss stiffened, making a 'fusing' outcome less likely. This has been supported by more recent research distinguishing between 'appetitive' competitors (looking to maximise gains) and 'aversive' competitors (looking to avoid getting behind on a deal) who were more likely to regard 'impasse' as an acceptable outcome (since it meant that at least they weren't losing anything).[48] Kahneman takes up the theme, too: 'For most people the fear of losing $100 is more intense than the hope of gaining $150. We concluded from many such observations that "losses loom larger than gains" and that people are loss averse. For this reason negotiations over a shrinking pie are especially difficult because they require an allocation of losses. People tend to be much more easygoing when they [perceive that] they are bargaining over an expanding pie.' It is because losses are always magnified for people, that I have described having a defeatist attitude as 'losing', even though I like to think of negotiation as being more about joining than winning or losing.

9. Defence mechanisms

Freud identified several defence mechanisms which we use to protect ourselves from situations that make us anxious. Other researchers have since added to his categorisations. Here are some examples of defence mechanisms and how they can distort our attitude in a negotiation:

Denial – a situation in which people are unable to admit an obvious truth about themselves (e.g. that they behave weakly in negotiations or that they are a bully). Could be used to perpetuate either a 'losing' or a 'using' attitude accordingly.

Displacement – taking out our frustrations on people and objects that are less threatening than the situation which caused the frustration in the first place. Could be the cause of a 'using' attitude in negotiations, e.g. punishing a junior contract partner because a major supplier gives us a hard time.

Projection – taking our own unacceptable qualities or feelings and ascribing them to other people instead. Could be used to justify a 'using' attitude to those people on whom we project.

Rationalisation – explaining unacceptable behaviour in a logical manner which avoids the true reasons for that behaviour, and so avoids any self-blame for those actions. Could be used to justify either a 'using' or a 'losing' attitude.

Idealisation – choosing to perceive another individual as having more positive qualities than he or she may have. Feeling that the sun rises and sets on someone else could support a 'losing' attitude.

Any of these 'confusing' states of mind may create an unhelpful attitude for you when you negotiate. Make sure that, when you are assessing the attitude you want to display during the negotiation, you have a realistic view of the other side and their view of you, otherwise you may end up wrongly assuming a 'using' or a 'losing' attitude, based on these kinds of misapprehension about the motives, history or reality of the negotiation. Don't be a confuser …

`SO — ARE WE ALL HAPPY ?`

Having identified the four main negotiating attitudes, we can now move on to look at how to ensure you carry the best attitude with you whenever you negotiate.

5

BARGAINING POWER

I Can See Clearly Now

Accepting that we want to be 'fusing' rather than 'using', 'losing' or 'confusing', what is the best way to capture that attitude?

One essential way to develop that confident mentality for negotiation which is one of the keys to success, and which fusers possess, is to have a proper understanding of the bargaining power the participants have. Many people get this wrong as it's very easy to underestimate the number of 'aces' you hold and to overestimate or fantasise about the bargaining power of the other team, while, as we saw when looking at 'confusing', there are also some people who exaggerate the strength of their own position. In reality, there are eleven sources of bargaining power which we will look at in this chapter and they are rarely arranged 11–0 in favour of one party or the other. It's often 6–5 or maybe 7–4 or, at worst, 8–3.

Some years ago a famous piece of negotiating research was carried out by Sainsbury's and Coca-Cola in relation to negotiations between them. Each company was asked 'who holds the aces' in the negotiations to sell cans of Coke into Sainsbury's. The sales reps from Coca-Cola scored it four aces to nil in favour of the buyers from Sainsbury's. They focused on what a disaster it would be for Coca-Cola if their brand was not represented on its shelves. The buyers from Sainsbury thought exactly the opposite – they scored it four aces to nil in favour of the sales reps from Coke. They could only see what a problem it would be for Sainsbury's if customers were complaining that cans of Coke were not available on their shelves. The reality was probably that it was two aces each – yet each company found it really easy to exaggerate the bargaining power of the other.

Counting Your Aces

So, getting an accurate picture of the balance of the bargaining power can either help to boost your confidence (or prevent you being overconfident and arrogant). You can't play your cards right if you don't know how many aces you are holding. Here are those eleven sources of bargaining power explained:

Information

We all know the expression 'information is power'. You may have information that the other party doesn't have about the transaction you are negotiating – for example, market data or financial information or information about competitors. This can give you an extra edge in the negotiation. Make sure you have as much information as possible when you negotiate – information about your market, your competitors, the people you are dealing with, your own product and services – it can be the difference that counts.

Here's another good example from media lawyer Paul:

Some years ago I was involved in a dispute between a songwriter and a performer who claimed, many years after the song was created, performed and recorded, that he, rather than the composer, had in fact composed the song. The composer had been regarded for many years as the sole composer and the performer had never had any song-writing credit, but was very belatedly claiming the greater part of the composition.

The composer wanted to avoid the worry and expense of litigation and we tried to negotiate a settlement. The problem was that the expectations of the performer were absurdly high and he was claiming at least twenty-five times the maximum amount that the claim would have been worth if it had been a meritorious claim, which it wasn't.

We had two or three meetings at which it was clear that the expectations of the two parties were so far apart that an agreed settlement seemed impossible. In a final attempt to settle, we had a meeting at which the lawyers on both sides and the clients were present. I decided that the only way to bring common sense to bear was to produce accounts, which showed in great detail the full earnings of the piece of work since its composition, together with supporting royalty payments and sworn statements from the publishers verifying the figures. These showed that the figures claimed by the performer were vastly greater than the entire earnings of the composition.

I produced the evidence at the meeting, so that I could be sure the performer would see it without any spin being put on it by his lawyer or anyone else. The performer was genuinely surprised by the level of earnings and, despite efforts by his lawyer to continue the proceedings, he called it a day and settled at a figure which was twice what the composer thought the claim was worth but a great deal less than the twenty-five times that figure which the performer was claiming originally. The caving-in was dramatic and shows the importance of having all relevant information available to support your position.

Expertise

You may have expertise that the other team doesn't have, such as, for example, specialist technical knowledge or access to industry experts. Or you may have a skill set which has been built up over years and is difficult to replicate or match – the kind of expertise which comes from experience. Don't discount that when measuring the mutual bargaining power. You may be up against someone who has other natural advantages such as market power or financial muscle but doesn't have the same expertise as you.

Here's a good example of the power of expertise from career and business coach, Liz:

I've negotiated with clients, teenagers and an ex-husband – but perhaps one of the most difficult negotiations was with the garage that serviced my daughter's car.

She had arranged a service by phone, enticed in by an apparent low price and not realising that lots of extras (that are essential to a service) would be added. The bill was blisteringly high.

We went in to complain and of course she had no written record of the agreement and could not recall the telephone conversation exactly, but the bill did seem outrageous.

One item in particular caught my eye, the price of the oil. Either they'd put ten litres of oil in or the oil was priced at current platinum prices. After stating that we thought the bill was unreasonable and we had no clear idea of what had been agreed they did concede that perhaps they hadn't communicated clearly what the final bill might be – but they wouldn't budge on price. So then I queried the oil price.

Me: So how much oil did you put in?

They told us.

Me: Reasonable for a one-litre engine, but why did it cost £42? That's more than it costs in a BMW.

Them: We use an extra-special rinky-dinky oil that helps fuel economy. (I paraphrase, they might not have said rinky-dinky.)

Me: Well, I've had bigger cars serviced and they didn't charge that, and anyway it's a Fiesta not a Lamborghini.

Then ...

Them: Just a moment, madam.

They disappear, come back and say they've spoken to the manager who in view of the fact that the initial phone conversation wasn't clear would reduce the price by £100. I accepted.

Moral? I had some expertise they hadn't anticipated. Firstly, I had the service bills of bigger cars to refer to. Secondly, I spoke with confidence on oil changes because as a child I'd watched my dad do so many. And we went in to complain on Saturday morning – right next to the busy car showroom!

Market Power

This is a source of bargaining power which is readily understandable. If someone dominates a market then that can give them bargaining power in a transaction. However, market power works in other, subtler ways as well. You may be a small player but have strength in a particular niche. That is still a source of market bargaining power. You may be small but have momentum from being cool or fashionable; that is an example of market power. In its early days Spotify was a very small music streaming service, but right from the beginning it created a buzz about itself in the market which made it seem much bigger than it was, which has helped to propel it forward.

The author Robert Cialdini, a major authority on influencing, has, in his book *Influence: The Psychology of Persuasion*[49] identified six principles of influence. These are favoured by what he calls 'compliance professionals' who wish to make us do or buy things. His book identifies and explains each of these principles in turn, and some of them are relevant to a discussion on bargaining power. His starting point is the same as those who believe that we have certain patterns of *automated behaviour* which cause us to respond in predictable ways to specific stimuli.

These responses mean that we don't have to catalogue, appraise and calibrate every decision we make (which would be far too difficult in a world of ever-increasing speed and complexity). One of the six automatic responses Cialdini has identified is 'the principle of social proof'. This suggests that one means we use to determine whether something is correct or not is to identify what other people think about it, and then go along with that. This is especially true in ambiguous situations – for example, situations in which groups of people witness what may be a crime or an accident. Generally, unless one person moves to help the victim then nobody will, as everybody assumes that the kind of indifference exhibited by the other bystanders is 'the norm'. If, however, one or two people make that commitment to get involved then lots of other people feel it's okay to get involved as well, as the emergency must be real. We all look for this vindication, and often its application makes sense in our daily lives; if other people are doing something it may well be the right thing to do. This phenomenon can be a source of 'market power' for a seller in a negotiation scenario. If everybody else thinks that a product or service is great, and it is really popular with either consumers or other businesses, then we may make the assumption that it is great, too, and be more inclined towards it.

Another example of market power arises if a product is 'scarce'. 'Scarcity' causes another of Cialdini's automated responses. Scarcity can influence people to want something more and so creating scarcity can be a great source of market-based bargaining power. As we have already seen in our discussion on negotiating attitude, people seem to be more motivated by the thought of losing something than by that of gaining something of equal value. Scarcity works as a motivator partly because we hate to lose freedoms (such as a freedom of choice) that we already have. If we think there will soon be less fish in the sea rather than more, the perceived value of fish goes up. So scarcity works especially well when something that was previously available in abundance becomes scarce. By way of an example, information that is banned or censored becomes much more desirable to know – just witness the furore on Twitter concerning the information suppressed by super injunctions. So if you own something of increasing scarcity (oil, gas, maybe water) this gives you bargaining power.

You can also create a sense of scarcity artificially. 'Deadline' tactics are a good example of the scarcity tactic at work – people often find themselves doing something they wouldn't normally do on the basis that the time to do so is shrinking (see Chapter 19, 'Different Behaviour Suits Dealing with Tough Guys', for how to deal with people who try this manipulatively on you). The real or pretend introduction of another potential buyer also evokes the scarcity principle as we become alarmed that we are about to lose something which presently we might have. Cialdini's own brother ran a successful business buying and selling cars by always ensuring that whenever he was selling a car three prospective buyers would turn up for the same appointment.

Creating 'limited offers' is another way of generating market power through the principle of scarcity. If something is only available as a limited edition or to a limited number of customers, that can create a sense of market-based bargaining power for whoever is making that offer.

Scale or Weight

You may have scale on your side. This is an easy proposition to understand in the organisational sense of the word. Large institutional organisations such as the BBC, and massive companies like Tesco or Microsoft, have a great deal of bargaining power.

However, scale is only an advantage if used effectively; scale can also make you cumbersome and slow to move or adapt to change; speedboats can be more zippy and fast-moving than tankers. Scale can also make you complacent; it can cause you to dissipate your bargaining power so that it is applied over too wide an area and is not brought to bear at a particular point, at a particular time. So, just because you are up against a larger player, don't assume they have all the bargaining power just because of their superior size. Size isn't everything. You may be able to utilise your own, smaller size by being nimble, quick-witted and flexible in a manner which is beyond them. Consider the USA, one of the largest and most powerful nations on earth. For all its scale across a range of criteria the US has not been able to impose outcomes satisfactory to itself on much smaller countries like Vietnam, Afghanistan or Iran – either militarily or through negotiation. By contrast, Luxembourg is tiny – less than 1,000 square miles in size. In many ways it has no right to exist – it ought to have been permanently gathered up by one of its powerful neighbours such as France, Germany or Italy. Only one-third of its 500,000 population was born in Luxembourg, so on any given day two-thirds of the inhabitants are 'foreigners'. And yet Luxembourg has made the most of its expertise in banking and taxation in order to negotiate a stable and secure identity for itself. It has one of the highest GDP per capita ratios in the world and, apart from occupation during the two world wars, has been independent since 1867. It has managed this despite the fact that it is tiny.

There is some evidence that 'scale' can work on a one-to-one basis – i.e. that physically taller or broader people have a slight advantage in a negotiation. However, once again that only works if the size is used effectively. Larger people may slouch or stoop or lack energy in their movements, or they may otherwise misuse their height or size and surrender the room to somebody smaller. Smaller people may move about a lot to 'fill the space' and make themselves appear bigger than they are. They may use their voice and gestures to make the most of their presence – speaking with authority and using hand gestures to increase the impact of what they are saying.

Here's a good example, from Michael Rust, attorney and mediator, of someone trying to use their physicality in a negotiation and failing:

I remember being placed in a difficult position in one of my first professional negotiations. I was representing an employer in a wrongful termination case and knew that the other party's attorney (Jessica) had a reputation for trying to dominate settlement meetings.

Once we were all seated together, Jessica almost immediately sprang to her feet and took a stance next to the whiteboard in the room. She was attempting to control the negotiation based upon her height (we were all seated) and her position of dominance (controlling the whiteboard).

However, because I was prepared for her tactics, I did not allow it to change my approach to the negotiation. Rather, I saw this as an opportunity. She had left her client alone at the table with me and my client. Now the numbers favoured us.

For the remainder of the negotiation I was able to keep Jessica busy at the whiteboard while my client and I negotiated the resolution to the case with her client. Through strategic body placement and making sure that Jessica always had something to do at the whiteboard ('Jessica, I think we should reword point two on your agenda'; 'Jessica, we have an agreement on this point, please write this agreement on the whiteboard') we were able to counteract her strategy and implement our own.

Also, due to the distance between Jessica and her client, there was no private communication between the two and her client was left without the assistance of counsel that could have greatly benefited him.

Ultimately, the resolution met all of my client's needs and was acceptable to the other party. It was not ideal for Jessica, but she had abandoned her client to stick with her strategy of trying to negotiate from a position of height.

Referral Power

Referral power is the ability to refer a decision in a negotiation back to someone who isn't in the room. This gives you bargaining power because it means that you can't be forced to concede by the other party – you always have the power to refer the decision to someone else. Many of us will have experienced how this source of bargaining power can work. You negotiate with someone and trade concessions to the point where it looks like you have a workable deal. Then they say, 'I'll just have to take that to [the board/client etc] for approval'. Or it may be the chairman who needs to approve it, or their line manager.

When they come back to you it's to tell you that this third party won't accept what has been discussed, or, worse still, requires further concessions in order to get the deal done. This puts you in some difficulty as you have already made more concessions than you wanted in order to get the deal to this stage. Furthermore, the other person, the source of the new requirements, is not in the room to argue with so you can't get at them in order to persuade them to accept your views. That's an example of referral power in action.

Network Power

This is the power to access a network in order to get more of what you want, perhaps access to a database of consumers, or access via social media to committed followers. This can give you an edge in a negotiation. When the music recommendation service Last FM was sold to CBS Interactive for US$240 million in 2007 it had not made a profit and its revenues from advertising were tiny. What it did have was access to thirty million signed-up users. That's a very powerful network and that is what CBS paid for. Alternatively your 'network' may make the other negotiator see you as more authoritative, expert or cool – we are often judged by the company we keep.[50] Latterly, the power of networks has been very evident in the unfolding of the Arab Spring which we mentioned in Chapter 2. You may also have access to an internal 'network' within an organisation which can give you extra bargaining power. All of us potentially have more 'network' power today in negotiations with employers, customers and suppliers because of our access to the information and data contained within the internet.

Numbers

Numbers can be a source of bargaining power. Everyone can understand how numbers in the traditional sense of financial strength can make a difference. In the English Premier League, Manchester City have spent almost £1 billion on players, management and facilities in order to transform themselves into league champions. Their spending power, deriving from the oil wealth of Sheikh Mansour, cannot currently be matched by any of their rivals and this gives them an edge in transfer negotiations. This not only affects the outcome when they bid against other clubs for the same player, it also affects transfers for other players in which Manchester City are not involved. If City put down a marker that they might be interested in a player, the selling club puts a higher value on that player when selling him to someone else.

It is worth noting, however, that while the power of numbers is undoubtedly a powerful bargaining source, it is not decisive in its own right because it is not the only bargaining ace. Players may choose other clubs because of their greater history (this gives clubs like Manchester United 'authority power') or because they think they are more likely to get game-time there (the reputation for playing youngsters gives Arsenal some 'market power' in the transfer market for younger players).

The power of numbers is not just about finances and commercial resources, though. It is also about the number of people you deploy in a negotiation. If you go into a negotiating room and you are outnumbered, you are automatically at a potential disadvantage. If there are four people on the other team and you are on your own, they have four times more thinking time than you have; four times as much mind power applied on their behalf. They can allocate one person to speak, another to observe, another to plan their approach, another to agree concessions – you have to handle all that on your own. So, if you go into a negotiating meeting and you are outnumbered, either get out of there or move to equalise the numbers. When you see footage of international treaty negotiations there are normally dozens of people lined up on each side of the table. Why? They can't all possibly have a speaking role, and how many experts does one side need? A lot of the time they are simply there literally to 'make up the numbers' so that one party doesn't feel at a disadvantage by being outnumbered by the other.

Relationship Power

If you already have a positive relationship with the person you are negotiating with, that is a source of bargaining power. This follows another of Cialdini's principles of influence, that of prior commitment.

When you have made a small commitment to a particular course of action you have an inbuilt desire to remain consistent to that course of action so as to justify your earlier decision. Once again, this is one of life's useful shortcuts which can enable people to avoid having to re-evaluate every decision constantly. This approach of consistency based on an initial commitment also works for two further reasons. Researchers have noted that it conveniently enables people to avoid confronting the consequences of making wrong decisions, by sticking with those decisions come what may. In addition, if people have made a commitment publicly, they are particularly inclined to stick with it so as to avoid losing face.

On this basis, professional salesmen and women wanting to sell you something try to get a foot in the door, knowing that if you will allow them this small commitment then a bigger one will follow. For example, perhaps retailers will ask you to enter into a written competition to endorse a particular product. They know that once you have done that you may well want to stick with that 'commitment' and go on to buy it. Written commitments are particularly valued by influencers (e.g. a written sales agreement) as this makes the commitment even stronger.

So, if you have an existing (positive) relationship with the other party – even if it's in relation to something quite small – you may be able to build on that commitment moving forward, because the other party will intuitively want to maintain that commitment.

Rules, Regulations or Standards

Having rules, regulations or standards on your side is a further source of bargaining power. It is always worth checking these as you may have the law on your side in a negotiation – for example competition law, or legal precedent, or a trademark, or you may have regulations on your side, such as a staff handbook. Have you ever heard an HR department sidestepping your request for a particular benefit by saying, 'We'd love to help but the staff handbook means we are just not allowed to'?

It may be that you have a standard set of terms that have become accepted in the marketplace, and you use this as your source of bargaining power. How many of us negotiate the small print of our mortgage or our insurance policies? Most of us don't bother because we anticipate that such terms have become institutionalised by the provider and so they will feel under no obligation to change them.

Here's a good example of the power of legal standards from technology start-up advisor and Biotech CEO Taffy Williams:

A syndicate of venture capital funds had agreed to a $16 million financing of a public company. They had conducted due diligence and negotiated the valuation of the company.

The final shareholder meeting to approve the deal was organised and all mailings of required documents took place in a timely and orderly manner.

The shareholders were enthusiastic even though they recognised the dilution would be significant.

The VCs had agreed to invest in the company due to a change in direction for the company – selling off old technology and devoting attention to new technology it had invented.

Three days before the annual meeting of the shareholders to approve all transactions and proceed to closure, one of the syndicate members contacted the company stating they would not fund the company! They provided no explanation. They were reminded that they had agreed and had executed all documents of the contractual arrangement. In addition, the syndicate was reminded that the shareholder meeting was only three days away and that all documents submitted to the shareholders and reviewed by the Security and Exchange Commission contained descriptions of the agreed deal.

A group of attorneys and shareholders began to explore syndication of a lawsuit for possible damages relating to the failure to close on the financing. Some rather strong discussions with several of the VC syndicate members took place over the following two months. The VC syndicate realised that a lawsuit was being considered and the funds to take legal action existed among the group of shareholders. It dawned on them that spending money in court on a case they might well lose versus funding the company as originally agreed were their only two options. In the end they agreed to stick by the original deal.

The standards that give you an edge may be less obvious than this. Most consumer-facing organisations will have Terms and Conditions, or other statements on their website, which will talk about customer satisfaction being a priority or putting consumers' interests first. Maybe they will have a vision statement or a charter for customer care. If you are having a dispute with a service provider it's worth taking the time to fish out these commitments as they also reveal an ace up your sleeve. A source of standards which you can then require the organisation to comply with.

As US negotiator Stuart Diamond points out in his authoritative book *Getting More* [51], sometimes these 'standards' are implicit rather than explicit. If you are in a restaurant there is an implicit standard that the staff will not be rude, that hot food will not arrive cold, that wine served will not be corked, that one set of customers will not be kept waiting longer than another. If you are in a restaurant and it falls short in any of these matters you could call it to account according to such standards. 'Is it your policy to serve customers with hot dishes that are stone cold?' would be a good way of expressing your dissatisfaction and negotiating a remedy. There are many such standards you can appeal to including punctuality, honesty, accuracy and non-discrimination. Appealing to standards to which the other party has previously committed also has the virtue of conforming with Cialdini's principle that we don't like to step away from a commitment we have already made – if we are already committed to a set of standards we want to maintain that position.

Be careful about assuming that matters such as 'fairness' or 'reasonableness' create enforceable standards of this kind, though. As we shall see when we look at Chapter 19, the problem with concepts like 'fairness' and 'reasonableness' is that they are not actually objective standards at all – we all have a subjective view of what is 'fair' or 'reasonable' in any particular circumstance.

I keep track of examples of the application of 'standards' in negotiations on my blog so you can read there current examples of this source of bargaining power, including its application to large organisations such as the one behind the 2012 London Olympics, LOCOG (the London Organising Committee of the Olympic and Paralympic Games).

Authority Power

Authority power is a further source of bargaining power. It stems from some kind of seniority that can be applied on your behalf. For example, you may have a small company but with a senior chairman who is a big cheese or a set of non-execs that makes people sit up. Having friends in high places would give you a source of bargaining power in your negotiations with others. You may have an unrivalled reputation for excellence either as an individual or as a company and this would give you a source of 'authority' bargaining power. Maybe it's as simple as having a respected qualification – an academic honour or a knighthood or a CBE. We have a natural respect for such badges of authority and this can translate itself into a bargaining ace for those who possess such authority. Again, this principle is supported by Cialdini as a deep sense of duty to 'authority' is another one of his six pillars of influence. Professor Milgram's famous experiment is also often cited as an example of this principle where, under the influence of an apparently approving authority figure, students were prepared to administer what they understood to be enormous electric shocks as a punishment to what they supposed were other erring students (who were in fact actors). Authority figures loom large in our life from an early age – parents, teachers, religious figures – and it seems that their influence persists into later life.

It is for this reason that con artists frequently like to pose as figures of authority – for example, as doctors, judges or professors, or even titled individuals. Uniforms also have the power to convey a sense of authority – even a civilian 'uniform' such as a well-cut suit. The trappings of authority have much the same effect. Apparently we are far less likely to 'honk' someone in an expensive car than someone driving a cheap one.

Authority can come in unexpected sizes and packages. Here's a good example of Charles Young, founder of the London Anti-Crime Education Service tipping the balance in a negotiation in court through his negotiating authority:

Jason Hill [seventeen] approached Charles Young with a request to assist him in his appearance in court, where he was appearing for breaching his youth-offending team order for the third time. Charles agreed to provide what help he could and attended Woolwich Crown Court as requested and introduced himself to the barrister. The barrister agreed to ask the judge if Charles could speak on behalf of Jason and explain the LACES programme and how this might help. The judge agreed to Charles speaking on behalf of Jason and Charles made the following points:

- I am an older version of J and have spent twenty years in prison as a result.
- Sixteen years ago I decided to set up the London Anti-Crime Education Service in order to prevent young people from following in my footsteps, using the benefits of the experiences I had been through.
- I currently tour schools and colleges and other organisations that cater for young people at risk of offending with a stage show centred around a mobile prison cell. This show demonstrates what prison is like and reasons not to go there.
- In recent times J has given considerable help with these shows, helping to erect the cell on stage and takes part as a serving young offender, wearing prison clothes and explaining his experiences that led him to imprisonment.
- I know that this is having a positive effect on him. Even though the youth-offending team have recommended that he is returned to a secure unit, I feel that with more time I can alter his train of thought and offending behaviour so that he can contribute in a positive way to his family, community and society in general.

Following an exchange of questions and answers, the judge agreed that he would revoke both court orders and defer sentence for four months, on the condition that Jason continued working closely with Charles Young and the LACES programme. This was agreed to and Jason was freed and remains free to this day.

Personal Power

Lastly, you always have your personal power as a negotiator. This is your *own* skill and ability as a negotiator; your skills at managing attitude, process and behaviour; your resourcefulness and creativity. In reading this book you are making an investment in your personal power as a negotiator. You will find you have more options, more choices and an ability to think through and plan your negotiations which those on the other team may not have. Even if all the other sources of bargaining power are ranged against you, you will still have your personal power as a negotiator – unless, that is, you choose to give it away.

I once negotiated a contract for a music producer with a young lawyer who I was dealing with for the first time. We spoke on the phone and when it came to discussing terms he said: 'I know all about your reputation as a negotiator, Clive, I don't suppose there's any point trying to negotiate with you ...' Actually, there *was* a point negotiating with me, because even if this young lawyer felt at a disadvantage I was open to negotiation, and he always had his personal skills as a negotiator to fall back on. But he chose to discount those skills and give them away in advance ... don't do that even if you think the bargaining power is ranged 10–1 against you, or you may get taken to the cleaners.

So, there you have eleven sources of bargaining power which, if you stop and analyse the situation, you may find available to you in almost all circumstances, and which will help you hold your own in negotiations.

Getting the bargaining power wrong can have costly consequences. Examples of this trait are readily found in contemporary business and you can read about them at www.cliverich.com.

One such example is AOL's purchase of the Bebo social network for kids for US$850 million in 2008. Just two years later the purchase had been such a disaster that Bebo had been sold to Criterion Capital Partners for less than US$10 million. The AOL/Bebo deal has since been branded by a BBC correspondent and economics and technology expert, Rory Cellan-Jones, as 'one of the worst decisions ever made in the dotcom era'. No doubt many things went wrong with the deal, but at its heart AOL must have incorrectly evaluated the bargaining power on both sides. AOL no doubt felt concern about missing out on the social networking boom and were anxious to tick this box. In this context, Bebo was perceived to hold a lot of aces – niche market power, network power (the power to access a network – literally, in this case) and expertise in this sector. But AOL also seemed to forget about the bargaining power it carried. As one of the world's largest ISPs it brought its own considerable scale, market power and network power to the table. No doubt there were other suitors for Bebo. Let us also not forget the frenzy that can build around hot digital properties. However, maybe AOL had sufficient bargaining power to negotiate a more competitive price for a company which had lots of users but had never turned a profit …

If you assess the bargaining power correctly then you may justifiably pick up extra confidence to tip you into a more positive mindset for the negotiation. When I hold seminars to coach negotiation there might be fifty or more people in the room. What's the bargaining power in the negotiation between me and all those people for their time and attention? They have the power of numbers – it's 50–1! If I was a black belt in karate I still couldn't physically stop them walking out if they wanted. They have scale and weight on their side. They have market power – there are other coaches they could go to if they wanted. However, I have some information and expertise they want. I also have my personal skills as a negotiator to rely on and some reputation in the market place. I would score the bargaining power in their favour but not by an unfeasible amount – maybe three aces to two. This helps give me confidence to handle the negotiation for their time and attention with the knock-on effects for the outcome from having a positive attitude. So, remember to marshal your bargaining power and use it effectively to counter situations where the other negotiator seems more powerful…

(PHYSICAL SIZE)

6

YOUR NEGOTIATING ATTITUDE, AND HOW TO CHANGE IT

Before we go further, have you filled in your attitude questionnaire at the app website closemydeal.co.uk? If you have, what did the results show you?

Which segment do you favour? Using, Fusing, Losing or Confusing?

Bearing in mind what you have read, and looking at your profile map, do you want to change your most common negotiating attitude? If you are a fuser, that's great. If you are displaying any of the other attitudes frequently it may be time for a rethink.

Some people look at their chart and say that they can't ever imagine changing their attitude. My feeling is that it's always possible to adapt and develop your attitude, and we shall look at that possibility now.

Turning Around a Bad Attitude

Maybe even looking at the bargaining power isn't enough to convince you to bring a positive attitude to the negotiation. Maybe you struggle with some of those anxious or hesitant attitudes that we identified under the rather blunt heading of 'losing'. Is there anything you can do about this? Yes, there is!

As we discussed earlier, whichever theory of psychology we subscribe to, these negative states of mind can be the result of our own filters operating on the way in which we experience the world. These filters can stem from patterns of thinking ingrained as a result of our upbringing or our experiences. As we have seen, we are more than capable of making cognitive mistakes – generalising wrongly from individual experiences and creating negative self-messages. For example, we might exaggerate the meaning of an event during a negotiation; or we might oversimplify events in previous negotiations as good or bad; or we might draw general conclusions which are not backed up by the evidence; or we might disregard important, positive aspects of an experience in favour of our negative view.

This applies in many situations, not just negotiating, as this brief example of my own about a friend illustrates:

I bumped into a friend of mine from college recently at a cricket match. It was great to see him again after many years, and we exchanged catch-up stories enthusiastically. It was as though there had never been a gap. I was surprised to find that several years ago he had moved to a neighbourhood very close to where I live – no more than a couple of miles away. He knew where I lived yet he hadn't been in touch. It turned out that he was apprehensive about contacting me. He told me that the last time I had seen him he had come round to my house with another friend on a Sunday evening and felt he had committed a terrible social faux pas by overstaying his welcome until late at night. We had very young children at the time who often kept us up at night so we needed our sleep. He had been so convinced that I would be cross about that that he had therefore avoided getting in touch, even though he had lived close by for a number of years. Not only was I not cross, I couldn't even remember the incident he was talking about!

Whether you believe our states of mind and our consequent behaviour are the result of cognitive processes, behavioural responses or a combination of the two, you have a *choice* as to the attitude you bring to negotiations. You are able to influence your own attitude. Your brain is not necessarily able to distinguish between 'states' which are 'real' and those which you *choose* to experience. Therefore it's perfectly possible to change your internal soundtrack and influence your own state of mind, and this is what you have to do first when you negotiate – influencing others begins with influencing yourself. What you need to do is deliberately substitute more positive messages for these negative messages and your brain won't spot the difference. NLP (neuro-linguistic programming) focuses a lot on that possibility – it is the 'programming' part of the discipline. However, you don't have to follow NLP to intuit that changing the way you think about something from a negative to a more resourceful approach can be helpful.

Challenging Internal Language

One way of doing this is to challenge your own language in thinking about a subject. Let's take the statement we earlier identified with losers – 'I always make a mess of this kind of thing – they must think I'm really stupid'. As we have seen, the thoughts which create this kind of pattern are often the product of generalisations, deletions or distortions of our actual experiences. We can challenge those thoughts with questions such as:

- 'Do I *always* make a mess of this?'
- 'Have I never negotiated successfully? Ever?'
- 'What kind of thing are we talking about?'
- 'What do I mean by a mess?'
- 'How do I create a mess?'
- 'How do I know I create a mess?'

- 'How well does it need to go in order not to be a mess?'
- 'Who are "they"?'
- 'Why must they think I am stupid?'
- 'How can I be sure of that?'
- 'What do I want them to think about me?'

These kinds of questions help reconnect a person with the reality of their experience so that they can recode that experience more positively.

Alternatively, you can recode your beliefs about a particular situation incrementally. I don't suggest that this is like turning on a switch from negative to positive, but you can get there if you take it step by step. Let's take that last message and see how we can go from 'I always make a mess of this kind of thing – they must think I'm really stupid' to a more positive message, through a series of replacement beliefs. To do this you don't even have to actually hold these beliefs – you can just presuppose that you hold these beliefs even though they are new to you. Imagine this sequence, starting from that negative assumption that you always make a mess of it:

- 'Although it may not be easy I can change my attitude to negotiation.'
- 'I don't have to do this for life, but I can try and do it for this one negotiation coming up.'
- 'I have prepared well for this negotiation.'
- 'I have some good people on my team – we are all well rehearsed.'
- 'I believe passionately in the product/service/proposition we are negotiating about – it really can add value for the other team.'
- 'I did have a successful negotiation just last month and I can draw some confidence from that – why shouldn't I have another one this time?'

- 'I believe the other team has overlooked a crucial piece of market information which I have. I also have a lot of expertise in this area. These two things give me some extra bargaining power.'
- 'Thinking about it, although I am right to be concerned, there is no reason why this shouldn't work out okay.'
- 'Even if things don't work out as I want it's not the end of the world and it doesn't mean I've failed.'
- 'In any event, they probably have plenty of other things to think about than whether I am stupid or not.'
- 'On that basis I'm going to give it my best shot and go for it.'
- 'I'm quite looking forward to it now – it's giving me a chance to show I've made progress as a negotiator.'
- 'I actually believe I can get what I want from this.'

You can try this sort of exercise to address any faulty internal message which is causing you anxiety. You can also use it to address internal negative messages if you are a 'user' who habitually takes advantage of 'the other side'. So, if your unhelpful starting belief is 'people who disagree with me in a negotiation are completely wrong and I should punish them by ignoring their needs' then you could use this kind of step-by-step exercise to move towards a more positive attitude:

- 'When I punish people it takes a lot of my energy, even if I'm right.'
- 'It also doesn't move negotiations forward and I do want this deal to work.'
- 'I could try just on this occasion to overlook my annoyance when people disagree with me.'
- 'Okay, I will make more of an effort to listen to them this time.'

- 'If that helps me get a better deal I've lost nothing.'
- 'I can still tell the other side I disagree with them.'
- 'Let's see what happens: it may be that if I listen more to them they will listen more to me anyway.'
- 'Okay, I'm going to experiment with seeing if I can get more of what I want in return for listening to what they need.'
- 'I'm quite looking forward to this now. I like this kind of challenge.'

Outcome Generation

You can also start from the other end of the process – the outcome you desire – and work backwards from there. NLP specialists are big fans of creating well-formed outcomes for themselves. If you programme yourself to think about a positive outcome, you are increasing the chances of that happening. If your desired outcome is a positive negotiating meeting, with everybody shaking hands and smiling and going out the door knowing that they have done a good deal, then focus on that outcome. Your unconscious mind does not distinguish between what is imagined and what is real, so the more effort you put into envisaging a positive outcome the more your mind may believe that is what is happening and the more it will enable you to act as though that is what you are obtaining.

It works the other way, too. If you worry about negative outcomes then you are programming yourself to make those happen. If you tell yourself *not* to worry the same thing will happen. Your unconscious mind cannot recognise a negative, so if you programme yourself not to worry about negotiating you are actually programming yourself to do just that. The operation of this kind of filter on the world is sometimes described as 'moving towards' thinking rather than 'moving away'. Those who hold positive outcomes move towards what they want by imagining what it would be like to achieve those outcomes. Those who focus on obstacles or problems in the way of a positive outcome 'move away' from what they want and are likely instead to achieve the negative outcomes they are worried about.

Anchors

Finally, you can also fire 'anchors' which bring about states of mind or attitudes that you desire. This is an NLP technique in which you link the attitude you want to access to a special signal which stimulates that attitude. Whenever you reproduce this stimulus you automatically go into that state. So, if you were seeking to reproduce a state of confident co-operation you might recall an experience when you felt this. It might have nothing to do with negotiating. Maybe you felt this attitude when you were part of a successful swimming team, or cooking a successful meal with other members of the family. By recalling the intensity of this experience (including the sights, sounds, smells and feelings associated with it) you can store that attitude. You can then access that productive attitude whenever you need it by linking it to a simple trigger (maybe pressing your thumb and forefinger together or imagining touching in your pocket that medal you won when you were part of the swimming team.) 'Firing the anchor' in this way immediately generates that positive attitude for you in the present moment.

So, whatever unhelpful attitude you are bringing to the negotiation, you can substitute that for a more positive approach and turn yourself from 'using' or 'losing' into 'fusing'. And if all that doesn't work you still have one or two other options. You can delegate the negotiation to someone else who has the attitude you need for a particular negotiation. This is one reason why people use lawyers, managers or agents to negotiate for them. They know that such people – for whom negotiation is a dispassionate experience – may bring a less anxious attitude to the task than they themselves can. Alternatively, you can bring someone in to be part of your team who displays the attitude you need. If their positive attitude is stronger than your anxieties, their presence will give you confidence and may help you shift your own outlook in the right direction.

You now have a grasp of one of the three links in the chain of success, negotiating attitude. It's time to move on to the second link in the chain, managing the negotiating process.

THE
NEGOTIATION
CHAIN

PART TWO

NEGOTIATING PROCESS

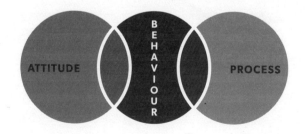

7

NEGOTIATING PROCESS – MANAGING THE STAGES OF SUCCESS

Negotiation process is the second part of the chain of effective negotiation. It is all about the overall 'structure' of the negotiation. Anyone can understand that a negotiation normally has a beginning and an end but most people don't realise that there are normally seven stages of any negotiation. People don't always apply them in the right order, and are often very confused about which stage they are at. This can create a rather haphazard negotiation in which each side is behaving as though it is at a different stage of the negotiation. Often people leave out some stages altogether. However, if a stage is missed out then the parties are usually doomed to have to revisit it until they get it right before they can move on. Where are you in the process? If you know this you will automatically have an advantage over someone who doesn't. If you don't then you may just operate one default stage throughout the negotiation – the chaos stage. Before we unpack those seven stages, if you haven't already done so I encourage you to go back to the closemydeal website and fill in the questionnaire on your own approach to handling negotiating process.

8

PREPARATION

Time-less

The preparation stage of any negotiation is frequently overlooked, as people feel they are too busy to invest time thinking about the deal in advance. One of the downsides of our interconnected world is that people are never 'off'. They are constantly available by mobile phone, text, instant messaging, email and Skype. They can participate in endless meetings either face to face, or by teleconference or video conference. I've seen colleagues on their BlackBerry at the beach and at family meals. I've had business calls from people who, judging by the sound effects, were clearly in the loo. I'm sure I have been guilty of similar behaviour, caught up in the apparent urgency of modern business communication. The demands of modern competition make us feel as if we should always be available and make us fear that we might be missing something if we are out of the loop. All of this militates against taking time out to think about preparing for a negotiation. However, if you miss out preparation, then you are preparing to miss out.

Here's a simple illustration from publicist Walter on the importance of preparation:

I walked up to a sunglasses stall at a street market in London. There was a particular pair I liked which were priced at £20. The policy was no refunds after purchase, but that didn't worry me. 'I'll be clever,' I thought, and went straight in – no preparation was needed. Or so I thought. 'I'll give you £15 cash. That's my final offer,' I said firmly to the trader. To my surprise he smiled and said 'Deal'. I was delighted. It was only as I walked away that I saw a big sign above the stall: 'Special Offer: All sunglasses £15 for Today Only.' Ahem …

The Bare Necessities

It is essential in negotiations to spend some time in advance planning. If you don't you set yourself up for a worse outcome.[52] If you just grope around in the dark you are likely to trip over. Here are a few things you might want to bear in mind.

First things first:

- Who is going to be on your team? Are there internal stakeholders who need to participate? Do you need any experts?
- What roles are your team members going to play? (e.g. is someone going to lead, someone else listen and observe, someone look out for opportunities to create solutions?)
- Who in your team is authorised to make concessions? This is essential: only one member of the team should be authorised to give points away otherwise confusion will soon reign.

- Do you need any materials prepared in advance, possibly to send to the other side?
- Who is on the other team and what roles are they likely to play? Have they worked together before?
- How would you describe the personalities of the people on the other team? What kind of behaviours do they tend to display?
- Is there any history (good or bad) between the parties which is likely to have a bearing?
- Is anyone on their team difficult? If so, why?
- What negotiating attitude do you want to bring to the negotiation and does that contrast with the attitude you think *they* will bring? Does anybody's attitude need to change?
- What climate or atmosphere do you want for the negotiation and will they want the same?
- Where will the negotiation take place and over what period of time?
- How will you create the agenda – on your own or with the other party?

In the thick of it:

- What are their objectives likely to be and what is motivating them (e.g. 'why' do they want those objectives?). Will different members of their team have different motivations?
- What are your objectives and what is motivating you?
- What concessions are available for you to give to them or for them to give to you?
- Are there any concessions available that wouldn't cost much but would be particularly valuable to them?
- What's the balance of the bargaining power? Who holds the majority of 'aces'?

Possible outcomes:

- What's your ideal position on the deal (price, quantity, delivery date, etc) and what's their likely ideal position? What's their likely bottom line?
- What's your bottom line, below which you would walk away? The space between ideal position and bottom line gives you your room in which to negotiate, or
- What will you do if you can't get a deal done – what's your Plan B? or
- What is the worst thing that could happen to you if the deal doesn't get done? or
- What is the worst thing that could happen to you if you *do* get the deal done?

Those last four items are really just alternative ways of looking at the same question – at what point would you walk away? It's much better to think about this moment when you are planning rather than when you are in the heat of the haggle. You will find it much harder to be objective then. Traditionally, people put together a 'bottom line' position based on likely points arising in the deal, beyond which they tell themselves they will stop negotiating. Others prefer to establish their 'best alternative to a negotiated agreement' as a benchmark against which to measure whether or not they should keep talking. Sometimes this is referred to by negotiating academics by the acronym BATNA.[53] They prefer it to having a 'bottom line' because it is not tethered to a predetermined set of issues arising out of the negotiation, and so can be compared to other potential outcomes of the negotiation that you hadn't anticipated at the preparation stage. Studies say that having a good BATNA can change both your own and the other team's perception of your value[54] – it can make them feel you have potential 'scarcity' value and so become a source of bargaining power for you.

Others prefer you to consider a WATNA – what's the worst alternative to a negotiated agreement that could happen to you if you failed to get a deal done with this particular partner? If the offer you are considering is worse than your worst alternative if the deal falls apart, you should certainly be taking that worst alternative instead. I actually prefer to consider the last of the above alternatives – what's the worst outcome that could take place if the deal *does* get done. I don't have an acronym for this, but I find it's a very useful way of looking at a deal. Many people enter into agreements without thinking them through all the way to the end. They focus on what they would like the outcome of the agreement to be, but not on what could happen if the deal gets signed but then goes wrong. Statistically, this is quite likely to happen, so it's worth giving some thought to the possibility of how you would feel and what you would do if the worst realistic outcome you can imagine came to pass. This doesn't mean being a pessimist – I am by nature a 'glass half-full' person. It just means making a realistic assessment of what could go wrong assuming that the deal is agreed. Now combine that possibility with the position on the table – say a 'take it or leave it' ultimatum from the other negotiator – and compare that combination to just 'leaving it'. Which sounds least attractive? Entering into the agreement on the terms proposed with the possibility of that worst outcome occurring, or just 'leaving' it? This is a very good way of knowing when to stop the negotiation – if the current deal offer and its associated worst possible risk sounds worse than just stopping, then bale out.

Here's an example of someone not considering the worst thing that could happen if the deal got done:

In 1973 Colonel Tom Parker went to RCA with a visionary deal. Parker was Elvis Presley's manager. He wasn't really a colonel, he was an opportunist. He had come to America as a penniless

Dutch immigrant and managed to acquire the title of 'Colonel'. Parker had decided he would sell all the Elvis masters to RCA in return for a one-time payment of US$5.4 million. No longer would RCA have to pay royalties to Elvis on each record sold; they would simply have to pay the one-off lump sum and that would be it forever. No doubt the Colonel was delighted when RCA accepted the deal, and the King was equally ecstatic about receiving his share of what by the standards of the day was a very large amount of money. Yet this was a classic case of not thinking a deal through right to the end. Elvis went on to sell millions of records. After his death in 1979 sales continued unabated. Had Parker negotiated the royalty rate upwards instead he would have earned far more than his share of US$5.4 million, probably right through to his death in 1997. Some estimate that sales since that buyout deal would have earned Elvis some US$500 million, of which US$320 million would have been earned since his death. Under the rather old-fashioned management deal which Parker had in place with the King, the Colonel's share of that would have been 50 per cent. Think through your worst possible outcome from doing the deal on the terms proposed – it will certainly help you judge when to stay in a negotiation and when to walk away.

As you can see, this kind of preparation exercise cannot really be done in the two minutes during which you are travelling down in the lift to the first negotiating meeting. Once you are in the negotiation live, you won't have either the time or the distance to think about these issues properly for the first time.

Out of this process of preparation comes your negotiating plan. This is your navigation tool through the negotiation. Note that this does not mean that you never *change* your plan. Clearly you can only anticipate so much in advance and you can only know what you know. Other factors may emerge during the course of your negotiation which make you want to change your plan in some way. That's normal. You may find, for example, that the ideal outcome you negotiated with yourself in advance of the negotiation needs to be altered because the other negotiator has raised issues you hadn't anticipated, or because an additional piece of bargaining power has emerged which sways you one way or the other.

The following contribution from corporate and regulatory attorney, Michael Garallek, shows how your original aims and desired outcomes may need to be adjusted as circumstances change:

My client in this story, Burt, was facing disciplinary sanctions from a financial regulator which would invariably involve a suspension from Burt being able to exercise his professional activities. It had been alleged that he had not acted in a client's best interest, a charge he denied. We decided that the best course of action was to negotiate a settlement with the regulator. From the outset, Burt wanted to play hardball and we planned that he should accept only a very limited period of suspension. It was clear that the period was well below what the regulator was seeking and, if we set it as our ceiling, we would have ended up in court. Instead of pressing the issue we asked for information to substantiate the regulator's version of events.

Unexpectedly, during the course of this information exchange Burt's company was sold and he found himself out of work. Burt suddenly had a lot more free time on his hands and now had an interest in serving a suspension as quickly as possible (which allowed him the time to find and secure a new job). We changed our plan and were also able to trade off accepting the suspension period suggested by the regulator for a lower monetary penalty.

So, plans can be adjusted. However, having a plan is still much better than not having one. By way of analogy, think about taking a long car journey before the advent of Satnav. If you were driving from London to Northumberland for the first time (a distance of some 350 miles) you would not simply have jumped into the car and said, 'Let's just head north and see what happens.' You would have planned your route. Of course, if you encountered road works or heavy traffic you might have altered your planned route. Maybe you would have taken an unscheduled break if you experienced adverse weather. You would still have been better off than if you had no planned route at all – as my wife and I once found out when we did actually head to Northumberland from London for the first time on a rainy Friday evening. A journey we reckoned would end at around 11 p.m. continued till 3 a.m. the following day, requiring our rather puzzled hosts to stay up until that late hour so that they could give us local directions over the phone and welcome us when we arrived …

Planning also encourages success because, by working out your desired outcome, you can just focus on getting what you need from the negotiation rather than being distracted by emotional outbursts from the other party or the need to prove who is 'right' in a negotiation.

Preparation *does* work. I know of a negotiation between two large technology companies where, for six months, one company ran a preparation room. In that room they appointed shadow negotiators to represent the other party. The shadow negotiators would rehearse regularly as though they were in planning meetings for the other team. They would consider what the other party might need, say and do. Many of the shadow negotiators had previous experience of working for the other team so they knew how it might think. The shadow negotiators would then run practice 'negotiation' meetings with those of their own colleagues who were actually doing the negotiation for real. This was fantastic preparation. You don't necessarily need to go to such lengths, but sustained, meaningful preparation is vital.

Preparation is especially important if you are engaged in team negotiations. It is vital that all the team members are equally well prepared. If they are not, the other party will almost uncannily gravitate towards the team member who is least well prepared, as they will correctly perceive that person as the weakest link in your chain. Or you will look as if you don't know what you are doing as a team – not a good look.

This story from Chris West, then a director of Industrial Market Research Ltd, illustrates how being equally prepared across your team is so important:

Two colleagues were negotiating a deal during which the potential client asked whether a specific and slightly contentious topic would be included in the project. In unison, one colleague said 'yes' and the other said 'no'. Amazed at their own contradiction, the first colleague tried to correct himself and said 'no'. Simultaneously the other colleague corrected himself and said 'yes'. End of negotiation …

When I asked other colleagues and friends whether they had any negotiating insights or anecdotes they wanted to contribute to this book, many of those I received were about the importance of preparation. I've therefore included a selection of them at www. cliverich.com if you want to be further convinced. Or you can listen to the wise words of my Russian grandmother who always maintained that 'an ounce of prevention is worth a pound of cure'.

9

CLIMATE SETTING

This is the second stage of negotiating, and, again, it's often a stage that is skipped altogether. In what atmosphere do you want the negotiation to take place? There are generally four choices:

(i.) A warm climate – very open and friendly, where the mood is relaxed and cooperative.

(ii.) A cool climate – very objective and data-driven, where a methodical process is what is important. There might not be much ill temper with a cool climate, but there won't be many laughs either.

(iii.) A hostile climate – very pressured and fast-moving. The atmosphere will be tense and may be emotionally charged.

(iv.) A cheeky climate – a bit wacky and off the wall. Anything goes in this kind of climate – the more exotic and unusual the atmosphere the better.

People sometimes find the subject of climate setting rather confusing. This may be because they are very used to operating in a climate they simply set by default, either because it's a cultural norm or because it's just a climate that suits their personal business style. However, each of these climates can be useful at different times and for different negotiations. For example a 'hostile' climate might suit disputes about contracts where one party is accusing the other of wrongdoing – there's no point being friendly and cooperative if you are going to make that sort of accusation. Industrial disputes and treaty negotiations often take place in a 'cool' climate – it's all about the process and the methodology. Climate treaty negotiators have, typically, chosen a 'cool climate' for their climate negotiations. If only they could achieve the same result for the rest of the planet …

Different climates also suit different types of individual – a cheeky climate might suit deals with highly creative individuals who could be bored by a cool climate and turned off by a hostile climate. 'Cheeky' might also work where you want to make a point that hits home without being aggressive. When the advertising agency Saatchi and Saatchi were pitching for the British Rail account, they famously started the meeting by keeping their prospective clients waiting in a dirty room, with inadequate provisions – a few curly sandwiches and stale crisps. When the client lost patience and was preparing to leave, the agency explained that what the client had just experienced was exactly how their customers currently perceived the British Rail brand – associating it with late service and poor delivery. It was a risky and wacky way of starting the negotiating meeting, but it worked and Saatchis got the account. 'Warm' climates are often favoured by individuals in 'informal' businesses such as music or TV. These businesses have often been constructed around a creative core which needs flexibility, trust and openness in order that creativity can thrive. That desired atmosphere then spills out into the rest of the business which supports the creative endeavour.

The point about climate setting is that you always have a *choice*. It is therefore worth thinking carefully about climate as, when climate goes wrong, or each party has a different view of what the climate should be, it has a very disruptive effect on people's behaviour and outcomes. It can make people very defensive and uncomfortable if, for example, they were expecting to attend a meeting with a warm, open climate and instead it turns out that the other negotiator wanted to create a hostile climate or a very cool, calculated climate. They might become very withdrawn and unresponsive, or even break off the negotiation altogether, believing that there isn't a 'fit' between the parties. It's also important to bear in mind that climate continues to be a factor throughout the negotiation. So, it can start off right and then go wrong subsequently – for example, if one party is revealed to have acted without integrity or to have told a lie.

When you can see that the climate has gone wrong, or hasn't been set appropriately, it's good to go back and reset the climate. This is an example of what I mean by the parties having to go back a stage until they have got that stage right.

Here's a story of climate resetting from my own experience:

I remember one joint venture negotiation I was involved with where the atmosphere had started warm and friendly, but a chill had then descended after one of our negotiators had inadvertently exerted referral bargaining power in order to disallow an important concession which the other team thought had been agreed. Cue some bad temper and recriminations. At the next negotiating meeting it was half-term and my six-year-old stepdaughter was at the meeting. Like many children she used to think that coming to the office was a very grown up and exciting thing to do. The other party had come in to the meeting looking very serious and rather grumpy, but they were unable to withstand the charms of a six-year-old turning cartwheels, climbing all over the sofas and asking them if they wanted to be a dinosaur. An unintentional shift in the climate to 'cheeky' changed the mood of the meeting. After that we were all friends again and were able to move swiftly to closure ...

Issues to Resolve at the Climate Stage

Whichever climate you choose, there are some important issues to be addressed at the climate-setting stage which shape the whole of the subsequent negotiation. These issues are:

- Who will attend the meetings?
- What is the timetable for the negotiation?
- Where will the negotiation take place?
- What is the agenda for the negotiation?
- How much negotiating authority does everybody have?

These issues sound obvious, but often negotiations lurch off without one or more of these matters being addressed, and the parties subsequently have to go back to square one and address them. You can imagine the confusion and uncertainty that is created where, for example, parties have different, unresolved views on what the agenda should be;[55] [56] or one party thinks the negotiation should only take a couple of two-hour meetings, but hasn't cleared this with the other, who thinks that a proper negotiation of the issues could take four months; or one party is completely unprepared for the attendance of someone on the other team who they weren't expecting. Confusion can especially be created if the issue of 'negotiating authority' is not resolved in advance. If one participant is seeking to exercise referral power by keeping a key decision maker out of the room then the other negotiating team needs to be mindful of that at the beginning of the negotiation. If they find out three-quarters of the way through that the person who needs to make the decision is not present, they are likely to be annoyed as well as dismayed at all the concessions they have given away without being any closer to the outcome they wanted.

In addressing these matters you can use a style which is consistent with the climate you want to create. For example, if you want to create a warm, open climate then these matters are best decided together. A good question to ask might be 'How would you like to handle the process of the negotiation?' In relation to location, if you are going for a warm and open climate you might want somewhere neutral and comfortable – a round table in an informal setting will make for a far more collaborative atmosphere than a large rectangular table in the boardroom. If you are creating a hostile climate then you might be far more peremptory about the way these matters are decided. For example, a statement such as 'My office, 9 a.m. on Monday – I'll give you the agenda then – and bring your cheque book' would probably achieve your aim of creating a hostile atmosphere. If you are creating a cool climate, then you would be addressing these issues in a very formal way – in writing no doubt, with lots of cc's to all the stakeholders. If you want to address them in a cheeky manner you are limited only by your imagination.

Here's an experience of my own with regard to a more unorthodox style of climate setting:

When I first applied for a job in the music business I had an informal interview with an idiosyncratic lawyer for one of the leading independent record companies of the time. When I walked into the room he was in the middle of a negotiating phone call with another lawyer. He ushered me to a seat and carried on his phone call. I was not a little surprised to find that he began to sing his proposed terms down the phone in a splendid operatic voice. This is the business for me, I thought, fresh from the Spartan and gloomy rigours of Bar school and pupillage as a trainee barrister ... In case you are wondering, that kind of behaviour would count as creating a 'cheeky' climate – even in the music business ...

Whichever climate you choose, just remember to pick the right climate for the right occasion ...

TOO MUCH WHALE MUSIC?

10

THE MORE YOU GIVE THE MORE YOU GET

Wants and Needs

Exploring wants and needs is the third stage of the negotiating process. Wants and needs are two different things. 'Wants' are organisational requirements that often drive the content of the negotiation. These may include requirements concerning delivery dates, quantities, cash, royalties, territorial rights, length of term and so on. 'Needs' are the personal drivers that underpin the negotiation. They are normally the answer to the question '*Why* do they want those things?'

'Needs' are more important than 'wants' because it is almost invariably the personal needs of the parties that will determine whether a deal gets done. This applies to almost all negotiations. That is one of the reasons why the surface issues – the normal 'content' of the negotiation – are the least important ingredients of the negotiation. That doesn't mean that organisational wants should be ignored. What it means is that the best way to address the organisational wants on both sides is to work out the needs that underpin them.

There are many reasons why someone might 'need' the things they say they 'want'. The humanist psychologist Abraham Maslow identified a general hierarchy of human 'needs' based upon self-actualisation which many readers will be familiar with and which looks like this:

> Achievement
> Respect
> Belonging
> Reassurance
> Survival

Maslow argued that these needs on the list have to be satisfied by each person from the bottom upwards. So we start off with survival needs, then move through to fulfilling our reassurance needs, then on to our need to belong to something. After that we move on to fulfilling our respect needs and, lastly, we look to fulfil our self-actualising achievement needs. Maslow located these needs primarily in the physical world – so survival needs revolve around food, shelter, clothing and warmth, and reassurance needs cover issues such as personal security, health and wellbeing and financial security. There has been much academic debate of this subject since the 1940s when Maslow first proposed his hierarchy and various different classifications and descriptions of human needs. Some academics[57] have argued that needs of the kind that Maslow described lie at the base of all concern hierarchies.[58] Some have argued that this hierarchy is too simplistic, and that in any event needs such as these are not necessarily satisfied on a strictly hierarchical basis. Professor Steven Reiss has created a longer list of sixteen human motivations, among them some from Maslow's hierarchy, but which also includes honour, idealism, order, power, social status, curiosity and vengeance.

Maslow's basic hierarchy of needs can be translated to the negotiating environment as well. Certainly other commonly stated negotiating needs can often be traced back to Maslow's classification. These include Reiss's list together with requirements such as stability, control, economic wellbeing, good relationships, social identity, ideological concerns, respect for tradition, and aversion to risk, as well as other commonly expressed needs like freedom or justice. We don't need to decide which of these academic theories is correct, and no doubt there are many other types and subdivisions of human need not catered for by these categorisations. What is important, though, is to understand that human needs drive negotiation as much as other forms of human endeavour. Let us take Maslow's original classification to illustrate this. If I am negotiating with a survival need I may be desperate – I may be worried that if this deal doesn't work I am going to get fired or my business is going to go bust. If I am negotiating with reassurance needs it may be that I want to be able to trust you, I will want to feel that if I work with you then everything is going to be okay. It may also be that I don't want to lose face – this kind of reassurance need is extremely common in negotiations as the parties struggle with the need to reconcile the content of the agreement with the preservation of their own self-esteem.

Sometimes the reassurance required can seem quite small to you, but still make a difference to the person you're negotiating with as this anonymous contributor indicates:

On one occasion a particular customer seemed more preoccupied with using a particular colour-coded spreadsheet for presenting the figures. We adopted the customer's spreadsheet, the customer agreed to use our figures. Everybody was happy.

If I am negotiating with belonging needs then I will want to feel that as a result of the deal I have joined something or become a part of some enterprise or venture. If I negotiate with achievement needs I may be looking to break boundaries as a result of the negotiation – maybe I will want to create some unique and innovative arrangement that has never been tried before. Entrepreneurs often have this particular negotiating need. If I negotiate with respect needs, I may need esteem or to be in the limelight as a consequence of the deal. Or I may need a much smaller sign of recognition – an apology, perhaps, or to know that I have been listened to, or just an acknowledgement that I am doing a good job. If you are negotiating with an official (a traffic warden, say, or someone in a public sector bureaucracy or a customer service role) then recognition can be a very powerful thing. Often these people receive a lot of abuse and complaints; they are only too conscious that they are small cogs in a big wheel.

A little recognition that they are doing their best or you appreciate their efforts can go a long way when you are negotiating with them. This story comes from PR expert, Anita:

My husband had booked for us both to go on the London Eye one Saturday afternoon, and, as part of our ticket, we would receive a glass of champagne on the 'flight'. Having arrived at the London Eye with plenty of time before our flight, we were greeted by a huge queue, which was moving very slowly. As time ticked on, others in the queue started getting very irate and as we neared the counter, a man in front started aggressively shouting at staff, complaining that he had missed his flight and 'what were they going to do about it?'. They apologised but he insisted that he wasn't waiting any longer and wanted to go on the next flight. He demanded a full refund, which they explained wouldn't be possible. They arranged for him to go on the next available flight (which required a short wait) and he angrily stormed off.

As we got to the counter, the employee apologised for the wait, and explained that as well as being extremely busy, there had been a problem with the card machines, causing an additional delay. We told him there was no problem. We were sure he had to put up with this abuse a lot and we felt a bit sorry for him. We just wanted to be able to go on the London Eye that day so we said we were happy to wait to go on the next available flight. The employee then apologised that there were also no more 'champagne' flights available that day – so he could only offer a normal flight or could put us on a champagne flight the following day. We agreed that we were happy to go on a normal flight, although my husband asked if we could be reimbursed for the ticket difference and if they could offer us anything for the inconvenience. Result? We were given a whole bottle of champagne as well as a refund of the difference!

Identifying Motivations

If two people are negotiating, one or more of these needs will be driving the agenda. Superficially the discussion may be about organisational wants such as price or the size of the advance, but underneath these needs will be the important factor. For example, if someone requests an advance of £50,000 there may be various needs underpinning that request. They may want £50,000 because it will solve a desperate cash crisis. Or maybe if they receive £50,000 it will provide reassurance and enable them to trust the other negotiator. Perhaps it will make them feel that they now belong to the club of partners or customers who are able to command an advance of £50,000. Maybe they will feel respected if they receive an advance of £50,000; or perhaps they will feel they have achieved something by getting £50,000 – maybe they will be the first partner with whom the other negotiator has agreed that, or maybe the £50,000 will be put towards some innovative and ground-breaking project. It may be that more than one of these needs applies at the same time, or that at a conscious level they are not aware of these motivations. The individual participant negotiating with them may have their own individual needs, and the organisation they work for may have some negotiating needs of its own.

If there are teams working on the negotiation for each party then different team members may have different underlying motivations. This means there may be more than one set of needs on each team and they may fluctuate as the negotiating proceeds – either because some needs become more of a priority than others or because others emerge as the negotiation progresses. Whatever the reason, if you understand the motivations of the people you are negotiating with you will be much better placed to cut through the usual arid debate about organisational 'wants' and focus on what will really get the deal done – namely, meeting those underlying interests of each participant.

A simple example from my own background may help:

When I was working on securing the sponsorship for a major TV show from a handset manufacturer it became apparent that the most important thing for them was membership of the same successful showbiz 'club' as the show itself. By belonging to this club they felt that they gained some of the attributes of the show; it made their brand seem even sexier, a talking point, a must-have product. They were right, too, as the association drove unprecedented demand for their handsets in the run-up to the Christmas selling season. So, integrating them in the body of the show was more important to them than the price, even though 'price' is often the main focus in sponsorship deals. This applied to the company as a whole and the executives negotiating on their behalf. This kind of 'belonging' need is often an important underlying feature of such sponsorship agreements ...

Here's another good example of needs being matched from wireless industry executive, Jeremy Copp – in this case a mutual reassurance need for risk management on both sides of the table:

We were looking to license a software component from a third party to include in our product. It provided an important piece of functionality for us, and potentially offered us a differentiator in the market.

Our preferred supplier was a relatively small start-up company for whom the project to develop and customise their software to meet our needs would occupy a significant proportion of their team. The upside for the supplier was in per-unit licence fees that would flow when our customers shipped product that included our (and the supplier's) software. There would naturally be a time lag before this happened and volumes built up.

All the technical and key commercial terms of the licensing had been agreed but the negotiation foundered on more of a risk management and strategic issue.

From the supplier's side they wanted reassurance about the future revenue streams; if for any reason we ended up using alternative software then the future royalties could be compromised. They were betting a significant proportion of the company's growth on this relationship. They therefore asked that we used their software for this functionality on an exclusive basis. This was as important to them as the development fees.

We were concerned to ensure our supplier would be in a

position to deliver successfully to us in the timeframes we required, and that if there were any issues in supply we could seek alternative solutions to safeguard our own customer commitments. This was as important to us as the level of their development fees and other normal issues in a software development and licensing contract.

The solution was to agree on bilateral exclusivity: we would use their solution for this functionality exclusively for all the time they provided the software to us on an exclusive basis; if they licensed to anyone else then we would be free to choose an alternative supplier. This offered benefits to both parties:

- It maximised the supplier's opportunity to see royalty revenue streams from delivering our product.
- We had the assurance that their (resource-limited) team would focus solely on development and delivery to us.
- A positive benefit for us was that it also meant that our competitors would not have access to the same technology; if they did, then we would be free to find alternative ways to differentiate.

A lot of people struggle with the idea that negotiating should be about meeting the needs of the other side. At first sight it is, of course, far removed from the traditional view of negotiation as being all about winning, often at the expense of the 'opposition'. 'Users' reading this will be scoffing that this sounds far too altruistic and that people who feel this way about negotiating should leave deal making to the grown-ups and go off and hug some trees instead.

However, for the reasons we discussed in Chapter 1, negotiation has changed, and if it was ever right just to try and push people around and take advantage of them, that time has now passed. We live in an age when partnerships are required and negotiation reflects that. Moreover, there is another, more selfish, reason for focusing on the needs of the other side. It helps you get more of what you want in return. The more you are able to focus on meeting the needs of the other negotiator the more you will be able to get back in return. The more you give, the more you get. That is a rationale for behaving differently that even the most selfish negotiator should be able to understand.

The exploring phase of the negotiation should therefore be concerned largely with understanding the motivations of both parties. Note that this is not the same as making our own assumptions about what the other negotiator needs, or making assumptions about what we think they ought to need. Often when people say to me that they are focused on the other person's needs, what they are really focused on is their own assumptions as opposed to the reality of that person's motivations. An understanding of those needs really has to come from the other negotiator so that you know you are dealing with authentic needs rather than some fantasy version of those needs which you have dreamed up. You genuinely need to put yourself in the shoes of the other negotiator and work out where they pinch, rather than guessing what they need because it's more comfortable wearing your own shoes. This means that in the exploring phase you will test some of the assumptions about their needs that you may have made during your preparation.

Focusing on underlying psychological interests is not just a productive way of progressing negotiations; it helps to avoid a number of the pitfalls of negotiating over organisational wants, as we shall now discuss.

Change: The Fear Factor

Many people dislike change; it can make them feel frightened or anxious or just irritated because they are perfectly comfortable where they are. Anyone who has tried to argue for dramatic change in a large organisation will recognise this tendency. When you negotiate you are asking people to change something – the status quo which existed before the negotiation began and which they may be quite wedded to. If you just talk about the organisational consequences of the deal you propose, you will trigger all sorts of anxieties which are likely to surface in objections to the change represented by those proposals. It is more plausible that you are likely to be able to overcome any resistance to change if you are working with the psychological interests of the people affected by your offer. Dealing with their requirements for e.g. reassurance may make negotiating your proposals for new structures, new approaches, new objectives, new measurements of success seem much more palatable to them.

Uncomfortable Positions

Furthermore, if you negotiate solely over organisational wants a number of things happen. First, people start by adopting 'positions' – I want this delivery date or that quantity. It all goes steadily downhill from there. Once they have adopted a position the negotiation between them can easily descend into a battle of wills – who can force the other into accepting their position. At that point the negotiation can arouse strong emotions which get tangled up with the substantive issue. The fact that someone opposes your will can give the impression that they are attacking you personally.

The negotiation can then move on to an unproductive cycle of scoring points, blaming the 'other side' and behaving angrily. The fact that they are adopting a particular position in their own favour gives you no comfort that they are interested in your outcome so this intensifies the potential for emotional antipathy. We saw earlier how easy it is to become a 'confuser' in a negotiation and to carry forward misconceptions about the other side's intentions and behaviours. If we have decided that someone is against us, it's very easy to view each instance of their behaviour as supporting that interpretation whether that is objectively the case or not. So, negative emotional judgements about the other side are very easy to perpetuate once made. Once we head down this path it becomes tempting to dredge up the past as evidence of bad behaviour from the other person. 'Blamestorming' takes over. Previous disputes are aired with each party blaming the other for previous failures to reach agreement, rather than focusing on the future possibilities of working together – unfortunately this happens a lot in international negotiations such as the various incarnations of Middle East peace talks.

Moreover, once we are adopting positions it's quite common to want to add strength to our position by having other people publicly support it. If the negotiation is all about being more 'right' than someone else, having other people say that we are right becomes important. This is when people start playing to the gallery. You see this a lot in political negotiations and industrial disputes. The participants brief the media on their position and take a swipe at the 'other side's' position – but they don't stop there. They accuse the other side of being 'unwilling to compromise', 'unreasonable', 'the cause of the conflict'. No doubt this creates short-term satisfaction as such expressions are duly noted and relayed over the airwaves or in print.

What happens when the 'other side' reads this kind of thing? Naturally, it flames emotions on their part, too. So they brief the media in turn, adding their own emotional rhetoric. Now the positions of all involved have been inflamed by emotions aroused by this kind of mutual attack. The next time the parties sit down to discuss their positions, is this likely to make it easier or harder to reach agreement? That is one reason why it is much better if discussions of this kind take place in private rather than through megaphone negotiating. Imagine how much more effective negotiations on industrial disputes could be if the participants were not slagging each other off in public? How much easier would difficult negotiations be over budget-deficit reduction in the US between Republicans and

Democrats if they did not take place against a running commentary of each party attacking the other's position in the media?

This is why in the seminal *Getting to Yes*, Fisher and Ury argue extensively in favour of the identification and addressing of underlying psychological interests as a way of resolving conflicts rather than negotiating from 'positions' or organisational wants, which simply create inefficient wars of words.

Once negotiation takes place on the basis of underlying needs rather than surface positions it's less likely that this kind of cycle will develop. If the negotiation is proceeding on the basis of our underlying psychological needs, what is there to get upset about? If you have a need to achieve something and I have a need to belong to something as a result of the negotiation, those needs are not threatening; they just describe our underlying interests from the negotiation. So neither party needs to blame the other. If emotional outbursts occur they can be framed as evidence of the intensity which one party feels about their particular motivation, rather than an attack which must be responded to in kind. When one negotiator is talking about the other's behaviour they can frame it as not meeting their own need rather than as an assault: 'That doesn't really address our need for a joint enterprise' rather than 'You just want to control everything'. The negotiation can focus on the future (What do we need to do to reconcile our respective interests?) rather than the past (I need to get back at you for the way you treated me last time).

Let's consider an instance that comes up a lot in contractual negotiations, where one party wants to renegotiate the original terms of the agreement on the basis of success. This may involve a distributor and a manufacturer who have an agreement for distribution of software or content or a product such as a toy. If this was just a typical positional negotiation, the manufacturer might say, 'We want a much higher royalty and guarantee going forward.' The distributor takes the position that they want to keep the terms the same. This is how the conversation might go:

Manufacturer: 'We are not paid enough.'

Distributor: 'We are already paying quite a lot.'

Manufacturer: 'We know that other distributors will pay more for a product this successful.'

Distributor: 'We know another manufacturer who will accept lesser terms for products of this kind.'

Manufacturer: 'It's unfair of you not to negotiate when the deal has been so successful for you.'

Distributor: 'It's unreasonable of you to expect that the terms you originally agreed to should now be renegotiated.'

Manufacturer: 'You are just playing hardball with us – you can easily afford this.'

Distributor: 'You are just being opportunistic – we can't afford to change contractual terms like this – what would happen if everybody did this?'

Manufacturer: 'That's just a lame excuse; not everybody else is as successful as we have been for you. You are only interested in your own profit.'

Distributor: 'That's very insulting – we took all the risk at the outset of this project by investing in the deal with the initial guarantee and you took none of that risk – you just want a free ride.'

Manufacturer: 'We agreed to lower terms at the beginning because we had to – now you want to continue to exploit us …'

Distributor: 'That's just the attitude you took last time – it was rubbish then to say you were being exploited and it's even more ridiculous now.'

And so on. If this was just a needs-based negotiation the manufacturer might say, 'Look, the product has been more successful than we both anticipated which is great for both of us. We would like to see that we have achieved something as a result of that. Can we revisit the terms on that basis?' The distributor might say, 'Yes, it's all gone really well. The only issue for us is that we take risk across a range of products – some of which work and some of which don't, so when it comes to looking at the terms of successful agreements we have to feel that we are not overextending our risk.' That already sounds different.

The manufacturer cannot really be attacked for expressing an achievement need in these circumstances. The distributor cannot be blamed for having a motivation based on reassurance. There will be individual needs on both sides as well. Maybe the manufacturer's representative is worried that if they don't improve the deal they will be judged for it back at their own company. Maybe the distributor's representative is very proud of his achievements so far with the product and needs some recognition for this. Focusing on the underlying motivations of the parties – *why they want the things that they say that they want* – sets up the negotiation for a much more productive and much less emotive outcome.

Looking for Cues and Clues

There is one problem, though, with focusing on the needs of the other side in this way, which is that people often don't disclose them. We are all so hooked on conducting the negotiation on the basis of organisational wants that we talk exclusively about these issues instead. Often entire negotiations will take place which are expressed purely in the lexicon of organisational 'wants': 'I want this price. I will give you that discount. There must be a £50,000 advance. You have to deliver this number of units. The term must not exceed three years. The territory can include the USA if we have exclusive rights. We will have an option to purchase the company, and the formula will be 'x'.' And so on .... People can be so absorbed by these surface issues that they won't even be aware of their own underlying needs. Frequently people will intuitively feel that they are giving something away if they disclose their motivations, and that it is better to maintain a 'poker face'.

Given how common this is, your job as a negotiator is to be a detective, looking for cues and clues as to what the other person's motivation might really be. Why do they want these things? If you can identify the underlying needs then you can move to meet those needs and get what you want in return. This is how deals get done. When deals fail it is usually because the parties are focusing on the 'content' of the deal and not these underlying needs.

So, what do you do in order to get those needs out in the open? One thing you *can* do is ask questions. This is an especially neglected aspect of the negotiating skill set, but if you ask a simple question like 'What do you need from the negotiation', or 'What would a successful deal mean for you?' it is amazing the kind of answer you sometimes get back. You may find that what you had assumed was a barn-sized need for respect driven by a massive ego is in fact a reassurance need borne out of a lack of trust. Or that what you interpreted as a belonging need to be associated with your organisation is in fact a much simpler survival need expressed as a request for instant commitment from you.

Open questions of this kind (as opposed to closed questions which simply elicit a 'yes/no' answer) can be really helpful in the exploring stage. Research[59] [60] has shown that those who ask for information about underlying concerns often get it. They can also ask the other party for an opinion as to the most objectionable parts of their own proposal, which helps them work out the other person's priorities. Asking people 'What priorities of yours prevent you agreeing to what we propose?' may be just as powerful and illuminating a question as 'Why do you say that you need that?' Generally speaking, the journalist's favourite questions of 'Who?', 'What?', 'Where?', 'When?', 'How?' and 'Why' are your friend during the exploration phase when you are trying to discover the other negotiator's needs. This is one instance where it *is* good to beat about the bush.

If you feel uncomfortable about probing into areas which can involve the uncovering of powerful or profound emotions for the other negotiator, you can inoculate yourself before you start by employing phrases such as 'Correct me if I'm wrong, but …' or 'I'm not an expert on this but isn't it the case that …?' Openings such as these are disarming and protect you from attack if you raise issues that the other dealmaker finds sensitive.

What if people avoid you when you ask a direct, open question of this kind? Well, then you have to be super-observant. Listen to what people say – ask questions when you are uncertain in order to get them to clarify what they mean and check your understanding by rephrasing the other's statements. Long-standing research[61] [62] has shown that this kind of reflective listening improves the other person's attitude towards you and increases their willingness to concede. Notice during the exploring phase the language people use. What issues make them excited, or anxious, what makes them annoyed, what makes them impatient, what makes them animated, which subjects do they avoid with their language? Which issues do they seem to prioritise? Listen to their voice – when do they raise their voice, or speak more quickly. What makes them speak more softly or deliberately, as though they are really having to think about something? What makes their voice sound forced or laboured? What makes them go quiet? What makes them hesitate?

Look at what they are doing with their body. You don't have to be a body-language expert or have eyes like a hawk to notice their gestures, posture and facial expressions. What makes them look relaxed, what makes them look taut and tense, what makes them look disinterested, what makes them look more aggressive – pointing a finger or leaning towards you? Are their facial expressions congruent with the words they are speaking, or does their face tell a different story?

We shall look at body language in more detail when we consider the third link in the chain of effective negotiation – the behaviours. It may not be as decisive a means of interpreting motivations in its own right, because it can sometimes be highly ambiguous. However, it is an important part of the meaning of what we say – usually far more important than the actual words used. So, it is worth observing verbal and body language to check your growing understanding of what the needs of the other negotiator might be. You can also continue to ask questions to check your assumptions as to what the body language might mean – for example, if someone looks defensive you can say 'I'm picking up that a sense of trust is very important to you in this negotiation. Tell me what you think about that?' These kinds of empathetic behaviours are crucial.

Research has shown that some negotiators are much better at empathy than others and they have been shown to achieve more 'integrative' or 'fused' agreements.[63][64] Here's Graham, the CEO of an economics research agency:

I've been in loads of negotiations with clients in my two years as managing director of an economics consultancy but the quirkiest one was when I swapped sides mid-discussion with my opposite number!

My deputy I and were negotiating an increase in fees for our second year of economic services to a big-name firm, with its director and her deputy.

Having set out the justice of our request for more funds to pay for the extra work we were now doing, her deputy was explaining with compelling enthusiasm how the current trading conditions meant none of their suppliers was getting an increase!

He was just getting into the swing with the line 'I will give you business introductions to our sister company instead of more cash' when his boss spotted my deliberate slight lowering of the head and shoulders as if to say 'Here we go again, how many more times am I going to hear that one?' The atmosphere seemed irretrievably solid and tense.

Perhaps the pathos was too much for her because his boss then said, 'They make a very good point, we can't expect all this extra for nothing ...!' To which I said: 'Hang on a minute! If you are going to swap sides and argue FOR us then it's only fair I should join forces AGAINST us with your deputy and remind you that you're supposed to be driving us down!'

Through that flash of mutual empathy, the tension was relieved, the smiles widened again and the lightly humorous symmetry of the situation was such that no one wanted to break the moment. Our fees were raised very reasonably, and quite rightly.

By the time the exploration phase ends you should have a pretty good idea of the underlying interests of all those involved. Maybe they now look different from when you were planning. That's okay: the exploration phase is there for testing such assumptions, just as you can test assumptions that you might have made about the other negotiator's attitude and tactics.

The important thing is to explore other people's needs, and not just ignore or make assumptions, however obvious you think the situation is ...

SO WHAT ARE YOUR MOTIVATIONAL NEEDS?

11

FINDING COINAGE

In 1688 Sir Christopher Wren was building St Paul's Cathedral and the Mayor of London had a problem. He was convinced the dome was going to fall down because it wasn't well supported and he was withholding a licence. Christopher Wren needed his permission in order to finish the structure. Wren recognised this need for reassurance by the Mayor and what he decided to offer was to build two extra pillars. The Mayor was absolutely delighted and blessed the rest of the project. Wren built these two pillars and it was only much later when the cleaners were cleaning the inside of the building that they noticed that the two pillars didn't reach the roof of the dome at all. They stopped several feet short of the roof and so in fact they weren't supporting anything at all, though from the ground it looked as though they reached the roof. It cost Wren virtually nothing to build the two extra pillars – he simply used the pillars to meet the reassurance need of the Mayor and get the permission he required in return.

Once you have identified the needs on all sides you can move on to the next stage which is to work out what 'coinage' there might be to bring to the table. 'Coinage' is a concession which has low value to the giver – it feels like loose change – but high value to the recipient because it meets a personal need. Coinage is the 'currency' that gets deals done. When negotiating, it always pays to look for opportunities of this kind. For example, going back to our example of the advance, if someone asks you for £50,000 in a deal and you would like to pay less, try and work out the need which underpins that request and (like Wren) you may be able to find other ways of meeting that need (using coinage) instead of letting them have what they originally wanted.

There are normally lots of different kinds of coinage available in any deal. Which coinage you select and how you deploy it is, of course, a matter of … *choice*. Here are some examples of coinage that might be available to meet different kinds of need. Can you frame concessions using these kinds of coinage in order to get back what you want in return? Remember, these concessions may not feel like much to you so they are easy to overlook, but they will mean a lot to the receiver – you are like an alchemist turning base metal into gold. Again I have used Maslow's needs classification here (see p. 105) but you could just as usefully do the same exercise with some of the other academic classifications of needs which we talked about earlier and I've indicated below how some of these types of coinage would meet other types of need.

As you are reading these lists, imagine yourself offering some of these things to the person who wanted that £50,000 advance you didn't want to pay. If you have correctly identified their underlying need, you may find they are prepared to reduce or abandon the request for £50,000 in return for the coinage you are offering.

Coinage for Achievement Need

If you encounter someone with achievement needs can you give them any of the following?

Freedom to act
Flexibility in the way that they work
A unique deal or structure
An opportunity to innovate or create

Development opportunities
A cause they can pursue
A problem to solve
An ideal to strive for

Giving any of the above as coinage may mean just as much or more to someone with high achievement needs as conventional measurements of value such as shares or money. Some of these types of coinage would also work for individuals with needs like curiosity, freedom and idealogical needs.

Coinage for Respect Need

When in negotiation with those who have a need for respect, are you able to give them any of the following?

Publicity or PR
Attention
Recognition
An apology
Your gratitude
An indication that you value their reputation
Displays of trust
A senior title or other symbol of status
A commendation, tribute or distinction
Opportunities to save face

Some of these kinds of coinage could also work for addressing motivations such as dignity or honour.

Coinage for Belonging Need

With those in need of a sense of belonging, the following might prove useful to have on offer in negotiations:

Office space

Joint ventures

A formal partnership

Board membership

A share of your time

Access to your experts, expertise or network

Being part of a team

Demonstrations of affection

Equal treatment

Cooperative marketing

Access to your infrastructure

Access to sales support from your organisation

Use of your trademarks, name or logo

Some of these types of coinage would also work for those who have a motivation such as a need for good relationships.

Coinage for Reassurance Need

If negotiating with someone who needs reassurance, can you give them any of the following to make them feel that dealing with you is going to be okay?

Guarantees

Cash flow

Support of legal or professional advice

Loyalty

Trustworthiness (e.g. an audit trail or other transparency)

Control or a sense of order

Commitments from you (cash, options, a fixed term etc)

A promise of focus or prioritisation

An exclusive relationship

Service level agreements

Risk reduction

Using their paperwork for the contract

Adoption of their methodology or systems

Recommendations from people or sources they trust

Longevity of relationship

A history of your successful cooperation with others

Respect for their custom and practice

A sense of justice

A promise of stability

Some of these kinds of coinage could also work with underlying motivations such as a need to see integrity, respect for tradition and aversion to risk.

Coinage for Survival Need

Can you give any of the following to those who may be feeling desperate? They may look trivial to you, but be a sight for sore eyes to your negotiating partner:

Speed of action

Speed of decision making

Immediate cash payment

Deferral of some pressing obligation

Quick solutions

The removal of risk or threat

Protection

Restructuring of debt

Some kind of indemnity

Forgiveness

The above are only lists of examples of coinage. Some of them may not apply in your sector or business. There may be many others which do apply which are not listed above. It's worth keeping a store cupboard of coinage concessions which may be available to you for your business or for negotiations with particular individuals in your life. Then, whenever you negotiate with them you can go to your store cupboard to find ready-made coinage that you may be able to deploy.

A word of caution. Be prepared to sense-test your coinage with the other dealmaker involved – don't make assumptions that they will automatically value it as highly as you do. On the seminars I teach we sometimes do a negotiating exercise where a landscaping company is negotiating with the owners of a stately home in order to acquire a piece of land from which to run a garden centre. One of the points in the brief is that the landscaping company has a swimming pool which they can install at virtually no cost. Almost without fail, participants negotiating for the landscaping company seize on this and start pressuring the owners of the stately home to accept the swimming pool as part of the deal. There is nothing in the brief of the stately home owners to indicate that they are at all interested in a swimming pool, so usually this attempt to foist attempted coinage on them is met with some bafflement. To have any value in the deal, coinage has to be of real value to its intended beneficiary, rather than just something which is convenient for you to give away.

This is a really useful example of the importance of finding valuable coinage from telecoms executive Elisabetta:

Whilst negotiating a deal with a potential Italian partner and getting to the final stages we got our CEO to meet the CEO of the other company. When our boss went to meet him in Rome the other CEO said he had prepared a 'surprise' for him: an exclusive visit to the Vatican, of which he was very proud. No doubt the Italian boss felt he had come up with a prestigious piece of coinage which would clinch the deal. Little did he know that our boss happened to come from a part of the world which had been torn apart by religious disputes and he really was not interested in anything religious.

At the same time, don't assume that just because something has no obvious value to you in the deal, it will also mean nothing to anyone else. That's the whole point of coinage.

Here's a short and sweet example from a contributor wishing to remain anonymous to illustrate the point:

My brother secured a big deal for double glazing by throwing in a date with his elderly widowed mother – she ended up marrying the client …

There you have it …

The critical aspect of coinage, once you have correctly identified it, is to use it in order to get something back that you need in return. This is the point at which coinage becomes currency. Very often people use their coinage too early in proceedings. They correctly identify someone else's need, and then match it with coinage which they feel able to concede. They then offer that coinage straightaway without obtaining anything back in return. This is often done because there is a sense that if coinage is offered early it helps to create goodwill. That may be true, but, as we shall see when we look at the 'bargaining' phase of a negotiation, the fact that goodwill has been created doesn't necessarily mean that the beneficiary will be minded to give you back something in return. The way to use coinage is to maximise its value to you by deploying it explicitly in return for something that you need.

'Coinage' is sometimes easier to grasp in theory than in practice, so here are a couple of stories from my past illustrating its use and its value in making deals happen.

When Robbie Williams first left Take That and sued his record company I was asked to try and get the dispute settled. The negotiations continued for weeks without a breakthrough. The looming court date, however, focused everybody's minds. In the end both sides deserve credit for recognising the needs of the other side and for realising that they each had coinage to bring to bear.

The record company naturally didn't want to appear to be in the wrong. This was a reassurance need. A simple statement from Robbie dealt with that, which didn't cost him anything – it was his coinage to give. Robbie decided he wanted to stop the action, and what he really needed was to be given the freedom to pursue his career elsewhere. This was an achievement need. It was in the record company's gift to meet this need easily as the record company was much happier if the action didn't proceed anyway, and the company had already reconciled itself to the likelihood that the artist would leave the label – coinage in action again. By recognising the mutual needs and deploying the appropriate coinage a deal was struck after an overnight session which ended at 9.30 on the morning the case was due to start. Phew!

Here's one last example:

When the iconic singer Morrissey signed to the RCA label it became clear that among the welter of other contractual requests there was one matter which was particularly important.

The artist wanted his records released on the RCA Orange label. This Orange label was a circular disc of paper which used to be affixed to David Bowie vinyl records released by RCA in the 1970s. This kind of need, to belong to the club of artists of which David Bowie was a member, was both appropriate and easy for RCA to fulfil – it didn't cost RCA anything to bring about, and yet it played an important symbolic role in getting the deal done on terms RCA was happy with.

12

BIDDING

How to Approach Bidding

The next stage is 'bidding'. This is where the parties put their offers to each other. Many people believe that the negotiation actually starts with bidding and so they jump in and make an offer almost as soon as the negotiation begins and the initial pleasantries have been exchanged. However, in our framework bidding is the fifth of the seven stages, so a lot of work will have gone on before we start chucking offers around. There will inevitably be a gap when bids are exchanged, but if the parties have been through the other previous stages of preparation, climate setting and (particularly) identifying needs and coinage, the gap should be bridgeable. The problems start when the previous stages have not been managed properly, if at all, and one party puts a bid forward which completely surprises the other. That's when the climate can go sour, people start making accusations of bad faith and the deal may collapse.

Exactly how you make your bid is – guess what? – a matter of *choice*. However, here are six crucial tips for bidding which will always help.

1. Get the timing right

Often people bid too early before the other stages of the negotiation have been completed or even undertaken. If that happens, in all likelihood their offer will miss the other side's needs and the parties will then be scratching their heads wondering how to bridge the unexpected gap. Equally, if people leave it too long to put an offer down, the other participant may not take them seriously enough when they finally bid. If you wait too long people may assume that you are hesitant about asking for what you want, or that you don't really believe in your offer, or that you don't know what you want. If they make any of these assumptions they may sense a weakness and start pushing you harder.

2. Ask for what you want

Too often people negotiate with themselves before they even start and put in a lower bid than they had originally intended. You can understand why this happens. Your proposed initial bid makes perfect sense to you when you are working it out within the comfort of your own boardroom. Perhaps your own side heatedly agrees that this is a fair and reasonable offer and so reinforces your own assumptions. However, once you are in the room with the other team you start to feel more doubts. Maybe they bring a very strong and robust attitude to the negotiating room. Maybe they start talking about other offers they have obtained from elsewhere. Suddenly you are having a debate with yourself about whether your initial offer is too bold. Maybe they will say it's ridiculous, or maybe they will really resent it or even walk out. Before you know it you are reducing your opening offer without even having tested it with the other party involved. Resist that temptation. If you have planned your opening bid carefully, run with it. At the point at which you make that bid it doesn't really matter whether they 'like' you. If you have gone through the other, previous, stages of the negotiation properly, the negotiation and the relationship will withstand the pressure of you asking for what you really want.

I like using negotiating stories for my kids and this one in relation to bidding works for adults, too:

Aladdin had a lesser known brother called Sadmanadin and it was actually Sadmanadin who found the lamp first. He rubbed the lamp, and out popped the genie and said, 'You have three wishes, Sadmanadin.' Sadmanadin said, 'Well, I'd like a new turban because my existing turban has been very bleached by the sun, and I'd like a new pair of sandals because my old sandals are worn out, and I'd like a new plough because my plough broke yesterday evening.'

The genie said, 'Very well, Sadmanadin,' and he granted the three wishes and disappeared back into the lamp. Then Aladdin came along and found the lamp and rubbed it and out popped the genie again, and he granted Aladdin his three wishes. Aladdin said, 'O Genie, I would like the earth, the moon and the stars, and the universe.'

The genie said, 'Why do you want all those things, Aladdin?' and Aladdin said, 'Well, O Genie, if I have all of those things I can show all of the creatures that exist how wonderful and bounteous your generosity is.'

And the genie said to Aladdin, 'Well, I can't deliver the universe, or the moon and the stars – would you settle for the earth?'

And Aladdin thought about it said, 'Okay then.'

And that's the story of how Aladdin ended up with the earth, and his brother ended up with a turban, some sandals and a new plough – always aim high.

A word of caution here. 'Asking for what you want' does *not* mean making ridiculous demands that are bound to upset and aggravate the other negotiator. Remember, we are talking about being a 'fuser' here. So your bid should have been constructed with the other person's needs in mind as well as your own. That should be recognisable in what you present. Even Aladdin appealed to the respect needs of the genie in making his bid. Asking for what you want is not a charter for being a 'user'. It is a reminder to make sure you protect your own underlying interests in shaping a bargain that recognises everybody's needs.

There is another reason for sticking with your planned opening bid. Generally speaking in negotiation 'the more you ask for the more you get' (or, if you are a buyer, 'the less you offer the less you have to pay'). If you open with a strong bid you will influence the expectations of the other negotiator and this effect can cascade all the way through to the end of the deal.[65] Asking for what you want at the outset also gives you more room for negotiating the deal as you go along. You can leave the door ajar and indicate if you like that you are open to negotiation when you make your bid. But do ask for what you want rather than negotiating with yourself.

Some people worry that if they ask for what they want, even if it is justified, it will still upset people they are dealing with, as it just sounds like too much. If that is the case you can break up your bid into multiple smaller bids.

Here's what writer and consultant Erik Brown has to say on that subject of breaking bids up:

During the 1990s, I ran a design consultancy. It was in the days when companies spent a lot on printed marketing material. We were almost always working with people in the companies' marketing team and their biggest fear was getting their arses kicked for overspending.

I borrowed a process map from the construction industry (we were doing a lot of work in that sector) that broke the entire process into a series of projects. So, the research and interviewing was one project, writing the first draft was another project, producing design visuals was a third project ... and so on. Each of these projects was fully costed and the costs were, with some caveats, fixed. After each project was completed we had a conversation with the marketing team about whether they wanted us to proceed to the next stage. We called them 'gateway' conversations.

The idea that they could stop the process at any time and were only committing to a single project payment reduced their anxiety, and meant that we normally ended up with the same amount of money as in the original estimate.

So, if it's too big to swallow, break it into bite-size pieces. This is a skilful way of making 'asking for what you want' seem palatable to your negotiating partner – but it would only work where, as here, there is an expectation on their part that there will be separate bids for different parts of the process. If they are just expecting one bid to cover everything, you have to ask for what you want at the outset and just hold on to your hat.

3. Sound like you mean it

'I want', 'I need' or 'I require' are all much better than 'Would it be okay if ...?' or 'Could I possibly have ...?' or 'What we would like is ...' We sometimes like to couch our offer in these conciliatory phrases because we think that sugar-coating our proposal makes it sound more palatable to the recipient. In fact, the use of such phrases is more likely to make them feel as though we are not really committed to what we want and they will therefore resist us more. Children between five and eight are absolutely brilliant at this aspect of bidding, as I can attest from personal experience. If I am at the supermarket checkout queue on a Saturday morning next to the sweetie display with my youngest son, he may well say, 'Daddy, I want a bar of chocolate.' This is a very effective way of bidding. He doesn't say, 'Look, Daddy, I know you are spending a fortune on the groceries and you only have a few minutes left on the parking meter but I was just wondering if I could possibly have a bar of chocolate please, if I'm a good boy this afternoon?' He knows that if he put it in that conditional way it would be all too easy for me to seize on one of those conditions and say, 'No'. So, he just says, 'I want a bar of chocolate.'

I'm not saying that this is the most polite way for him to ask but it is an effective way of bidding. Why? Because it sounds as if he means what he says. This is one of the most critical features of effective bidding – whoever you are negotiating with has to believe that you really want what you are asking for. If you use softer expressions such as 'I would like' or put your bid as a question ('May I have?'), the message you are sending out is that you don't really mean it. If you sound like you don't believe in what you want, why should anyone else believe in it either? When you are bidding I'm not suggesting you should be childish, but be direct and to the point, as children naturally are. I'm sure you always did that before adults coached you out of it by telling you 'I want doesn't get'. This may have made you more polite and more sociable as you grew up, but it messed up your bidding technique as a negotiator.

If you bid unconvincingly you will not get what you need from the negotiation. Here's an illustration from my own experience:

Once I was negotiating with a well-known international broadcaster who was licensing some DVD rights to Bertelsmann. There was a negotiation going on about the length of the term – how long they should grant us the rights for. I wanted the term to be as long as possible. The negotiator I was dealing with took so long to put his proposal forward that I felt he was being squeamish about bidding. That automatically made me less inclined to accept his bid when it came. He finally said in a very apologetic way, 'Well, how would you feel about a term of seven years?' I immediately concluded that he didn't mean it and in the event we swiftly moved to an agreed term of twenty years.

In my website blogs I often focus on effective bidding because it is less common than you might think. You can read various stories there about it – including a series on the travails of the Euro, a cautionary tale about inadequate bidding by the Eurozone Governments and institutions (such as the European Central Bank) in their ongoing negotiation with the financial markets.

4. Make sure your voice and body support what you say

If they don't, you won't sound convincing. We will discuss more about this when we come to look at behaviours and body language. In the meantime suffice it to say that when you are bidding your voice needs to be strong and maybe a little louder than normal. You also need to sit up straight first rather than slouching, and then lean forward a little as you bid. Bidding is all about pressing your own agenda on to the other party and leaning forward can help to 'push' the other negotiator back.

5. Don't be afraid to bid first

This is somewhat controversial because you will come across some negotiation experts who tell you that it is better to bid second, so that you know what the other negotiator's expectations are and you thus avoid making misjudgements about what your own expectations should be. My feeling is that it generally pays to go first as you will end up getting more of what you want.[66] Plenty of research shows that agreements fall significantly closer to first offers than counter offers. It's better to be first out of the starting gate. The reason for that is that if you go first you set the parameters for the negotiation and influence the expectations of the other negotiator. In *Thinking, Fast and Slow*, Kahneman describes this as 'anchoring' the bidding. For this purpose let's take a straightforward positional negotiation on price, simply because it illustrates the point.

Say I want to buy a piece of jewellery from you. I think it is worth not more than £500, so I open the bidding with a suitable low offer – say £200, to give myself some negotiating room. Let's say that you think that piece of jewellery is worth not less than £800 and you had decided to make an opening bid of £1,200. When you hear my opening bid is only £200 that may unsettle you. You may think, 'Well, if he thinks it's only worth £200, there's no way I'm going to get £1,200 for it – I'll just bid £900 and see how it goes'. Now, as a result of bidding first I have made you reduce your opening offer by £300 to only £100 above your bottom line. By contrast I have stuck to my planned opening bid and I still have £300 between that opening position and my bottom line.

There are exceptions to any rule and I would not suggest that you go first if you don't know the negotiating terrain of the sector you are dealing with, or you haven't really thought through what you plan to bid. In the example above, if I knew nothing about jewellery, or I had not planned the negotiation and was being asked to make up a bid on the spot, I would not go first. Equally, you would make an assessment of the person you are dealing with.

Some people just look like they are happy to negotiate with themselves, and if that's the case you may as well let them go first and do your negotiating for you. Here's a good illustration of that from record company executive James:

We went to negotiate for the rights to some classical music videos we wanted to sell. It was my first week in the record business, so I figured I didn't have to say much. My colleague Guenter and I sat down with the owner of the video rights after watching some of the merchandise.

Both sides were very friendly and non-adversarial. However, when it got down to pricing the following exchange was heard:

Owner: 'Well, now that we've settled on which products you want, let's talk about price.'
Guenther smiled at him and didn't say anything.

Owner: 'What sort of rate do you think you'd pay?'
Guenter: (Long pause, then speaks very slowly, still smiling) 'Well, it's your work, I was thinking you'd have a price in mind.'
Owner: 'Well, we typically get 18 per cent ...' (Looking for a reaction)
Guenter: (Smiles, looks directly at him.)
Owner: (Fidgets) 'We could give you a discounted rate, as you are a major label ...'
Guenter: (Looks down at his hands) 'Hmmmmmm.'

Every silent period (and there were a lot of them) was excruciating for me, and I wasn't even an active participant.

Owner: 'What about an advance?'

Guenter: (Silent, looking down)

Owner: 'Well if you pay an advance the rate will go down.'

Guenter: (Looks up, back at the man, smiles but says nothing)

Owner: 'If you'd give me a $25,000 advance, I'd knock the rate down by 2 per cent, say, to 16 per cent.'

Not to bore you with the details, but every time Guenter didn't say anything, the guy would feel obligated to fill in that dead air, as they call it in the radio business. The owner was truly 'negotiating with himself'. When we got out of there, we were paying about a third less than we expected, while cherry-picking the best material ...'

6. You only need one good reason to support a bid

Some experts say that it's important to state your reasons before you make your bid, to prepare the way, otherwise people will not listen to your bid; they will just be seething because it seems to be all about what you want. I don't agree with this. When people take this approach they often come up with twenty reasons to justify what they have asked for. There are two reasons for not doing this. The first is that, as a general rule, when you're bidding the more you say the more you give away. If you give people long-winded explanations and lots of data you give them more ammunition which they can potentially turn against you.

The second reason is that when you give a long list of justifications the other party normally stops listening anyway after the first one or two, waits till you give the last one on the list (which is normally the weakest), demolishes that and causes all the other reasons to be ignored. It's very tempting to elaborate and supply all sorts of explanations to support your bid. Don't do that. Once again, little children provide us with the example of how to do it right. If you are having a negotiation with them about what time they ought to go to bed, they will only give one good reason at a time to support their bid. The negotiation might go like this:

Parent: 'It's 7.30 p.m. – bedtime now.'
Child: 'No, I don't want to go to bed yet.'
Parent: 'But 7.30 p.m. is your bedtime.'
Child: 'No, not yet, I'm not tired.'
Parent: 'Well, you will be tired if you don't go to bed now.'
Child: 'But it's still daylight.'
Parent: 'Well, we'll close the curtains then.'
Child: 'But my friend Alfie doesn't go to bed till 8 p.m.'
Parent: 'Well, it doesn't matter what happens in Alfie's house, what matters is the rule in this house which is bedtime at 7.30 p.m.'
Child: 'But I'm thirsty.'
Parent: 'Well, we can bring up a glass of water.'
Child: 'But there's a goblin living in my wardrobe.'
Parent: 'I'm sure there isn't, but let's go and check together.'
Child: 'But I have a stomach ache ...'

And so on. By only using one good reason at a time to support his or her bid, a child ensures that the parent has to deal with all the reasons rather than just the first or last. By using the reasons one at a time the child also doesn't give too much away. The child may also manage to delay bedtime to the time when it wanted to go anyway!

So, the moral is make your bid, give one good reason and then shut up. A caveat, though – the reason you give has to be one that would seem reasonable to the other negotiator. If we are working on the basis that the psychological needs of both parties need to be met, it's not enough that the reason just seems like a good one to you. Of course it would, since it's your bid. The reason must also seem justifiable to your negotiating partner, so that they can see that even if they disagree with the bid, you are considering what they need from the negotiation. This is another way of avoiding extreme and provocative bids at the outset of a negotiation. If you know that the one reason you give to support your bid has to be something that the other negotiator might agree with, that will be a good discipline to ensure that your bidding does not get out of hand.

Once you have made your bid, don't be afraid if there is a silence at that point. This is a great story from CEO Steve on the effect of silence *after* bidding:

As a young pup I was with a salesman called Chris and we were negotiating the biggest computer licence deal that the company had had up to then with a guy called Eddie. Before going into the room Chris looked me in the eye and said, 'Look, when I have finished the pitch don't say anything, under ANY circumstances.'

The meeting then went as follows:

Four people in the room: me, Chris, Eddie and Eddie's FD.

1) Warm welcomes.

2) Very short pitch by Chris finishing with term and price and the comment, 'That's the deal, are we going to do it?'

3) Silence ...

4) Silence ...

5) After five long minutes Eddie's FD got up to clear up the tea cups and biscuits, then sat back down.

6) More silence ...

7) After ten minutes (which seemed like a lifetime) Eddie said, 'You want me to agree to this deal, don't you?' Chris said one word. 'Yes.' ... a little more silence ... 'Okay, let's do it,' said Eddie.'

So, make your bid, give one good reason to support it and then sit back. Silence may be a good sign; you don't have to fill the airwaves in support of your bid. And ask for what you want – as

long as you can think of a reason that would genui
to the other party. For children negotiating with their
unspoken reason is often 'Because you love me …'

13

BARGAINING

Bargaining is the sixth stage of the negotiation, the haggling stage, where counterbids are swapped in an attempt to reach closure. Once again, this is a stage at which negotiations can go wrong if the other stages have been skimped on. If there has been little preparation, and not much exploration, the bids may well have come out with a significant gap between them. If an inappropriate climate was set (or even if the right climate was set initially) there may be climate-related problems now. 'That's outrageous,' says one party. 'How can you possibly think that's a sensible offer?' 'What are you talking about?' says the other indignantly. 'It's an incredibly generous proposal.' Cue much huffing and puffing as each negotiator blames the other for the impasse. What to do now? If the parties haven't thought about the real needs of the other negotiator, and established the coinage they may have to give away, they will be short of currency to bridge the gap between the bids. The only solution will be to go back to the stage of the negotiation where it first went wrong and start again …

Let's assume that the previous stages have been reasonably well handled and we are now reaching the bargaining stage in the right order and with the negotiation in reasonable shape so far. Some people think that bargaining is overrated and that it's much easier just to split the difference between the two parties' positions 'since most negotiations end up somewhere in the middle anyway'. They feel this saves time and avoids having to deal with complicated issues like exploring and meeting underlying needs. If that was always the case, this chapter could be fairly short. However, splitting the difference isn't always the most effective strategy. One danger of this is that, even if it works, it can make for very inefficient outcomes.

There is a famous negotiating example of two sisters arguing over the last orange in the bowl. They can't work out who should have it. So, after a bit of a haggle they decide to cut it in two and have half each. This sounds like a good deal until they work out afterwards that one sister needed the peel of the orange in order to bake a cake and the other needed the juice of the orange in order to make a drink. Positional negotiating often yields these less than optimal outcomes. Attempting to split the difference can also get you into trouble. When you offer to split the difference the negotiator you are dealing with may not agree with you – but since you have just offered to give away half your negotiating room they will take your offer as their starting point when they make their counter-offer. So, even if you end up reaching agreement from there, you will be much closer to their position than yours.

Let's take a more sophisticated view of the bargaining phase. How you choose to bargain is up to you. It's another of those areas of negotiation where you have a *choice* and there is no right way to do it. But here are a dozen key suggestions to help you along:

1. Try and keep some points open, even if you are prepared to agree to them

This is so that you can create packages of points to 'give and take' with the other dealmaker. This makes trading easier as there is always something you can give away in return for what you need. If you negotiate and agree everything point by point as you go along, what tends to happen is that you end up leaving the difficult points till last. At that stage you may find you have nothing left to bargain with as all the concessions which each participant feels able to make will have been given earlier in order to settle the easier points. This doesn't mean that you should not agree anything until you get to the difficult points, as quick agreements on some easier points in the early stages of bargaining can create a positive feeling of momentum in the negotiation. However, if you leave some of the easier points open you can then create packages along the lines of 'If you agree points (a) and (b) then I'll agree points (c) and (d)'.

2. Offer concessions of decreasing size as the bargaining continues

If there are big gaps when the bids first appear on the table and you make tiny concessions at that stage, this may be interpreted as a lack of willingness to reach agreement. However, if you make smaller concessions as you go along, this can be a good thing to do as it increases the pressure on your deal partner to move and/or come up with creative solutions of their own. It also enables you to manage your stockpile of concessions so that you don't run out.

3. Remember the value of taking a break in a negotiation

Such breaks might be either short ones of, say, twenty minutes or an hour, or longer ones of a few days or weeks. Breaks can be particularly useful at the bargaining stage, as the atmosphere can get quite pressured and fast-moving. Some people love the energy of the bargaining stage – they were born to haggle in Berwick Street fruit and veg market in London. Other people find it quite draining. If you are feeling tired or worn out, take a break; this will give you the chance to refresh yourself and re-energise. Regardless of whether you are a natural or not, you are unlikely to be at your best after ten hours of negotiating, so be prepared to take a break after long sessions in any event. There is no obligation on you to keep going till you drop.

Breaks are also useful if you get stuck in a negotiation in the bargaining phase. This can be very frustrating to all parties and sometimes continued proximity to each other heightens the tensions and encourages the parties to start blaming each other for the impasse. Taking a break can enable you and your team to regroup and get creative in order to generate new solutions to move the deal forward. In addition, there is research[67] suggesting that taking breaks can help switch the mood of the negotiation from competitive to collaborative (as long as those taking the break have a 'pro-social' attitude which is geared towards finding solutions of joint benefit).

Finally, breaks create the opportunity for off-line corridor conversations, where people quietly sidle up and let someone on the other party know informally what it would take to move forward.

I have been involved in a number of negotiations with unions such as the Musicians' Union and Equity. Face to face, the atmosphere can often be rather unyielding and on the union side the negotiators are unwilling to give anything away. But if you take a break, sometimes they feel able to step away from their formal position during that interval in order to give you a hint on how progress could be achieved. When I was in Hollywood helping Syco negotiate its agreements with Fox in connection with Simon Cowell's appearances on *American Idol*, I found that negotiations primarily took place during such breaks. In the formal meetings with everybody in the room the atmosphere would be highly cordial, but often not much progress was made. As soon as everyone was out of the room you would find quiet conversations taking place between the studio and the agency or the US lawyer in which participants seemed to be happier to cut to the chase.

So, taking a break can be really useful. Just remember before the break to allocate responsibility to one party or the other to come back with the next proposal. If you don't, you may both return expecting each other to have come up with the breakthrough idea.

When I first started negotiating, I never used to take breaks. I have since discovered the pitfalls of negotiating relentlessly …

`SO - GENTLEMEN — ARE WE ALL AGREED THAT IT'S TIME TO TAKE A BREAK ?`

4. When you get stuck try and increase the size of the pie

You can do this by finding additional items to negotiate which potentially create more value for the parties than those items on which you are stuck. This creates an incentive for negotiations to continue and is a really useful approach to adopt when bargaining. Maybe you and I are divided on what the royalty rate should be on a licence agreement for some software and we are just not making progress. It is the last open point on the licence agreement. However, as licensor I would be prepared to agree to you paying me a lower royalty if I had an opportunity to invest in your company and acquire some shares. So I raise this as a possibility and I find that, coincidentally, you have been looking for funding and you would be really enthusiastic about exploring that idea with me. I am keen to explore that idea, too, since strategically I am looking to move into distribution and I really rate your company as distributors. Suddenly there is a whole larger conversation going on which is much more positive and makes the issue of the royalty seem much less important than it did before. Focusing on the underlying needs of the other negotiator will often throw up these previously unnoticed opportunities to change the negotiation by enlarging its scope.

Here's a good example from record label CEO, Martin Goldschmidt:

One example I am quite proud of is the negotiation I did for synchronisation licences with David Lowery for the band Cracker. [Synchronisation licences are those granted to broadcasters, filmmakers or advertisers to use recordings in synchronisation with moving images such as a movie or a commercial.] He procured a $10k sync opportunity with a user and brought it to us to do the contract, as contractually any synchronisation licences had to be granted by us to the user. The band were unrecouped $90k at the time. [This meant that Martin's company had spent US$90,000 more on the band in recoverable costs than they had recovered from royalties on the sales of records and downloads – so the band 'owed' their record company $90,000.] Not unreasonably, David asked how he would benefit from this synchronisation licence, since as things stood the $10k fee would just go towards paying off his debt to us. I thought about it and offered him either a pay-through of 15 per cent of the proposed fee, which he could keep (in lieu of an agent's commission), or to credit his unrecouped balance with a notional 150 per cent of the income. [Theoretically this would bring closer the time at which the band would recover their unrecouped balance and start receiving royalties again, though, as Martin points out, 'At the time I believed that he had no chance of recouping.']

He chose to credit his unrecouped balance. Something wonderful then happened. This incentivised him so much that he got several more synchronisation licences and cleared the unrecouped balance totally! He was so happy at the result that he then asked us to represent his music publishing also.

So what started off as a disaster and big unrecouped debt led to a big joint benefit and a strengthening of our relationship.

By being prepared to expand the pie to include the unrecouped balance, Martin transformed a sterile zero-sum conversation about dividing the US$10,000 synchronisation fee into something that was much better for all parties.

Sometimes expanding the pie is just about reframing the issue. Many negotiations which seem to be about a fixed amount of money can be opened up in this way. All over Europe, governments are presently negotiating difficult public spending cuts. The arguments are rigid and are all about fixed pies – reducing the level of current public sector deficits. Because the negotiations involve 'losses' to workers the opposition is even more intense than if the negotiations involved lack of 'gain'. If these debates were re-framed it could make a big difference. 'How can we provide the public services we want for the next generation at sustainable cost?' would be a question which gets everybody on the same side of the table and opens up many other avenues to agreement – including spending linked to innovation, productivity, entrepreneurial initiatives and process improvements.

5. Be patient
Not only are we often in a tearing hurry to get to the haggle in the negotiation (regardless of whether or not we have covered off the earlier stages such as preparation and exploration), we often want to rush through the bargaining phase as well. In doing so we often make premature judgements about what our options are, and what the other party's options are.

We don't allow enough time for the other party to work through any emotional issues which may be influencing their judgement. We don't allow enough time for our behaviours to be effective. We will look at choices of negotiating behaviour next, but at this stage it's enough to note that whichever behaviour we select it may take time for it to be impactful on the other negotiator. We don't allow enough time to consider altering our plan in the light of the new information which emerges. We don't allow ourselves time to work out the team dynamics of the other party – maybe there is one key target we should be focusing on who is more prepared, more open to persuasion; maybe the key decision maker isn't even present but we are in too much of a hurry to notice this. We don't allow for time to change the negotiating partner's point of view. Often this is a gradual process that does not happen in one go. We have already noted that once people have made a commitment to something they are often reluctant to change that commitment because it makes it look as if they got something wrong. So, if they are committed to a particular point of view in a negotiation it may take time to change that. Allow for that time in your negotiation planning and in the bargaining phase.

6. Create more than one solution

There is a temptation when negotiating to believe that the process is a quest for 'the answer', a single approach that both parties can agree to. It's much more likely that there is a range of options that would be appropriate. Creating such a range of possibilities makes it more likely that you will reach an effective solution. We live in an age of huge individual choice (certainly in the West). People often like to make individual choices about what they will and won't do. If you give them some options (rather than just one solution) you can appeal to this contemporary trait. Doing this also helps people select priorities among their own needs.

One very effective way of achieving this is through creating joint solutions. Breaking off from the formal negotiating process with the express purpose of coming up with potential solutions together is a very powerful way of making progress in the bargaining phase of a negotiation. In order to do this it may be a good idea to choose a different environment from the one in which you have been negotiating, so there is a clear division between the joint problem solving and the negotiating process which has preceded it. There also needs to be a ground rule that each party will suspend its critical judgement of the solutions contributed by the other, and take them at face value as potentially viable solutions to be worked on. Perhaps add that neither party can use what is said during the brainstorming session against the other later – this may encourage wider disclosure of ideas. This kind of activity works. For instance, research has shown that 'team incentives' encourage information exchange and the creation of collaborative solutions where each party benefits.[68] [69] Anticipation of cooperation has also been shown to lead to improved interpersonal and intergroup relations.[70] [71] Creating joint solutions also has the additional benefit of ensuring that the other party feels wedded to the outcomes proposed because they have had a stake in crafting those outcomes.

7. Think carefully before you give away something for nothing

So-called 'goodwill' concessions may create goodwill but – particularly if you are dealing with a 'user' – they may also convince people you deal with that they can get something more for nothing. Or they may just pocket the concession and not feel inclined to reciprocate, as people often feel they deserve whatever benefit you confer on them in a negotiation anyway and 'users' will almost certainly feel that way. People don't always feel that one good turn deserves another.

Robert Cialdini's views on influencing might seem to contradict this idea since he argues that the rule of 'reciprocity' is one of the six great sources of influence. This rule tells us that we feel we have to repay in kind what another person has provided us. If someone buys us a birthday gift, we feel obligated to buy one for them, too. If someone invites us to their party we feel obligated to invite them to ours. 'Much obliged' has become a synonym for 'Thank you' in English and in other languages, too – it literally means 'I owe you something because you did something for me'. The principle is particularly effective when what we are responding to is a 'concession' made by someone else. So, argues Cialdini, skilled influencers (e.g. encyclopaedia salesmen) might propose a large price first, and then retreat to a more reasonable proposal, knowing that the act of making a concession is more likely to induce in the customer a sense of obligation and responsibility to make a concession in return by buying something. Small wonder, then, according to Cialdini, that many companies are so keen to provide us with free 'samples' of their goods – these samples may create an unconscious sense of obligation which makes it more likely that we will buy something in return.

My practical experience is different. In negotiating, concessions made in isolation may well generate goodwill, but they don't necessarily spark reciprocal concessions. A retailer giving away free samples is not negotiating – it is actually trying to create goodwill. It anticipates that as a result of that goodwill some of you *may* buy something later – enough to make the cost of the giveaways worthwhile – but it has no intention of negotiating with you over price at that point. Genuine negotiation is a specialist form of influencing and I'm not convinced that people are inclined to reciprocate a concession unless you specifically make it part of the bargain. People will understand the principle of reciprocity applying explicitly as in 'If you give this to me then I will give that to you', but in a commercial negotiation they may not respond in the same way if you say to them 'I gave you something for nothing earlier … would you care to reciprocate now?'

Academic research on this point is mixed. Some shows that people 'match' cooperation and non-cooperation by the other party in a negotiation – but in the middle part of a negotiation (which would normally be the bargaining phase) there is a tendency towards undermatching – i.e. people offer back less than the value of what they have received. For example, analysis of prisoners' dilemma scenarios has found that the amount of cooperation returned by someone who was the beneficiary of cooperation by the other side was not proportional to the amount of cooperation received – people gave back less than they got.[72] [73] Matching is more prevalent where the negotiating partner is perceived as powerful or tough, but this in a sense supports the argument in favour of not giving away something for nothing. If you do that you will not be perceived as powerful or strong and so the other negotiator is less likely to be inclined to match your concession.

Accordingly, concessions are best offered on a 'tit-for-tat' basis.[74] [75] Negotiators who follow a tit-for-tat strategy are perceived to be stronger than those who follow a softer strategy (e.g. of unilateral concessions) and fairer than those who follow a firm policy of no concessions. The consequence is that the other deal partner feels there is no mileage in trying to exploit such negotiators and decides to reciprocate the concessions made on a tit-for-tat basis. There may be some negotiations where goodwill concessions are less of a risk – e.g. if you have established that the other negotiator is a 'fuser' who is not looking to take advantage, or perhaps in intimate relationships where the 'norm' might be expected to be a 'giving' one rather than one solely based on exchange of favours.[76] [77] As a general rule, though, make it clear that you expect something back when you give something away, or the other party may try to take advantage ...

8. Lead with your conditions and not your concessions

If you lead with a concession that's all the other side will hear – they will have stopped listening by the time you get around to asking for your condition. So, if you want to give something away and get something back for it in return the way to say it is 'If you do this for me, I will do this for you'. If you put your condition first the other negotiator will understand that in order to get the concession they have to give something. If you put it the other way round – 'Okay, I will concede this – will you give me that in return?' – they will be less inclined to play ball because they will feel able to stop listening as soon as they hear the words 'Okay, I will concede this ...'

Another good children's story illustrates the point:

The Emperor of China was invading a small kingdom to the south. He swept in with his army and arrived at the city gates of the capital. As he was about to go into the negotiations with the rulers of this kingdom he said to his adviser, 'How shall I handle this negotiation?' and his adviser said, 'Listen, and respond to

155

everything you hear.' So the Emperor said to the rulers of the
kingdom, 'I want the whole northern part of your kingdom,'
and they said, 'Well, you can have the whole northern part of
our kingdom if you give us 10,000 camels and 50,000 bars of
gold.'

The Emperor duly occupied the northern part of the
kingdom, but he never gave them the bars of gold or the
camels. The following year he invaded again. He arrived at the
city gates and this time he said to the rulers, 'I want the whole
of the western half of your kingdom.' And they said to him,
'Well, you can have the western half of our kingdom if you'll
marry the daughter of our ruler so that our two kingdoms are
united.' And the Emperor took the western half of the kingdom,
but he never married the princess.

The following year he arrived yet again with his army at the
city gates and he said to the rulers, 'I want the whole of the
remainder of your kingdom,' and they said, 'You can have the
whole of the remainder of our kingdom if you spare our lives.'
The Emperor duly took the whole of the rest of the kingdom
and he beheaded all the previous rulers.

Afterwards his adviser said to him, 'Congratulations,
O Emperor, and do you feel that you listened and did you
respond to everything that you heard?' And the Emperor
said, 'That's exactly what I did. The problem is, each time
they offered me what I wanted I felt I didn't need to listen to
anything else, so I didn't hear anything after they agreed to
my demands ...'

When bargaining, state your conditions first and then your
concessions, not the other way around, otherwise people won't
listen to what you want.

9. When you get stuck and you want to see if something will work, use hypothetical questions

This is a very good way of testing out options in a risk-free manner. Let's say that we are stuck in a positional negotiation on what the length of term should be in a contract. I want it to be five years, you want it to be three. I have a feeling that if I added an escalation in your revenue share from the deal on the basis of sales targets being achieved, you might agree to extend the term by an extra two years. If I make that proposal directly you may reject it – but you may note with interest that there are some circumstances in which I would be prepared to increase the revenue share I am prepared to pay you, and start putting pressure on me in that area of the negotiation. What about if I make that suggestion to you hypothetically? I might say, 'Would you be prepared to increase the term if I considered improving your rev share based on sales escalations?' If you say 'yes', that's great, and we can start exploring that idea further. If you say 'no', I have lost nothing by floating the idea. I haven't actually offered to increase your revenue share and so there is no basis for you trying to push me harder in that direction.

Hypothetical questions are a good way of testing the water without giving anything away. They also give the other negotiator an opportunity to respond without feeling that they may be committing to something. If you ask a question as a hypothetical, your potential deal partner can answer hypothetically as well: 'Hmm, it's possible that might work if the sales escalations were attainable.' At that point they have not committed to your hypothetical proposal; they have simply indicated that it might provide a way forward – they haven't given anything away either.

10. Don't negotiate beneath your bottom line

I hope it's self-evident that this is not a good idea! However, it is quite common to find people negotiating below the point at which they had previously said they would walk away. That may be a bottom line, or a BATNA, or a WATNA, or risking the worst that could happen if the deal takes place. It's as though they get so committed to the mission of closing the deal that they lose track of what a worthwhile deal would be. This can happen especially where there is a competitive element to the negotiation and one party wants to deny a competitor the opportunity of doing this particular deal. In these circumstances beating the competition seems to become even more important than doing a deal that makes sense. You can adjust your bottom line if the circumstances of the deal change or developments prove that your original assessment of your bottom line at the preparation stage was incomplete. But be careful about doing this. Often your objective assessment made before the negotiation started will be a much more reliable guide to when you ought to stop than any judgement made once the heat is on. If you keep negotiating below your bottom line you are likely to end up with a deal you resent.

Here's a candid contribution from Tony Kypreos, social impact investor and entrepreneur, who negotiated in Eastern Europe on behalf of a technology SME:

Always be ready to walk away – many companies are desperate to close the deal – it's a time-critical opportunity, after all! It is much better to walk away from a deal if it does not feel right.

In this case our business was forced to instigate commercial litigation that we finally won but the process was costly and lasted many years. It would have been much better to walk away from this deal.

11. Be prepared to take small steps on the way to success

Remember, you may get another chance to come back for more.
You may aim high and bid high, but as long as you are above
your bottom line, be prepared to consider settling for less if
circumstances suggest that is the *only* realistic outcome. Getting
things perfect may seem super-crucial at the time, but you often
get the opportunity to improve that deal over time or even to
renegotiate it.

This is a good illustration from Tim Clark of IE Music:

I remember being with legendary Island Records founder Chris
Blackwell when he was negotiating a licensing deal and we had
had to concede a point or two. After the meeting, as we walked
out he turned and said to me, 'Tim, never forget, the signing
of a contract is the first step in its renegotiation.' I have never
forgotten his advice!

I have blogged on this issue many times and you can find stories
on the website taken from real-life situations where people have
simply tried to achieve too much too quickly. These include former
Chelsea (and now Tottenham) manager Andre Villas-Boas in
his negotiations with his senior Chelsea players about changing
tactics. They also include former Olympus CEO Michael Woodford,
a newly installed reforming leader of the Japanese corporation
who may have pushed too quickly to address the consequences
of the corrupt historic dealings he discovered and was fired for his
pains.

Sometimes when you negotiate you have to recognise that
change must be made in small steps. You may well get a second
bite of the cherry later.

12. See if there is a way of making what the other negotiator wants seem counter to their own interests

I hope it is also self-evident by now that if you appeal to what people need in a negotiation, you will get more of what you want. The same is true if you hold out the prospect of them getting the opposite of what they need unless you get what you want. Needs are just as powerful in a negotiation whether we are looking for something positive or are trying to avoid something negative.

Here is a telling example from a lawyer, Nathan, of doing exactly that and putting the other negotiator on the horns of a dilemma. It's a longer story but a compelling one:

A wealthy client was being blackmailed by a woman, let's call her 'A', who claimed to be carrying his child. My client felt aggrieved because A, who had a history of drug abuse and related medical problems, had told him she was sterile.

Having failed to persuade my client to break up with his long-term girlfriend and invite A and her unborn child to move in with him, A had made increasingly wild threats against my client. These included a paternity test, litigation, telling my client's girlfriend about his infidelity and getting members of A's family to seriously assault or even kill my client – unless my client agreed to make her a generous financial settlement.

My client asked what he should do. Whilst the threats of physical violence were credible, my client felt he and his family could deal with them. His principal concern was to preserve his long-term relationship with his girlfriend. He also wanted to avoid a paternity test, and neutralise A's threats.

At first sight, a paternity test seemed to be a no-risk strategy for A. It could show one of three things:

i) that A was pregnant by my client,

ii) that she was pregnant by another man, or

iii) that she was not pregnant at all.

If i) she had a legal claim against my client. If ii) or iii), she would have no claim, but there was no evident downside for her. However, the wide range of threats she had made suggested that A was not confident of the outcome of a paternity test. It seemed she was making any threat that came to mind in the hope that my client would pay her some money to go away.

In order to call A's bluff, we had to make the paternity test seem as risky for her as for my client. So I advised my client to say that, if a paternity test showed him to be the father, not only would he support the child, he would demand custody of it, on the grounds that, whereas my client had a secure home, steady income and a stable relationship, A was an unemployed single mother with a history of drug abuse, and unfit to bring up the child.

This created a paradox for A – whilst A needed a positive result in the paternity test to pursue any claim, it would leave her no better off, because she would lose custody of the child and the improved material circumstances she hoped would go with it.

At first my client was reluctant to adopt such a potentially high-risk strategy, but, when he thought about it, he agreed that, in the unlikely event that he had fathered a child, he would want to bring it up himself rather than leave it full-time with such an unsuitable and unstable mother. So he went ahead with the plan. It worked perfectly.

The strategy was successful partly because it was completely unexpected – A had anticipated that my client would do almost anything rather than face up to his responsibilities – and mainly because it turned a positive paternity test into a potential Pyrrhic victory for A, that would not address her no doubt desperate need for money to pay for drugs.

Perhaps most importantly of all, the strategy preserved my client's relationship with his girlfriend. Whilst it did not prevent A from telling my client's girlfriend about his infidelity, it removed any incentive for her to do so. There was no advantage to A in telling my client's girlfriend of his infidelity. Her only interest was how much my client would pay to avoid it. Without addressing it directly, the strategy convinced A that my client was confident in his long-term relationship, thereby neutralising A's threat to it.

To this day, my client has heard nothing further from A, and continues to live happily, and faithfully, with his girlfriend who is blissfully unaware of the whole episode.

It is to be hoped that, with all of these options at your command, you will never get stuck in the bargaining phase again. If you do, remember there is (almost) always a way to get the deal done – you just have to look for it. When a door is stuck, brute force isn't always the answer. Sometimes it just needs a little pressure applied in the right place to open it. These 12 techniques will give you all the leverage you need – you just have to use the right amount of the right one. As a negotiator from Texas once remarked to me, 'Small hinges can open big doors'...

14

CLOSE AND REVIEW

Reaching Closure

If all the other stages are completed successfully, you will get to the closure stage.

How do you know when the closure moment is approaching? You can look for clues as to whether the other team may be ready to close. Do they look a bit more relaxed? Are they starting to speak more about the future than the present or the past? Check for consensus by asking 'Are we all agreed that ...' This acts as a signpost to closure and also provides a summary of the agreement. That is always useful as, without it, people often get up from the negotiating meeting thinking they have reached agreement, only to find later that they each had a different idea of what the agreement was. If there is paperwork to be done, move on to that quickly, so that there is not a long gap between agreement and formal closure. Offer to draft that paperwork first if you can. That is a bit like the equivalent of bidding first – it helps you to shape the parameters for the paperwork.

Too many people mess up this stage of the negotiation by continuing to haggle over points in the deal. This can be tempting. The negotiation process can be very absorbing and, once you are in it, it can be difficult to know when to stop. This is why having a plan at the outset is so important. That way, you can measure your progress against the objectives you set in your plan. Are you well above your bottom line? Is the proposal on offer better than the best alternative to doing this agreement which you identified for yourself at the outset? Is it better than the risk of the worst thing that you envisaged could happen if you didn't do this deal? If the answer to those questions is 'Yes', this could be the closure moment. Resist the temptation to keep going and negotiate further concessions just because you can. Closure is a fluid moment and needs to be bottled as soon as possible so that it does not slip through your fingers.

Here's a good closure story from artist manager and entrepreneur Michael:

I was thinking about a house I had in the South of France. I mentioned to my gardener I was selling it sometime next year. The next thing I had a phone call from a complete stranger and an offer at the price I mentioned to my gardener. Then I had a phone call from an Australian superstar artist – let's call him Mitch – who asked if he could have a look at it. He came round with a female superstar companion. Mitch made a better offer the same day, all this without an agent and before I expected to sell it and the only person I had mentioned it to was my gardener!

I called the first bidder to tell him I had had a substantially better offer and was of a mind to accept it. He upped his offer by £200,000. I called Mitch to tell him I was of a mind to accept the higher offer when he upped his own previous offer by £200,000. This was fun. I realised that in theory I could keep going back and forth like this for some time, but I was already well above the price I would have accepted at the outset of negotiations. I called the under-bidder to tell him I had accepted the offer from Mitch and would not go back on my word. Ironically, he then told me that he would not have felt inclined to go any further anyway. I'm sure I closed the deal at exactly the right time.

The motto of the story is 1) always tell your gardener what is going on, and 2) that sometimes negotiating is about feeling the temperature of a deal and trusting your instincts to close. If I had not closed with Mitch when I did it could all have gone back to square one.

Missing Closure

If you hesitate or prevaricate the other party may change its mind and get cold feet for any of a number of reasons:

Deal fatigue – they are so exhausted by the process that they lose interest in the deal or decide it will be too difficult to work with you after the deal is completed.

A key party leaves the scene – maybe the sponsor of your deal on the other team takes a new job or is fired or made redundant, or someone else takes over the deal who doesn't like you so much.

The other party restructures – maybe a different division is now responsible for the deal with you. You will have to start the process of convincing them of the merits of the deal once again, and maybe they will come to a different conclusion

The other party has a change of strategy – a deal with a partner like you is no longer a priority.

Economic factors blow the deal off course – maybe a change in interest rates makes the other party decide to hoard cash rather than spending money on the deal with you.

An operational change of direction – maybe a poor financial quarter makes the other party decide to cut back on investment temporarily.

They change their view of you – maybe if you keep haggling they decide you are a 'user' who doesn't share their interests and it would be better to move on.

They come across a competitor who they believe could do the job better or cheaper than you, and decide to switch horses while they can. So, when you get the chance to 'close the deal', make sure you get it closed, otherwise the opportunity can simply disappear. Don't be too greedy. As the saying goes, 'pigs get fat, but hogs get slaughtered'!

An example from my own experience of this follows:

When we were negotiating to acquire the recording rights for the Pop Idol TV series in 2001, we got to the night before the final without the agreement yet being signed. Gareth Gates was to face off with Will Young in the final and there was huge national interest in the outcome. Battle buses were travelling the country to drum up support for each contestant. Everyone could sense this was the beginning of a phenomenon and the contracts had therefore been robustly negotiated on both sides. There was a competitor lurking in the wings so I was convinced that we could not afford to allow signature of the agreements to wait until after the final had taken place. I got the lawyer for the other side to agree I could go over there at four o'clock that Friday afternoon and I remember the long night of negotiation that followed, the patience required by both sides to work through the remaining points, and the debris building up in the office as the night wore on, from paper plates with curly pizza crusts to half-finished cups of coffee.

I remember the sense of elation when we emerged at 2.30 in the morning with a signed agreement, and the sense of relief as both singles subsequently raced to the top of the charts. Will Young's 'Evergreen' sold a total of 1.7 million copies and holds the record for the fastest selling UK single of all time (over 400,000 sold on its day of release). Gareth Gates' 'Unchained Melody' sold 1.2 million copies. The Pop Idol franchise (including American Idol) has generated millions of sales worldwide –

American Idol winners alone have sold over sixty million albums around the world and fifty million single downloads, and that excludes the winners from all the other series around the world. Looking back on it, I'm still glad we closed that contract when we did.

By the way, 'closing the deal' means taking the deal all the way from agreement in principle to signing the contract (if there is one). It does not mean shaking hands and then leaving it to the lawyers to sort out the paperwork on their own. If you take your eye off the ball at that point the paperwork can trip everything up. Lawyers are paid to make sure that paperwork minimises all risks, covers all eventualities and doesn't allow for any ambiguity. Sometimes deals get carefully negotiated so that there is a balance of risk, an acceptance that the deal can't cover everything and a tolerance of some ambiguity. If there is a conflict between the aims of the negotiated agreement and the legal aims of the paperwork, then all that previous hard work in setting a climate of trust can fall apart.

Failure to Move from Bargaining to Closure

What if the problem is the opposite – not that you fail to seize an opportunity to close, but you just can't get from bargaining to closure, no matter what you do? What if you have managed the process correctly, brought the right attitude and used all the tips on bargaining that we talked about earlier and you still can't get there? Sometimes in these circumstances it's worth checking whether the people round the table are the people to get the deal done. Sometimes there is just not a meeting of hearts and minds, and this will usually become apparent during a (failed) bargaining phase in which everybody gets stuck.

When this happens it's worth considering whether either of the teams need to change. Maybe you need to substitute someone on your own team who is simply winding up the opposition. Maybe you need to take yourself out of the equation – sometimes it's best to accept that we are the problem in a negotiation and that the outcome would be better served if we are not directly involved. Maybe there is some history that you just can't get past, or you just find the negotiator on the other team infuriating even though your colleagues are getting on fine with him or her. Maybe there is a person on the other team who is genuinely an obstacle because of their attitude or behaviour. If so, it can be worth raising this, diplomatically – 'I wonder if it would help if we mixed the teams up a bit – bring in some fresh energy to see if we can move forward?'

Hopefully, you will not encounter this kind of obstacle too often; you will correctly interpret the closure signals during the bargaining phase from people you are able to work with, and you will move smoothly into the closure stage. There is one other tip on closure to take note of as you near the finishing line – 'last-minute nibbles' from the other party. Often when a deal is close they will chance their arm and ask for one extra concession. They do this opportunistically, sensing that you may be so relieved that a deal is at hand that you will nod that last point through in order to get the deal done. If you feel that is what is happening, just say no. If it was a tactic they will drop the point. If it was a genuine issue you can then have a proper negotiation about it. It is unlikely to be a point of such substance that they blow the deal, otherwise they would not have waited until the last minute to raise it.

This story is from early on in my career:

Once we settled a long-running audit claim with an artist, worth hundreds of thousands of pounds. The proposed settlement was well within our bottom line and the other team seemed comfortable as well. As we stood up to shake hands the artist's manager said to our chairman – 'Oh, by the way, you will be paying the audit fees for our accountants, won't you?' As he extended his hand to shake, our chairman immediately said, 'Oh yes, of course we will'.

That last-minute nibble cost £50,000. Watch out for them ...

In summary of the 'process', get closure when you see the opportunity, but don't forget about the other six stages of the negotiation. If you miss any of these out, you will not obtain a mutually beneficial outcome.

'SORRY, I FORGOT TO ASK – HOW WOULD YOU LIKE TO HANDLE THIS NEGOTIATION ?'

Review

There is one other stage after closing, which should follow on as night follows day. This is a stage which takes place so rarely that it almost never happens. That is *reviewing the negotiation*. How often do we sit down and review our negotiations? Thinking about what went well, what went badly? What we can learn for next time? Almost never, I suspect. The temptation is just to move on to implementation and focus on the next deal instead. This bypasses a major opportunity for learning.

When you next conclude a deal, take a few minutes out to review how it went. How did you execute against your plan? Did you stay above your bottom line? How accurate were your predictions of the other party's characteristics? Did you bring the right attitude to the negotiation? Did they? What could have been done to change their attitude if it was unhelpful? Did you select the right climate? Could you have prepared more? How successfully did you identify the underlying motivations of everyone involved? Did you find some hidden gems – some coinage that helped you get the deal done? Did you bid and bargain successfully?

In short, go back to all the matters you considered in your preparation phase and see how they went. To the extent that things went well, give yourself a pat on the back. To the extent that they could have gone better, make a note to learn from that for next time. Reviewing is useful in many situations, not just negotiating, but it is a key way of developing your skills as a deal maker.

Ideally it should take place just as soon as the deal is done, so that the impressions and recollections you have of the deal are very present for you. If you review it some weeks or months afterwards, your memories may be less accurate and your feedback to yourself may be influenced by how the deal is actually turning out in practice – that's useful to monitor as well, but it may not tell you so much about how you should have negotiated at the time, since you could not have been aware of all the factors that would impact on the implementation of the deal. So, close and review should go together at the end of the negotiating process.

Your Profile

Before we close the process stage of this book, and while we are on the subject of review, what did your profile map at the closemydeal website tell you about the way you handle negotiating process? Taking an overall look at your profile and considering both your own answers and others' feedback, how much do you focus on preparation or exploring needs and coinage when you negotiate? How much do you practise the key tips on bidding and bargaining? How sensitive are you to the closure moment? All the stages of the negotiation are important. Is there anything you could be trying to do more frequently?

Keep this profile, and come back to it in a few months' time. Maybe by then you will find you are giving each of these stages of the negotiating process the appropriate priority.

THE
NEGOTIATION
CHAIN

PART THREE

NEGOTIATING BEHAVIOUR

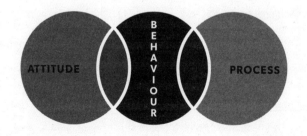

15

CHOICES OF BEHAVIOUR

Behaviour is the third link in the chain of effective negotiation and, again, it's about the 'structure' of the deal (rather than the 'content' which people normally spend most of their time discussing). How do you select which behaviour to use and what behaviour works best on which occasions? Select the right behaviour for the right context and you are much more likely to get a deal done, whatever the state of play regarding the 'content' of the deal. As we shall see, there are at least sixteen possible negotiation behaviours to select from, so it's all a question of – *choice*!

Once again, before you read this chapter, I would urge you to go and fill in the questionnaire at the closemydeal website about how you currently handle these sixteen negotiating behaviours.

The Framework of Useful Behaviours

There are many different kinds of possible negotiating behaviour in a negotiation, and any attempt to classify or summarise them inevitably risks leaving some possibilities out or not covering all the possible shades and variations of different types of behaviour. However, it's useful to have a basic framework you can utilise, so here is the model I work with which you too can work with. It is clustered around four basic behavioural styles, with a number of possible choices within each style. Don't worry if you can't absorb them all at once. There are plenty of examples in the next few chapters, and there is a useful graphic summarising the behaviours at the end of this chapter.

(a) 'I' behaviour

This is all about my agenda and what 'I' want from the negotiation, irrespective of what the other side may need. Examples include:

'Proposing with reasons'

For example:

- 'I propose this, because ...'
- 'I need this because ...'
- 'I want this in order to achieve x ...'
- 'I've put together this spreadsheet which supports what we have asked for ...'

'Using incentives and pressures'

For example:

- 'If you do this for me, I will do that for you ...' (the incentive)
- 'If you don't do this for me here's what will happen ...' (the pressure)

'Stating expectations'

For example:

- 'I don't respond to threats ...'
- 'You must come up with a better explanation ...'
- 'The advance has to increase ...'

'Testing and probing' what the other negotiator is saying

For example:

- 'Why do you want that?'
- 'How do you justify that rate when the market rate is 10 per cent lower?'

- 'What is the difference between your suggestion and the one I made an hour ago?'
- 'Why haven't you mentioned x when you know we need that information?'
- 'How does this compare to the standard of full disclosure which we agreed would govern this negotiation?'

(b) 'You' behaviour

This is all about working with the other negotiator's agenda and putting them at their ease. Examples include:

'Active listening' (which means showing that you have been listening by summarising or rephrasing what the other party has said or seems to be feeling)

For example:

- 'I see, so what you are saying is ...'
- 'If I could summarise what you have been saying ...'
- 'So, to put it another way, your argument is ...'
- 'I sense you are very unhappy about that ...'

'Exploring' by asking open questions

For example:

- 'How would you feel about this?'
- 'Help me understand that.'
- 'Tell me more about that your feelings on that.'
- 'Would it work if we did it like this?'

'Focusing on common ground' (drawing attention to what is agreed which shows the other party that progress is being made on their own agenda)

For example:

- 'At least we are all agreed on these three key points ...'
- 'Even though this last point is difficult, we've now covered

nine of the ten points on the agenda …'
- 'Well, we all want a deal which benefits both of us, so there must be a way forward.'

'Disclosing' (either feelings or information, which makes the other party feel valued or trusted)

For example:
- 'Let me tell you this in confidence …'
- 'I'm feeling this is not going too well – how are you feeling?'
- 'I shouldn't show you this really, but I want you to feel as though you are already part of the team …'

(c) 'We' behaviour

As its title suggests, this is about showing what 'we' can achieve together by doing a deal. Examples include:

'Visualising' (painting a positive picture of what the future together could be like)

For example:
- 'Just imagine what could happen if we can get this JV off the ground …'
- 'Let me set the scene for you, as we pick up the award together for best new product development next year …'

'Checking for consensus'

For example:
- 'Are we all agreed that …?'
- 'Let's summarise what's been agreed today …'

'Sharing problems'

For example:
- 'We seem to have a shared problem here.'

- 'We both face the same challenge.'
- 'Your difficulty is really just the flipside of ours.'
- 'Shall we identify the difficulties on both sides which arise from that potential plan?'

'Sharing solutions'

For example:

- 'Why don't we brainstorm some options together?'
- 'Let's make a list together of all the potential ways forward.'
- 'Shall we lock both our experts in the room together and ask them to come up with a joint plan?'

(d) 'Parting' behaviour

This is about taking contact out of the negotiation through recessing for a short period or adjourning for a longer duration, or through falling silent or terminating discussions. You can use any of the other behaviours to 'part'. Here are some examples:

'Pit-stop'

For example:

- 'I need a short break.' ('I' behaviour.)
- 'How would you feel about a quick break?' ('You' behaviour.)
- 'Just imagine how refreshed we will feel after a five-minute break.' ('We' behaviour.)

'Longer break'

For example:

- 'Can we come back to you in a couple of weeks?' ('You' behaviour.)
- 'I expect this will go better if we resume in seven days' time when all our research has been concluded.' ('I' behaviour.)

All these behaviours can be used positively. As such, they are much more use than negative behaviours. Negative behaviours make the other negotiator seem small and will very quickly create emotional tension and resentment, perhaps even immediate retaliation or withdrawal from the negotiation. They include being sarcastic, patronising, dismissive, insulting, dishonest and manipulative. Not to mention going over the other side's head or blaming them. These are to be avoided. Agreed?

Here's just one example from Paul Atherton, a producer with Simple Productions:

My girlfriend wanted to buy a new car. She did her research, compiled a list of attributes she wanted in a car, what size, mpg, insurance category.

She'd drilled her final decision down to a Renault Clio. Having been patronised for being a woman at the Renault dealership ('What colour would you like, love?', etc) she asked if I could come and negotiate the price on her behalf.

I'd learnt never to negotiate on price but on finance.

I knew what she wanted to pay on a monthly basis and put this to the dealer. The inevitable departure to the manager occurred but when the salesman returned he said they couldn't get anywhere close to her figure. In fact, he said sarcastically, the only place we could possibly pay that money was if we bought a Skoda.

We hadn't even put Skoda on the list. An oversight on our part as Skoda had just been bought by VW – we immediately went off and got an amazing deal from the Skoda dealership – way below her budget and far more car for her money.

We both took great pleasure in returning to the Renault dealership in her brand new Skoda Fabia a few days later to thank the manager for his salesman's recommendation!!!

Thanks to his patronising and then sarcastic comments we went somewhere else to buy a car. No idea if he kept his job.

Getting Stuck on the Wrong Behaviour

If you accept that your behaviour is not the product of the situation you are in, or the people you are dealing with, but a conscious choice that you make as a negotiator, it ought to be possible to use the full range of the positive behaviours outlined above and pick the right behaviour for the right occasion. However, here's the problem. We all tend to rely predominantly on our favourite behaviour, regardless of the circumstances and of whether it is working or not: we can get stuck in the same gear, regardless of the gradient. In fact, when things are going badly, and we really need to come up with a new approach, that is when we are most likely to rely on our favourite kind of behaviour. Sometimes when things are not going well in a negotiation the very best thing to do is *vary* your normal behaviour. It may surprise the other deal-maker, and push the negotiation forward. At the very least it will interrupt a negative pattern in a negotiation.

I once negotiated for the purchase of a music publishing catalogue containing songs written by one of the leading British art-house bands of the 1970s. The catalogue was owned by two wily older men who had been around the block a few times. It was late at night after an all-day meeting and things were not going well. My natural style as a negotiator is collaborative and I don't normally do a lot of shouting. On this occasion, partly because I was tired and partly because I was generally irritated with them, I gave myself permission to lose my temper. Everyone was shocked – including me. From that moment on the negotiation proceeded smoothly towards a satisfactory outcome for everybody. That's not an argument in favour of shouting, but it's important to be prepared to mix things up a bit with your behaviours from time to time, rather than always proceeding down the same behavioural route. If you do that you limit your options, you become predictable to the other negotiator and you are limiting your outcomes.

Here's a good example of getting stuck using the wrong behaviour for the wrong occasion:

I was once sent to Italy by Syco to negotiate with an Italian singer who was being considered for Il Divo. We journeyed to a furniture warehouse on the edge of town where the singer lived with his parents above the store. It was a cold day and there was a hole in the roof with snowflakes floating gently down on to the furniture. The young man's parents were there. The father was a quiet, small man who said nothing. The negotiation was driven by the singer's mother – a very strong character. She was determined to push for every possible benefit for her son. Nothing was too much for her bambino. She wanted him treated better than any other member of the group. No doubt this all proceeded from the best of motives and it was this achievement need which drove the consistent 'stating of expectations' – an 'I' behaviour.

As the record company, however, we needed to make sure that the group members were all treated the same – otherwise it would be very difficult to create a stable group. This was a reassurance need which required more 'you' and 'we' behaviour – listening, exploring, sharing the problem. Result? We didn't sign that particular singer. He has gone on to have a fairly successful solo career, but at that point he wanted to be in the group, and twenty million Il Divo album sales later it is worth considering whether the right behaviour was chosen for the right occasion on that day in Italy ...

You can find many other examples of behaviour being used questionably at the website – from the British government's well-intentioned handling of its reforms of the National Health Service, through to Apple negotiating its licensing deals with the music industry.

In the next three chapters we shall look at how to avoid getting stuck like this and how to make the most rather than the least of your behavioural options. Meanwhile, here is a summary of these 16 behavioural choices.

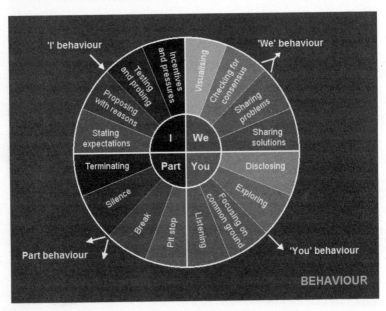

16

BODY LANGUAGE: THE KEY TO MODELLING SUCCESSFUL BEHAVIOUR?

Whichever behaviour you select, you want to model that behaviour convincingly. There are a number of different aspects involved in this. Part of it is simply your choice of words. Part of the impact of what you say is conveyed by the way you use your *voice*. Part of the impact is conveyed by the way you use your *face* and its expressions. Part of the message comes from the way you use your *body*.

All of these constituent elements may have both a voluntary and an involuntary element. Some experts suggest two-thirds of the meaning in any social situation is conveyed by body language.[78] Some experts argue that only 7 per cent of the meaning of what we say is conveyed by the actual words.[79] The other 93 per cent is conveyed by the 'music' and the 'dance'. The 'music' is the way you use your voice – its pitch, its rhythm, its loudness, its expressiveness, where you place the emphasis, your vocal power and tone, its speed, where you use pauses. The 'dance' is the way you use your face and body – your facial expressions, eye contact, your posture, whether you are fidgeting, your use of body space, your gestures, your proximity, the use of touch and movement.

Such experts argue that all three elements – words, voice and body – need to be in alignment for your behaviour to be impactful. If they are not, others may not believe you mean what you say.

This is not to forget about the impact on your message of other non-verbal cues such as the way you dress and the surroundings you choose (e.g. what does placing ultra-modern furniture in your office say about you, as opposed to using only antique furniture? Or wearing loud clothes, a punky haircut and overlarge, colourful glasses rather than a sober suit, a more traditional hairstyle and modest spectacles?).

There is no doubt that non-verbal communication forms an important part of our messages to each other. Before human beings developed language they communicated non-verbally. Newly born babies and infants do so before they learn to speak. Allowing for some cultural variations, certain behaviours such as smiling, crying and pointing are almost universally understood. As former Home Office psychologist, Len Curran has noted,[80] non-verbal communication can be used deliberately to reinforce a spoken message, to mock, to criticise silently (e.g. a headmaster's frown or sarcastically raised eyebrow in a classroom). It can be used to convey dominance (e.g. standing too close to you), or formality, or intimacy (e.g. mirroring someone's posture or touching). Certainly, when used deliberately to reinforce your own messages, it must be helpful to ensure that your body language is consistent with the words that you use – not least when you are negotiating. If it is consistent there is no absolute guarantee that you will be properly understood, but there is less scope for misunderstanding than if your face, voice or body are not congruent with what you are saying.

'I' Behaviour

Let's look at some suggestions of how that can work. For example, if you want to make a bid:

- Use the right language ('I want', 'I require', 'I need').
- Keep it brief, don't waffle.
- As well as using strong words to make a bid, you can

use your voice and body in a way that supports this 'I' behaviour. So make sure your voice sounds strong and maybe a little louder than usual, and speak slowly and clearly. Metaphorically, this will help 'push' the other side back.

- In addition, as we noted earlier when we were looking at bidding during our discussion of process, you might also want to lean forward towards the other negotiator (which may also have the effect of pushing them back).
- Your facial expression should be serious – no smiling.
- You should try to look them in the eye. If you find that difficult or disconcerting, focus on the point on their brow between the eyes or just choose one of their eyes to focus on. You may find that a bit easier and from the point of view of the other person it will still seem as if you are looking them in the eye.

If you do all these things, you may notice that the other negotiator shifts backwards in the chair a little. This would be a good physical sign that your 'I' behaviour has worked and 'pushed' them in the direction you want the negotiation to take. If you don't do these things, don't be surprised if the other negotiator doesn't take your bid seriously. If you slouch back in your chair, or your body is curled up, or you are looking at the ground or using a hesitant, quiet voice, or speaking too quickly, or mumbling, that sends a signal to the other negotiator which is at variance with the words you are using, so even if you say 'I want this' or 'I require that' the message will come across far less strongly than the words you have used.

'You' Behaviour

Conversely, if you want to use 'you' behaviour, with some exploring language must go appropriate alignment of body and voice. 'You' behaviour is all about working off the other person's agenda so you need to put them at their ease, like this:

- 'You' behaviour is frequently characterised by the use of questions, and questions which open up the dialogue are best. Closed questions are not so useful because they merely get you a yes/no response (e.g. 'Do you agree that we should focus on the negotiating process?'). Open questions are better because they start a conversation (e.g. 'How would you like to handle the negotiating process?').

- Once again, though, you need to make sure that your body and voice support this approach. With regard to your voice, you might want to use a softer tone, which is more relaxed. You don't have to be so clipped and to the point as when you are bidding. You can take longer to make your points when you are exploring. You want the other party to feel they have as much time as it takes to explore everything thoroughly. Your rhythm and pace can be slower.

- One tip on tone which I picked up from the coacher's coach, James Stokes, is to make sure your voice descends at the end of the question rather than rises. When you ask a question with a rising tone at the end it makes it sound as if you are much less certain about what you are saying. When you ask a question with a descending tone at the end, it sounds more like a statement and the other party will feel more like they ought to answer it because the question has been asked with some authority.

- From the point of view of supporting this use of language with your body, it can be good to lean back slightly. This can subconsciously make the other party feel as though they have permission to fill the space – it's as if you are 'pulling' them towards you.

- Your facial expressions can be more welcoming and less stern – a smile is all right as long as it doesn't turn into a fixed grin.
- Look alert and attentive, as though you are actually interested in the answers to the questions you have asked.

If you can manage to put all of this together when using 'you' behaviour, the physical result on the other negotiator might be that they involuntarily shift in their seat towards you, which could be a sign that the behaviour is working. If you don't align all these elements properly then you can guess what the result will be. If you ask exploring questions in a loud, boorish manner, with a barking voice, that will not open up the discussion. If you lean forward in a menacing way rather than leaning back in order to invite dialogue, it doesn't matter what words you use: the other negotiator will not feel comfortable or confident about exploring with you. If you have a thunderous expression on your face, or look like you are chewing a wasp, or you are staring out of the window, the other person will not pick up that you are genuinely interested in what they have to say.

'We' Behaviour

You can see the pattern now, so let's turn to 'we' behaviour:

- 'We' behaviour is all about what can be achieved by joining together, so you would expect the language used to have lots of references to 'we' and 'us' rather than 'I' and 'me'. You would also expect lots of references to togetherness – use of expressions such as 'hand in hand' or 'in partnership' or 'joined at the hip'.
- If you are visualising, you would need to be using metaphors that can inspire and excite the other

negotiator: 'Together we can conquer the world' or 'Side by side the sky's the limit'.

- Your voice will need to be animated and energised to convey the excitement of what you are talking about.
- You may want to speak a bit more quickly than usual to support that and with fewer pauses, as we tend to do when we are in a state of excitement. Equally, your voice may need more variation in tone and be pitched a little higher which are also characteristics of an animated person – just think how football commentators sound: they can get excited describing a throw-in.
- As before, your use of your body and facial expressions should be supportive. When you are using 'we' behaviour it's often helpful to sit next to the person you are negotiating with rather than on the opposite side of the table. This can help convey that you are both 'on the same side'. You can also lean sideways a little towards the other person to emphasise this.
- Your facial expressions should be animated and alive, and the excitement should be visible in your eyes.
- This is one instance in which fidgeting could be acceptable: all of us fidget sometimes when we are in an excitable state.

If you can manage all of this, the other negotiator may well be more convinced by the image you are portraying. If your body and voice don't support the words, they are unlikely to be moved. If your voice is downbeat and dull, if you speak very slowly and quietly, you are not going to convince anybody, even if you start off by saying 'Let me paint a picture for you…' If you are leaning back as if you are stretched out for a nice quiet afternoon nap, you will not come across as inspiring. If your face suggests you could get a job as a funeral director, and you look bored, you are not going to succeed in getting the other negotiator to share your vision.

So far so good. Deliberate use of congruent body language to support your own message can make your behaviour more impactful. If you are on the receiving end of such deliberately enhanced messages, that may increase the effectiveness of the communication to you.

Inadvertent Body Language

It's harder to evaluate the usefulness of reading 'inadvertent' body language coming from the other negotiator. For example, some people interpret involuntary *facial* cues, such as blushing, or dilation of the pupils, or sweating, as signs of stress and certainly these cues can be associated with anxiety or the initiation of 'fight or flight' responses. But that is not the guaranteed interpretation. I may just be flushing because I am hot, or have recently been exercising. My pupils might dilate because I have come from brightness outside to a darker room.

It's the same with use of the *body* – it is quite easy to misinterpret involuntary cues. For example, some experts believe that:

- If hands are clenched, gripping the chair, or the arms are crossed over the chest, that indicates the person is 'clinging' to their position or 'holding on', or is defensive or angry.
- Drumming the fingers is a sign of boredom.
- Hands folded neatly in the lap suggests submission, or following the rules.
- Stroking your beard or chin, or smoothing your hair, can be a learned behaviour to calm anxiety.
- Closeness of body can indicate a desire for affiliation.

The problem with all of these assumptions is that they may or may not be correct. I may stroke my chin out of habit, or for the sake of comfort, or because I am thinking about something, or because I am about to make a decision – it may have nothing to do with my being anxious. I may be drumming my fingers out of boredom, or it may be a deliberate pressure tactic to show that I am feeling superior to you, or maybe I am a musician and so I frequently exercise my fingers when I have nothing else to do with them. Maybe I hold my hands in my lap because my nails are a bit scruffy and I don't want to show them, or because I have lost a button off my cuff and I want to disguise that – it may have nothing to do with being demure. Maybe if I am standing closer to you than you would expect it is not to do with a specific desire for affiliation but because that is what a lot of people in my country do – there is a generalisation that this applies, for example, in Indonesia.

Detecting Deception

In a similar vein to those previous potentially misleading signals, here are some examples of supposed involuntary signs of deception:

- When we want to 'smile' to show we are happy about something we find it hard to control 'dependable' muscles which reveal our true feelings. So, even if we are smiling:
  – The eyebrows could rise and come together, and the forehead might wrinkle, suggesting fear or anxiety.
  – The smile may 'look' false – because it's too quick or too long (like a frozen smile) or because it is crooked.
- Equally, if we say 'yes' we may make gestures which indicate 'no'. For example, if we are asked to do something we don't want to do we may say 'yes', but accompany that with an incompleted shrug or raise the palms of our hands to indicate we are saying 'yes' only because we feel powerless to say 'no'.
- If we are lying we may touch our mouth or parts of our

face close to our mouth (like the cheek or the nose), almost as if we were trying not to speak an untruth.

- We might close our eyes or rub an eye vigorously or look down to avoid eye contact with the person we are deceiving.
- We might rub our neck or scratch the back of it or pull at our collar as though we are very uncomfortable with the lie we are telling.
- Liars are said to fidget in their chairs a lot, perhaps leaning one way then another, as if trying to get away from the situation.
- Some experts such as psychologist Paul Ekman[81] believe that we give ourselves away with micro-expressions lasting less than a fifth of a second which are then replaced with a contrived expression. So if we are lying we might replace a momentary genuine look of discomfort with a practised smile. It is argued that the other person picks up these genuine momentary expressions unconsciously, which may explain why we feel uncomfortable, without quite knowing why, if someone is not telling the truth.

Again, the problem with all these insights is that the same actions may be explicable in other ways. Maybe we just don't have an even smile; maybe our forehead is naturally furrowed when we smile; perhaps we touch our cheek or our mouth because we feel nervous or because we have an itch. Maybe we rub our eye because we have hay fever or are tired. Perhaps our shirt collar is too tight or it's a hot day and our neck is sticky and that's why we rub it. Maybe we are a naturally fidgety person who never sits still. Perhaps any micro-expression picked up by the other side is an indication of our genuine feelings about some other situation which has popped into our head and which has nothing to do with expressing deceit. I may just be avoiding eye contact because I am shy, or because eye contact is considered invasive (as we shall see, there is a generalisation about Japanese culture that eye contact is avoided – bowing rituals help support this custom). Or maybe we are dealing with a genuine liar who is very practised at concealing all of these 'clues' to deceit, so their absence doesn't signify that we are dealing with someone who is telling us the truth.

Unless you are highly trained in reading body language, if you want to detect deceit it may be better to go back to the spoken word to do it most effectively – for example, by phrasing questions in a variety of ways to see if you get consistent answers, or by asking questions to which you already know the answer.[82]

Matching Verbal and Physical Messages

What can be said positively about interpreting the other side's *inadvertent* body language is that it may certainly give some *clues* as to what is really going on. As we have already noted, one of the challenges about negotiating is that the other negotiator often doesn't tell you what they are really thinking or feeling, so you become something of a detective looking for evidence as to their real state of mind.

Paying attention to involuntary body language can provide one set of data to take into account – *especially if it is inconsistent with the spoken mes*sage. Just as deliberate, congruent body language can enhance the effectiveness of a message, so inadvertent, incongruent body language may point to a discrepancy with the spoken words. This can be combined with cues taken from the actual words people use, the way they behave, the priorities they express, the needs they seem to be focused upon, in order to create a composite picture of what may be happening. If you don't just rely on one snapshot of these elements, but calibrate them as you go along, adding more data all the while, you will end up with a more accurate view of what you are dealing with than if you ignore the non-verbal signals.

Having looked at how to make the behaviour you choose as impactful as possible, let's now look at how to choose the right behaviour for the right occasion.

17

MATCH THE BEHAVIOUR TO THE RIGHT STAGE OF THE PROCESS

One thing to bear in mind when choosing your behaviour is that *different behaviour* suits *different stages* of the negotiation process. Let's examine each stage after the preparation stage in turn and give some examples.

Climate

The right behaviour here depends on which climate you wish to create. If you want to create a hostile climate then a spot of 'I' behaviour, focused entirely on your own expectations and demands, would probably be just right. For example, 'I propose that the meeting takes place in my office' (stating expectations), or 'Unless we finalise the negotiations by Tuesday, we can't continue' (using pressures).

If you want to create a warm and open climate, more cooperative 'you' behaviour is far more likely to be helpful. 'How would you like the agenda to be agreed?' (exploring) or 'I'd feel more relaxed if the meeting took place in a neutral setting' (disclosing).

If you are going for a cool climate, maybe a spot of proposing with reasons would work: 'I suggest the agenda is agreed in writing by a jointly convened committee because that will ensure that all interests are formally noted.'

If you want a cheeky climate, some 'we' behaviour may work, for example, 'Let's organise a karaoke night for our two teams to have a joint brainstorm on creative ideas' (sharing solutions).

Exploring Needs and Wants

(a) Listening and exploring

'You' behaviour is more commonly useful in the early stages of a negotiation, when you are exploring and trying to identify the needs of those involved in the negotiation.

As a starting point, it pays to concentrate on the other negotiator at this stage, so you will want to be asking plenty of 'exploring' questions. You will need to be actively 'listening' very carefully to your deal partner's responses. This involves classic 'you' behaviour – showing that you have been listening by nodding, focusing your attention on the other side, summarising and paraphrasing. Focusing your attention means genuinely paying attention and not just planning what you are going to say next or worrying about your next meeting while giving the appearance of listening. Active listening also means checking your understanding regularly – 'Have I got this right, then, you are saying (x, y and z …)?' Summarising what people say means doing that genuinely, even positively, not just with a spin that belittles its importance or tries to make it suit your own arguments. You are not giving anything away by showing that you understand what they have said. If you don't do this, the other negotiator will worry that they have not been able to get their point across and they will be fretting about that when they should be listening to you.

Active listening also involves reflecting emotions back to the other party. In order to do this you first have to be able to notice emotions accurately. Researchers have concluded that differences in the accuracy of emotion recognition may be linked to negotiation performance, because the ability to comprehend subtle communication signals is a beneficial skill that provides relevant information to negotiators.[83]

Having noticed the emotions being expressed, it's important to show people that their emotions are acknowledged – often they want that even more than any concrete outcome or response. If someone is upset, simply saying 'I can see you are extremely upset by this' is really helpful – certainly more so than just brushing aside their emotion because it makes you feel uncomfortable.

Legitimising their emotions in your active listening is also very powerful; this is the other part of acknowledging emotions – it lets people know it's okay to feel the way they do. So 'I can see you are extremely upset by this and, putting myself in your shoes, I can see why you feel that way' is even more effective. There is nothing weak about doing this. Quite the reverse. Whoever you are negotiating with, and however irritating they may be they are probably just doing their best as they see it – even if they are the mouthpiece for positions that you don't wish to hear. Recognising that they may have emotional stakes in the deal is likely to get you far further than if you ignore that.

Genuine listening is very difficult to do in practice. We often prefer to speak instead, but there is a good maxim for negotiating which is to use your ears and your mouth in the proportions in which God gave them to you. On that basis, two thirds of your time should be spent listening and only one third talking. If we listened more, we would all achieve better results as negotiators. Maybe international treaty discussions should be called 'Listens' rather than 'Talks'… Don't feel that negotiations are won by the person who talks the most.

'SO THOSE ARE THE FIRST TWO HUNDRED
MAIN POINTS ABOUT ME — NOW, HOW
ABOUT YOU ?

(b) Focusing on common ground

It is also useful to 'focus on common ground' at the exploring stage of the negotiation as it reminds the other negotiator that their own agenda is moving forward. Just saying, 'Well, at least we both want to extend our agreement as soon as possible,' can transform the feelings around a long list of apparently irreconcilable points that each party wants. Now we are both on a positive track rather than just focusing on the distance between us, because we both want the same thing. Focusing on common ground is often a good way of re-framing challenging differences and replacing them with a positive context.

Here's a story from John Royce, an organisation consultant and negotiation trainer, showing how focusing on common ground – however tenuous – can be the pivot for a positive negotiation. John was one of the people who inspired me to be a better negotiator, and some of the ideas developed in this book were first introduced to me by him and his colleague, Kevin McKee, twenty years ago:

A managing director was concerned that one of his manufacturing plants for telecoms equipment was underperforming. Two
departments were stereotyping each other. The marketing group
saw production as inflexible, stubborn and unaware of customer
requirements. Production, on the other hand, saw marketing as
out of touch with reality.

I was asked to mediate between the two groups in order
to produce a working agreement. The scene was set in the
conference room on location, where I arranged a small circle
of chairs for the three most senior production people and the
three most senior marketing people, plus a chair for myself. The
production trio were the first to arrive and proceeded to rearrange
three of the chairs into a straight line. The marketing people
arrived, observed the situation and arranged three more chairs
opposite the production team. I felt like the umpire at Centre
Court, Wimbledon!

I decided on an approach that they would not expect. 'What
do you think you all have in common?' I asked. There followed
a period of seven minutes of total silence, during which you
could have cut the atmosphere with a knife. Eventually, one of
the production people sat forward and said, 'I suppose we're all
human beings.' Laughter filled the room, which turned out to be
the breakthrough. Both parties apologised for their past childish
behaviour and put their minds to a serious resolution of their
differences. Within two hours, we had an agreed action plan.

Focusing on common ground can also involve identifying and ring-
fencing the thing that you both *don't* agree on. This can have the
positive effect of making such issues seem more manageable. 'It
seems to me that if we could just reconcile our respective needs for
protection we would be able to get this done pretty quickly – would
you agree?'

Finally, focusing on common ground can give you a common 'enemy' against which it makes sense to unite. This encourages people to work together collaboratively because the thing they are working against is more important to both of them than the issues which divide them. The common enemy does not need to be that dramatic. It might be a regulatory process or some red tape which both parties would rather avoid, a factor that causes costs to rise for both of them or prevents increased mutual profit, a competitor who stands to outpace both of them, a legislative requirement which wastes both sides' time. Focusing on these common obstacles can help minimise the distance between them on those issues on which they disagree.

(c) Disclosing

'Disclosing' is a further 'you' behaviour that can also be useful in the exploring stage of the negotiation. Disclosing your feelings or confidential information can make people feel that they are in some way privileged to be hearing something which might normally be private. 'I don't know about you but I am finding this really hard going. It seems that whichever way we turn we are running into obstacles. How are you feeling?' This sends a message that you value and respect their involvement – it's a vote of confidence in them and their own agenda as well. It may also invite them to disclose something back which can be very helpful to you in your own quest to identify the real interests on each side. They may respond – 'Do you know what, you are right, I feel the same – my board is giving me a lot of grief, too, over the amount of time this is taking ...' This would be a further example of the principle of 'reciprocity' we looked at earlier.

(d) 'You' behaviour and likeability

There is another reason for using 'you' behaviour in the exploring phase of a negotiation, which is that it makes us more likeable.

Cialdini cites 'liking' as another one of his core sources of influencing. We tend to be influenced more by people we like than by those we don't. Sadly, in making 'liking' decisions we often rely on shallow factors. We like people who are good-looking – hence, for example, the supra-popularity of good-looking sports stars over ordinary-looking ones. We like people who are more 'like us', because they share our interests and passions. We like people who compliment and flatter us – even when we know that the flattery is probably not genuine.

We like people with whom we share cooperative exercises – consider why companies send employees on outward bound trips where they have to bond over team exercises in which cooperation is required. Moreover, we like things that are 'associated' with people we like – we assume that the products and services they are associated with must have the same positive attributes that we assign to them, and we want to link ourselves with that good association because that also makes us feel better about ourselves. All of us can be influenced by sales reps who take the time to find out about our background and interests and then present their own background so as to seem more like us. It may emerge that, spookily, they have the same interest in golf or some other sport, and know very well the part of the country we come from, and that predisposes us towards the product they are selling.

You don't have to be manipulative about being likeable and it is not advisable: people often see through this kind of artifice, even if they enjoy it. However, showing a genuine interest in the other person, asking them questions about themselves, demonstrating that you have been listening to what they have been saying, focusing on the points you have in common, sharing confidences appropriately – these are all 'you' behaviours which can make us seem more likeable to the people we are negotiating with, and help set up the later stages of the negotiation positively.

(e) 'You' behaviour and trust

One other reason for utilising 'you' behaviours in the exploring stage is that it helps people trust you more. Trust is a key component in successful 'fusing'-based negotiations. Trust has been found to encourage the exchange of information.[84] [85] Trust has also been shown to encourage cooperation. Trust is also a key element of positive relationships between people – 'truth in signalling' thought or feelings is often cited as one of the most important attributes of positive working relationships and, once lost, it is hard to reverse.[86] [87]

(f) 'You' behaviour and bad relationships

Of course you may well be negotiating with someone with whom you already have a *negative* relationship, perhaps as a result of a previous dispute or disagreement. How do you have a productive exploration phase with them? The answer, once again, is to focus on 'you' behaviours as there is evidence that these kinds of behaviours can turn such relationships around. Researchers recommend maintaining open communications to improve relations, and engaging in active listening.[88] If you do this while maintaining a 'fusing' attitude it can make a difference (e.g. openly expressing concern for the other's welfare and demonstrating a real interest in problem solving). Be prepared for any such process to take time, though, during which you must behave consistently. Negative relationships can be turned around but they take much longer to reverse than to create.

'I' behaviour is often less appropriate in the exploring phase as it's all about your own needs and therefore doesn't encourage dialogue or openness. 'We' behaviour could be helpful in the exploring phase but you have to be careful with it, as it assumes an intimacy and a desire for togetherness which the other party may not yet be ready for. If you 'join' too early you may put the other side off. I remember my father facilitating a job interview for a former Disney music executive, a lovely man and naturally very extrovert and effusive. When he was introduced by my father to his prospective new employer he was so overfamiliar, and so excited so quickly, that it was actually off-putting to the employer and he didn't get the job.

Finding Coinage

As you would expect, 'you' behaviour is also useful when you are trying to find coinage on both sides. This requires patience, curiosity about the other party and an ability to actively listen and observe. None of these attributes is particularly associated with 'I' behaviour. The other negotiator is far less likely to be disclosive about their needs or the coinage they have if you are exerting pressures or stating your own expectations. They may not feel comfortable enough to be disclosive, or they may not feel they can get a word in. Once again, 'we' behaviour could be useful at this stage, too, as long as you do not put people off by being too gushing or intimate too early.

Bidding

I'm sure you've already worked out that 'I' behaviour is generally more suitable for the bidding stage of a negotiation. 'Proposing with reasons' ('I want this because …') is made for bidding and 'stating expectations' can be useful as well ('We expect a 50 per cent increase in your current royalty rate to us'). Softer behaviours associated with 'you' just don't do the job. We have already seen how, if you present bids as exploring questions ('How would you feel about …?' or 'Would it be okay if …?'), that is not impactful on the other negotiator. 'We' behaviour doesn't really work either as in the bidding stage you are necessarily prioritising what *you* want. 'Parting' behaviour, such as use of silence, may occasionally be helpful tactically: remember the story from Steve whose boss used silence to enhance the power of his bid.

Bargaining

'I' behaviour suits the bargaining phase as well. Gaps can be closed through the use of 'incentives and pressures' ('If you agree to x then we can agree to y,' or 'If you don't agree to this proposal then we will do z'). 'Testing and probing' is also useful during the bargaining phase as you probe away at the bid(s) made by the other party ('That's ridiculous, why do you want that?'). In addition, the bargaining phase also frequently features lots of counterbids for which 'proposing with reasons' and 'stating expectations' are appropriate. 'Parting' behaviour comes into its own in the bargaining phase as well. As we've already mentioned, it can be great to take a break during the bargaining stage in order to regroup, re-energise and think up creative solutions. 'Parting' behaviour is precisely about calling for those shorter or longer breaks.

'We' behaviour can also be great for breaking deadlocks in the bargaining phase – for example, 'visualising' and so inspiring people with a vision of future success to carry them over stumbling blocks in the deal which are preventing closure. 'Sharing problems' and 'sharing solutions' to those problems are also 'we' behaviours which are tailor-made for the bargaining phase, by which time such gaps will be clear.

'Sharing problems' is a great way of getting parties to put their personal animosity aside for a moment and consider the challenge they face jointly. You and I may not like each other that much and we may have exhausted each other with positional negotiating, but if we can both acknowledge that we have a shared concern with, e.g. getting the deal done before the end of the tax year, the sharing of that challenge is likely to encourage both of us to work constructively on its resolution. Sharing my problems with you is also a way of empowering you in the negotiation, of making you feel as though you co-own the problem and the solution. This can be helpful in resolving many conflicts, not least industrial disputes.

Consider this example from telecoms executive Elisabetta:

SITUATION: some seven to eight years ago I was working for a technology consumer products company in Europe. We were commercially very successful and we were the clear number one in the market, commanding a price premium for our excellent quality product and brand.

COMPLICATION: we started getting some strong competitors from Asia who were offering similar, though more low end, products at lower prices. While these new competitors manufactured their products exclusively in Asia (mainly China) we were the only player manufacturing our products exclusively in Germany even though in a very modern factory.

As business leaders we realised that we only had two options: 1) Move our factory to Eastern Europe or China, or 2) Get the manufacturing costs down in our German factory.

SOLUTION: we negotiated over the two options with the trade unions. The move to China would have meant the loss of all jobs in the factory in Germany and also a loss of flexibility in delivering products to distributors at short notice directly from the factory due to the distance to China.

With this in mind, all management functions (sales and marketing, manufacturing) and the unions looked together at ways to address the problem and make an already automated factory more competitive. They had a shared interest in a positive outcome. The only way to do this was to reduce personnel costs, e.g. to reduce salaries and some extra benefits of all staff in the factory against a commitment from the company not to relocate the factory. After long negotiations this was the result and salary adjustments were made. In addition, sales and marketing decided that from now on they would also market the products as 'Made in Germany' as a differentiators against 'cheap' competitors.

CONCLUSION: the strategy worked and the factory is still thriving today. Other manufacturing companies in Germany have followed the same example.

This is not just an example of the power of sharing problems but also one of the power of finding a common enemy (in this case potential competition from China) in order to minimise the negotiating differences between the parties.

'Sharing solutions' works the same way as 'sharing problems' – brainstorming collaborative answers to problems can help create outcomes which cut through bargaining difficulties, as we saw when we looked at the bargaining stage of the negotiation.[89] Academic research points to creativity arising from negotiators sharing priorities and making joint decisions as a key element in successful negotiation.

Closing

You have choices about how you get to closure but, generally, it would be with either 'we' or 'I' behaviour. 'We' behaviour is good because you want the emphasis to be on togetherness as you approach the finishing line. We have talked before about the need to 'check for consensus' when you believe you have reached the closure moment: that is a 'we' behaviour. Equally, effective 'visualisation' about how you are going to work together may carry you over the line to closure. Alternatively, if you feel closure is near but the process needs a shove you can 'push' your way to a close with some 'I' behaviour.

For example, asking a question like 'I think we're all done now, aren't we?' (with your voice coming down at the end of the question) is effectively 'stating an expectation' and may do the trick.

Sometimes people find this focusing on 'I' behaviour during the latter stages of the negotiation a bit confusing as they feel it is inconsistent with a collaborative negotiating stance. However, it makes sense if you remember that negotiation is a process with its seven stages. This book advocates a 'fusing' attitude to negotiation where you try to combine the agendas of the two parties. In the early stages of exploring and identifying coinage that means focusing on the other negotiator and ensuring that you fully understand their needs and demonstrating that you are interested in their motivations.

Having worked that out, the balance of the seesaw switches during the latter stages of bidding and bargaining so that the emphasis is more on what you are going to get back in return for meeting the other negotiator's needs – i.e. their needs have not disappeared, it's just that in the later stages you are prioritising what you get back in return for addressing them. If you only focus on these later stages and only use 'I' behaviour throughout, you might be perceived as a bit of a 'user'. If you only focus on the early stages and only use 'you' behaviour, you might be casting yourself as a loser. The ideal 'fuser' understands that the negotiation process is a seesaw and balances their focus on the other negotiator during the early stages with constructive usage of 'I' behaviour during the later stages of the negotiation.

18

MATCH THE BEHAVIOUR TO THE PERSON

If matching your behaviour to the right *stage* of the negotiation is one key to making the best behavioural choices, the other is matching the right behaviour to the right *person*. People are distinguished by their different personalities. They are not all the same, so it would be surprising if one type of behaviour suited everyone you deal with. So what kind of person are you dealing with?

Defining Personality

Psychologists have created many different theories and classifications of personality. Some work with very broad 'types', for example Type A and Type B. Impatient, achievement-orientated people are classified as Type A, while easy-going, relaxed individuals are designated as Type B. In looking at typologies analytical psychologists such as Jung distinguished two broad attitudes:

- **Extroversion** – outward looking, action orientated, people orientated, seeking breadth of engagement.
- **Introversion** – inward looking, thought orientated, happy to spend time alone, seeking depth of engagement.

Overlaying these attitudes are the four functions of *sensing* and *intuition*, and *thinking* and *feeling*. Individuals who prefer sensing are more likely to trust information which is concrete and tangible, or factual, whereas those who prefer intuition tend to trust information that is more abstract or theoretical, or that might be based on a flash of insight. Individuals who prefer thinking make decisions on a rational, logical basis, which matches a set of rules, and without emotion. People who prefer feeling come to decisions by empathising, looking for harmony or balance, and relying on personal values. Combining the two attitudes with the four functions gives eight possible personality types, each with a different dominating function that informs the personality – for example, people may be 'extroverted sensing' types or 'introverted thinking' types or 'extroverted feeling' types, and so on.

Criticism of typologies of these kinds as descriptors of personality has tended to be based on the fact that the categories are so broad. This has led to the development of *trait* theory which describes personality by way of narrower behavioural tendencies, with central traits forming the building blocks of the personality. Cattell[90] identified sixteen such traits which measure our degree of personality features such as warmth, reasoning, dominance, liveliness, social boldness, rule consciousness, self-reliance, sensitivity to others, tension and openness to change.

Current thinking among psychologists revolves around the so-called 'big five' traits. These are:

- **Extroversion** – the extent to which we are talkative, expressive.
- **Openness** – to experience, creativity, new ideas.
- **Conscientiousness** – how organised, self-disciplined we are.
- **Agreeableness** – how trusting, tolerant, compassionate we are.
- **Neuroticism** – the extent to which we are anxious, not able to deal well with stress.

Neuro-Linguistic Programming and Personality

NLP does not articulate personality in this way but, as we have seen, draws on patterns of thinking, or 'meta programmes', to explain behaviours which make us different as individuals. These are the most powerful of all the 'filters' through which we interpret our experience of the world. There are many different such patterns or ways of 'sorting' our experiences. Such patterns may be discernible from people's use of language and other cues.

For example, NLP practitioners recognise that, in the first instance, some people sort by reference to their *emotions* or *senses*, some by reference to *picture images* which they form in their mind's eye, others by reference to *auditory cues* such as voices, words or noises. This classification has found its way into teaching models as a way of describing how students can learn more effectively (as in Neil Fleming's so-called 'VAK' model of learning). You may be able to tell where people may fall in this classification by the language they use. 'Visual' people will use expressions such as 'Let's look at it this way' or 'I see what you mean' or 'My view is' or 'Seeing is believing'. People who work with sounds will also use language which indicates their preference. They may use expressions such as 'I hear what you say' or 'That sounds right' or 'Tell me more about that point' or 'Listening to what you've just said ...' People who are 'kinetic' and work with their senses may use expressions like 'That feels better' or 'That smells a bit fishy' or 'We're within touching distance now' or 'That leaves a nasty taste in my mouth'.

Some NLP theorists believe that you can also spot these typologies by reference to people's eye movements. If people look up when they are talking to you, they may be visual thinkers who are seeing pictures in their mind's eye. If they look to the side when they are speaking to you, they may be working with auditory cues. If they are looking down, they may be working with their senses, feelings and emotions. In each case whether they are looking to their left or right could be revealing as well. If I asked you to imagine being lost in a public place as a small child and you worked with 'pictures', you might look up and to your left if you were *remembering* a picture of what that was like when it happened to you, or up to your right if you were *imagining* a picture of what that must have been like for some other child. You might look sideways to your left if you were drawing upon a remembered auditory representation – for example re-hearing in your head a news bulletin about a missing child, or sideways to your right if you were creating an auditory representation. If you were looking downward to your right that might indicate you were experiencing feelings and emotions aroused by the scenario. If you were looking downwards and to your left that might indicate some internally constructed dialogue going on as you analyse and try to make sense of the scenario. In each case the right/left indicators could be reversed for someone who is left-handed.

In addition to differentiators based on language and eye movements, here are some other NLP categorisations of patterns of thinking:

- *Some people like to move towards solutions*, others are more tentative and are happier exploring the same problem from several different angles, or focusing on the difficulties with a proposed solution. You might find more academics among the latter category. We looked at the importance of 'towards' thinking rather than 'away' thinking when we considered negotiating attitude.
- *Some people like to work with the big picture*, others are more interested in the detail. When you shake hands on a deal, do you like to just get on with this exciting new venture, or is the small print of the long-form contract and all its schedules more important to you? As with most of these patterns, people who like detail will often

reveal themselves with their language – you will find them talking about the importance of 'the nitty gritty' or being 'precise'.

- *Some people are very 'associated'* – very emotionally engaged in what they are doing and living in the moment, others are 'dissociated' – they seem rather detached and unemotional, almost as if they were somewhere else when they are talking to you. Like all these patterns there is no right or wrong about this. Sometimes it's very useful to 'associate' so that you can fully experience the emotions and feelings of a situation. For example, being in an associated state might be very helpful when you are 'exploring' as a negotiator. Sometimes being 'dissociated' is helpful – for example, if you want to deal with tough guys without experiencing the hurtful emotions they might arouse by being threatening or aggressive.

- *Some people are very focused on the past* and dwell on their previous experiences. Again, their language may give you a clue. They may say things like 'Do you remember when …' Or 'Did you hear what they said …' or 'This happened the last time we dealt with this point …' Others are very experiential and live only for the present, with no thought for the future. Still others are always focused on the next thing ahead of them and preoccupied with their future options. They may say things like 'What's next on the agenda?' or 'In future I would like this handled differently …' This is the space where you might find those with a strong achievement need. They are never satisfied with what they've achieved, and are always looking to the next big thing.

- Some people *like to look for similarities in a picture* (called 'matching'), others instinctively look for what is missing ('mis-matching'). I am not necessarily talking literally

about a painting though you could spot this difference
in the way people react to, say, a landscape. 'Matchers'
might say 'I just love the way the sky and the sea meet –
the colours blend perfectly just like in that other picture
she painted of the harbour'. 'Mismatchers' might say
'What a shame that she didn't use more pink for the
flowers'.

- *Some people remember by reference to time, others by
  reference to place, others by reference to an object, others
  by a person, and others by an activity.* Let's say you are
  asked what you were doing when you heard that John
  Lennon was shot. In fact you were having breakfast with
  Sam and Janet at eight o'clock in the morning at Café
  Italiano in Putney and the meal was absolutely shocking.
  You might remember that moment in any one of these
  ways:

  - I was with Sam and Janet (people).
  - I remember it was eight o'clock in the morning (time).
  - I was having breakfast (activity).
  - I was at Café Italiano in Putney (place).
  - I was having one of the worst meals I can remember
    (object).

I am sure you can think of many other personality variations which
are not covered by any particular psychological theory but are
recognisable on a day-to-day basis. For example:

- *Some people are very self-reliant, set their own standards,
  and don't need approval from others,* others feel insecure
  without that kind of approval. If you don't get invited
  to a party by some friends do you see that as an
  opportunity to stay home and get on with a good book

or a blight on your social reputation? If you do a job at work is it enough for you to know that you've met your own standards or do you need evidence of validation externally – the praise of a manager or colleagues, or evidence that customers or suppliers value what you have done? Internally referenced people are more likely to be individualistic, and make up their own minds about something – many adopters of new technology might fit into this category. Externally referenced people prefer to take the advice of experts or conform with what everyone else is doing.

- *Some people are naturally optimistic*, others run a 'catastrophe' pattern, always expecting the worst. We came across the importance of this kind of distinction in working out who might have the attitude of a 'loser' in a negotiation.

- *Some people love to have lots of options*, and hate routines, others are more comfortable with a very linear process in which the steps are all laid out for them, so they don't have to think too hard about the next one. When you are in a supermarket looking at all those choices of different brands of food, do you revel in the choice or are you pleased if someone makes that choice easier for you by highlighting the offer of the week?

- *Some people are very decisive*, others find decisions harder to take and feel less comfortable being put in a position where they must decide something, in case they get it wrong. You may find more of the latter operating in a bureaucracy where there are plenty of other people to help take or share a decision.

- *Some people are very comfortable with risk*, others are more risk averse. Entrepreneurs are well represented in the former category.

- *Some people are quite impulsive* while others are more considered. What kind of shopper are you? Do you see something you like and buy it, or do you research a number of websites and compare prices, functionality and styles?

    When you buy an electronic gadget and get it home, what do you do first? Tear off the packaging and start pressing buttons until you work it out, or spend forty minutes reading the instruction manual first?

- *Some people lead with their head when making decisions and are very rational*, others lead with their heart and make decisions based much more on their feelings. How do you book your holidays? Based on the most persuasive travel literature or on what you fancy that year?

- *Some people love confrontation and thrive on all that negative energy*, other people seek harmony in their dealings.

- *Some people have a very practical sort of mind and are very comfortable with 'doing', e.g. handling new processes or new technology*, others are more comfortable thinking about things and living in their heads – don't ask these people to carry out any DIY for you as it is likely to be a disaster.

You get the picture. However you choose to classify and categorise them, there are numerous different types of people in the world. Thank goodness. None of them are inherently better or worse than others, they are just different from each other.

I am not suggesting that you make these judgements about people in a flippant way. They require careful observation and checking of your initial instincts. Furthermore, people may display several of these characteristics at any one time and different characteristics at different times depending on the situation in which they find themselves, so I am not advocating that you take a simplistic view of people's behaviour. Whether you are working with typologies, traits, NLP classifications, or your own day-to-day experiences of differences in personality, in watching out for these patterns you need to 'calibrate' – make sure that your initial observations are correct before assuming that you are right.

However, these different patterns of personality may be observed and if you can spot them you can begin to work out why people negotiate in the way that they do and what triggers they may have which encourage them to buy, sell or make any other kind of negotiating decision. Moreover, *if you observe these patterns correctly and then you communicate with people in a way that is congruent with the way they relate to the world as individuals, you are more likely to be impactful on them and trigger the desired response.* This is because you will be conveying messages in the same code through which they interpret the world. This applies to the language you use and also the behaviour you choose to select.

Behaving Differently

This creates an imperative to negotiate differently with different people, rather than approaching negotiations the same way with everybody – making no allowance for the different kinds of people you are dealing with, and simply pursuing your own default behaviour patterns on auto pilot. There has been much research as to personality in the workplace and how different traits relate to function or workplace values.[91][92] However, understanding different personalities is just as important in evaluating your negotiation behaviour. Behaviour is another aspect of negotiation in which you have a *choice*. Many of us fall asleep at the wheel when we are negotiating, and just do the same thing every time. However, it cannot be right to treat all seven billion people in the world in the same way.

Here are some examples of how you can pick the right behaviour from our negotiating framework to suit the personality you are dealing with. Get the decisions right, and your negotiating partner is more likely to feel 'this is my kind of person' and agree with you:

- If, from an NLP point of view, you are dealing with a '*visual*' thinker, you can use '*visual language*' – 'The way I see it' or 'Picture this …' or 'I'm a bit hazy about that point'. If you are dealing with an '*auditory*' thinker, you can use '*aural language*' – 'Can we speak more about this …?' or 'Talk to me about that …' or 'Just listen to yourself'. If you are dealing with someone who processes the world through their *senses*, you can use appropriate '*sensing language*' for them, too – 'I was very touched by what you said …' or 'That feels like the best approach to me …' or 'I didn't grasp that point …'

- Beyond this, NLP advocates speak extensively of the importance of 'matching' as a way of creating rapport, literally taking on someone else's style. In her book *NLP at Work*,[93] Sue Knight speaks of aiming to match:

    – Posture (e.g. position of the arms, legs, body and head).

    – Expression (e.g. direction of gaze).

    – Movement and gestures.

    – Voice (e.g. intonation, loudness).

    – Values and beliefs.

    Knight also advocates 'pacing' – respecting the state or feelings of others as you match over a period of time. So, if you are dealing with a thinker who interprets the world through their senses and they are feeling uncertain about a deal, you can consistently address that as you go along, by matching – e.g. 'I can understand that you feel uncertain – how would you like to feel?' This approach helps build 'rapport' which Knight describes as 'the ability to relate to others in a way that creates a climate of trust and understanding'.

Now, you don't have to be a follower of NLP to see
that rapport-building can be useful and, indeed, essential
during the exploration phase of a negotiation. Literally
matching the other side's behaviours demands a lot of
concentration, and may seem a bit daunting or over
the top, but you can certainly use behaviours that are
'complementary' to the way other people interpret the
world. The same applies during the later stages of a
negotiation such as bidding and bargaining where you
may not want to 'match' but you certainly want to pick a
suitable behaviour for that kind of person. Here are some
examples of how to do that.

- During the exploring stage of a negotiation, if you are
dealing with someone who is naturally *pessimistic and
always looking for problems* then active '*listening*' would be
particularly useful for this person – all that summarising
and paraphrasing shows them that their concerns have
been listened to. Ignoring their concerns or telling them
to chill out is unlikely to work very well with these
people, because it conflicts with the filters through which
they interpret the world. 'Focusing on common ground'
may not work either, even though it is normally a very
effective behaviour at the exploring stage. If you say
to this person, 'Well, at least we've disposed of five out
of the six problems,' they will just be focusing on the
remaining problem which may loom much larger to them
than the five problems you have already solved.

- If you are working with someone who likes to have
external validation then using *disclosive behaviour* can be
just the thing – the intimacy implied by you trusting them
with confidential information may be just what they need
to feel comfortable. 'Disclosing' might not be so helpful
with someone who is 'internally' rather than 'externally'

referenced and is therefore more interested in their own internal emotions and dialogue rather than whether someone else is showing them approval.

- During the bargaining phase, if you come across someone who processes the world in accordance with '*big picture*' thinking, a 'we' behaviour like '*visualisation*' may work – painting a big and positive picture for them. If they are '*small chunk*' thinkers and focus on detail then they are more likely to be influenced by a behaviour like '*proposing with reasons*' which could involve the production of lots of supporting information and data. People who like a fine tooth comb approach will love all those spreadsheets and annexes with which you justify your proposal. This kind of behaviour wouldn't work so well with someone who likes 'big picture' thinking, because they would just find it boring.

- If you have someone who is very '*linear*' in the way they interpret the world, '*stating expectations*' for that person may be perfect – it's very clear and there is no ambiguity. For someone who prefers lots of '*choices*', stating an expectation may seem like a narrowing down of their options. Better to deal with this person by making *more than one proposal with reasons*: 'We could offer this or if you prefer we could do it that way …' Or maybe use some 'we' behaviour and create some *shared solutions* with them so they feel they had a hand in the choices you come up with.

- During the 'closing phase', if you are dealing with someone who is very *focused on the 'past'* then painting an exciting visualisation for them of what the future will look like after the deal has been done may be less effective than *showing them a picture of how this deal will fit in with their past successes*.

- If you are dealing with someone who looks for '*matches*' rather than 'mismatches', '*checking for consensus*' would be a good 'we' behaviour to use for that person, as they will naturally want to confirm what's right about the deal for them.

- If you are dealing with someone who *avoids decisions*, the use of behaviour employing '*incentives*' may be just the thing to help them get off the fence in the bargaining phase. If you use negotiating 'pressures' with this sort of person they may well feel paralysed and make no decision at all.

' I DON'T WANT TO PRESSURISE YOU INTO DOING THE DEAL, BUT YOU NEED TO GET OFF THE FENCE '

I once met a client for the first time in a boardroom. I was there first so when she came in I offered her a cup of tea. There was a box on the table with about twenty varieties of tea. She leafed through them all, going 'No ... no ... no ... they don't have the one that I like'. I realised that she might be someone who looks for what's missing in a picture rather than what is right about it – and so it proved. Whenever I needed her to approve something after that (a mini negotiation in its own right), I would send her a proposal and ask her what was missing. Normally she had nothing to add. However, working with her pattern rather than ignoring it made it much easier for her to accept my advice.

As you can see I tend to use practical or NLP examples of personality types when I am engaged in this exercise, but you could equally as well use the psychological types and traits outlined above. Nobody is asking you to be an expert psychologist; you are just collecting as much data as possible about the person with whom you are negotiating in order to come up with the most effective deal for both of you. For example, using the 'big five' trait analysis you might feel that, if you are dealing with someone who has a dominant '*conscientiousness*' trait, a logical behaviour like '*proposing with reasons*' may work and more emotionally based behaviour (e.g. visualising) would not be so effective. Someone with an '*openness trait*' might respond very well to 'we' behaviours such as '*problem sharing*', '*shared problem solving*' and '*visualisation*'. Those scoring highly in the *neuroticism* trait are unlikely to respond very well to tough-guy pressure tactics as these may make them very anxious and provoke a fight or flight response – 'you' behaviour such as *listening* is much more likely to be reassuring for these people. Those with a strong '*agreeableness*' trait will be very happy to '*focus on common ground*' and are likely to be comfortable with the Q and A associated with '*exploring*'. If you want to work with Cattell's traits theory, those who score high on the '*dominance*' trait would probably respond well to use of '*pressures*' since it's likely to be a tactic they use themselves and recognise. Those who score high on the '*liveliness*' scale may be a bit put out by extensive use of parting behaviours such as silence but will engage with '*exploring*' behaviour. Those with a high degree of '*openness to change*' will embrace a behaviour like '*visualisation*'.

All too often when we encounter people who have different behavioural patterns from our own we get frustrated with them, or don't understand them, or even dislike them. From a negotiating point of view (however you go about labelling the differences), identifying their difference creates an opportunity for you to appreciate that difference and you should work with it rather than against it so you can get more of what you want in return.

Adapting your behaviour to the person you are dealing with can make all the difference in persuading them to agree to what you want in a negotiation. It really is important to have the capacity to be all things to all people. This kind of skill is especially important when you are finding suitable behaviour to deal with 'tough guys' in a negotiation, as we are about to find out.

19

DIFFERENT BEHAVIOUR SUITS DEALING WITH TOUGH GUYS

Name the Bad Behaviour

When you are dealing with tough guys, you may need to employ different behaviour from normal to influence them. Although negotiating the modern way involves collaboration rather than confrontation, not everyone has yet cottoned on to that. So you will still encounter many people who are looking to take advantage of you, looking to make you feel small, and believe that successful negotiators should be 'users'. You can't ignore this group of people; they will be around demonstrating 'the dark side' for as long as humanity exists, so you need to be able to deal with them.

Tough-guy behaviour may consist of use of threats, aggression, complaints, unreasonable deadlines or many other forms of intimidation. Most tough-guy behaviour is deliberate. It is a manipulative form of 'I' behaviour designed to make you feel bad and to put you under pressure. So, in dealing with tough guys the important thing normally is to *make their behaviour the issue*. Don't continue the negotiation until their bad behaviour has been raised and addressed, or parked safely so it can't hurt you. Once you have made it clear that you know what is going on, it is very likely that their tactic will be dropped, as once they know they have been rumbled there is no point continuing with the tactic.

Some people find this counter-intuitive and feel that they ought to be 'professional' and ignore the bad behaviour that is going on around them. 'I'm not going to stoop to their level' might be the internal message. However, this is like sticking your head in the sand. If you allow tough guys to get away with their bad behaviour, they will just keep doing it, making it harder and harder for you to get what you need from the deal. Often people find the idea of confronting tough guys a bit frightening, but tough guys trade on that. They frequently use pressure tactics in the same way that bullies do, assuming that you won't stand up to them. If you do stand up to them, then, like many bullies, they will back off. Besides, we are not saying that you have to be unpleasant – quite the reverse: if you reciprocate the pressure tactics that they apply, or make your response personal, you are likely to escalate the tension. What we are saying is that you make the behaviour the issue, not the person – as we shall see, you don't necessarily have to be confrontational to confront a tough guy. Often the use of carefully worded questions will do the trick – a sentiment expressed as a question is usually seen as less provocative than the same sentiment expressed as a statement.

Here are my bottom twenty typical tough-guy behaviours and some of the responses you can use to deal with them. You will see that making the bad behaviour the issue or otherwise sidestepping it is a consistent feature of these responses. Incidentally, although I refer to these people as 'tough guys' by way of shorthand, they may include either men or (less often) women. One further note. I have divided this chapter into two sections. The first section deals with behaviours which are undeniably tough-guy behaviours and the second deals with issues of 'fairness', 'reasonableness' and 'principle', which are sometimes invoked unscrupulously by negotiators to support their position, but may also be the source of difficult and genuinely held disagreements.

Genuine Tough-Guy Behaviours

1. Threats – direct or veiled

If someone is threatening you in a negotiation, you don't have to sit there and take it. You normally have the choice of using any of the behaviours to make their behaviour the issue. So if someone is threatening you, you could say, 'We don't negotiate on the basis of threats – shall we start again?' That would be 'I' behaviour – 'stating' an expectation. Or you could say, 'Is it standard in negotiations with your company for each side to threaten the other?' That would be to try to get the other side to accept a standard of behaviour which excludes threats. If all that sounds a bit confrontational you could try 'How would it be if neither of us threatens the other in this negotiation?' ('exploring'). Or 'How would it be if we both used this tactic? Would it be helpful to both of us?' ('exploring'). Or you could say, 'Just imagine how much easier this negotiation would be if neither of us was threatening the other' ('visualising'). Or you could just stay silent ('parting' behaviour). This is not as direct, but pushy people certainly hate silence as it gives them nothing to push against. If you stay silent long enough the tough-guy behaviour may just evaporate.

Whichever method you use, you will find that those who make threats will normally back off if you make their behaviour explicit. It may put you in a cold sweat at the time, but you will only have to do it once and that is almost certainly a better alternative than having to deal with the prospect of their ongoing and repeated threatening behaviour.

2. Aggression

Again, you don't have to sit there and take aggressive behaviour. If someone is shouting at you or otherwise being hostile you can address that.

Once again you have a choice of which behaviours to use. You could say, 'Why is the atmosphere so hostile?' (that would be 'testing and probing'). Or if that sounds too forceful you could try 'Is there a rationale behind the atmosphere being so hostile?' ('exploring'). Or, more softly, 'I'm sensing a very hostile atmosphere here' ('disclosing'). Or you could use 'we' behaviour: 'Can I just check we are all agreed that neither of us is going to be hostile to the other?' ('checking for consensus'). Or you could call a break every time they do it (i.e. using 'parting' behaviour). Or you could ask them what they would do if they were in your shoes and were feeling very uncomfortable with the ferocity of the climate (a loaded 'exploring' question).

Getting the other side explicitly to put themselves in your shoes is a skilful way of dealing with a number of different difficult situations in negotiations, and this particularly includes dealing with tough guys as it invites them to say whether they would be happy to be treated in the same way as they are treating you. The answer is unlikely to be 'yes', in which case you have *set a standard* for their behaviour which you can hold them to going forward.

Here's an example from Giles, now a marketing executive for comeround.com, of how making the behaviour the issue can work when someone is being aggressive:

I can remember one particularly amusing incident when I was in Business Affairs at EMI; it was in the early days and so I would have been a young, enthusiastic lawyer in those days. I was up against a partner in a leading music law firm (no names, of course ...).

We were negotiating over the signing of one of his artists to EMI. The meeting was in a huge boardroom (big long table – the usual thing) at his firm's offices.

Despite outdoing me on experience, seniority (and age!), for some reason this partner still found it necessary to shout, bang his fists on the table and even – at one point – lean across the table and in quite possibly the most patronising manner I have ever witnessed, touched me on the forearm muttering something along the lines of 'You young lawyers are always obsessed with that clause ...'

In response to his shouting and fist-banging on the table, I simply replied in the most pleasant and calm tone I could muster: 'This is your boardroom and table and you're of course free to shout and bang your fists as much as you want but please don't mind me if I don't join in.'

His tactic was obviously to try to evoke some sort of response on my part, leading to me becoming distracted from the deal points in hand or, indeed, simply to unnerve me through a somewhat embarrassing display of aggression. It didn't work, of course. After my response, he could see I was not going to take the bait and so he calmed right down. From that moment onwards, any inequality there may have been in our respective levels of experience and negotiating powers was quickly brushed aside. We concluded the deal on terms which were extremely agreeable to us.

3. Personal attacks

Tough guys may make personal attacks on you designed to undermine your 'state' of mind and make you feel more vulnerable. They may comment on your competence or your appearance; they may seek to undermine your status; they may deliberately choose to misunderstand you so as to try and make you trip up; they may keep you waiting; they may choose an uncomfortable seating arrangement or a venue where you feel at a disadvantage. Again, the answer is to make their behaviour the issue: 'Is there any particular reason why I have been seated in the least comfortable chair and you are sitting in a chair that's higher than mine?' Or 'What would be your response if you had been kept waiting forty-five minutes for a meeting?' Or 'Let me check that we agree we are going to be tough on the issues today and not on each other ... am I wrong about that?' Make sure you maintain a strong state of mind – the same positive attitude with which you walked into the room. One thing that can help here is to imagine difficult situations like this arising when you are doing your planning. If you imagine yourself dealing with the problem then it will be less uncomfortable when it happens in practice. Using a professional sportsman analogy, their mental preparation will encompass not just positive thinking about the outcome, but also encountering imaginary problems and overcoming those problems in their heads in advance. That makes the challenge seem like less of a challenge when it actually happens.

4. Complaints

Sometimes people put forward complaints opportunistically. They do this to try and gain the moral high ground in the negotiation, regardless of whether or not the complaint is bogus.

Once again you can confront them with this: 'I propose you stop asserting this fanciful claim, because the negotiation will go a lot better if it's grounded in reality.'

Alternatively (whether you think the complaint is real or not) you can get them to repeat it. People often invest their complaints with a lot less energy the second time around, so this will take the volume down. You can then reduce the volume further by summarising the complaint yourself ('I see, so what you're saying is ...'). By now the complaint is assuming manageable proportions. You can then cut through it entirely by asking the other side to state their suggested remedy. This often takes the wind out of their sails completely, as they have been so focused on their complaint that they haven't even thought what their remedy could be.

This approach works equally well if the complainer is genuine about their complaint.

5. Good cop/bad cop

A lot of people use this tactic, thinking it's quite clever, but in fact it's very irritating and can quickly be overcome. The 'bad cop' tries to beat you up in the negotiation. Meanwhile, the 'good cop' is very reassuring and even disapproving of the bad cop. The good cop then tries to soft-talk you into concessions on the basis that if you go along with that the bad cop will leave you alone. You can lance this tactic by making their behaviour the issue.

'I'm very confused here. One of you is being very pleasant and the other is acting all tough. Why don't we stop for five minutes so you two can agree a common approach. Then we can start again.'

That should sort it out ... What's the point of them continuing with the tactic after you have made a statement like that?

Alternatively, you could ask 'How necessary is it for one of you to be very nice to me and the other to be nasty?' That will have the same effect.

6. The salami slicer

The subtle tactic of the salami negotiator is to keep coming back for more – but in such small amounts that you are tempted to agree with them each time, because they don't seem to be asking for a lot. They keep taking slice after slice until you suddenly realise that virtually the whole salami has gone. The way to confront this behaviour is to say 'Is that it?' when they come back for more. If they say 'yes', hold them to that agreement. If they say 'no', you know they will be back for more even if you agree to this latest round of concessions and so you can negotiate strongly on those points without feeling as though you are preventing the deal from closing.

7. Upstairs referral

We have talked before about the significance of 'referral power' – the ability to refer a decision in a negotiation to someone else who isn't in the room. If the other party is able to engineer this situation it gives their negotiator in the room a lot of protection because *they* can't be forced to agree to anything, but they can extract concessions from *you* knowing that their boss *may* not agree to the solution they discuss with you. Some people use this tactic disingenuously by not disclosing that the deal they discuss with you will require approval. They then spring that on you and, of course, the deal comes back from the approver requiring further concessions from you. So, it's a way of getting more out of you than you would otherwise have given. That is why it's always good to ask at the climate-setting stage, 'Do we have everybody we need in the room in order to reach agreement?' Asking that question prevents this tactic from being deployed because the other party will have to be upfront about their negotiating authority.

8. Deadline pressure

This is the typical refuge of a pressure negotiator. They try to hurry up your decision in order to pressure you into making a mistake or a concession that you would otherwise not have made. This is often done by creating the spectre that if a decision is not made quickly the opportunity will be lost. 'Buy while stocks last' would be the mantra of this kind of tough guy. They invite you to climb on board now 'as the train is leaving the station'. Sometimes this sense of panic is intensified by the other negotiator ignoring you for a while both before and just after they have set the deadline, to exacerbate your anxiety that you may not get the deal done.

There is some evidence that exerting time pressure can lead to lower demands, and greater concession making, so you need to be sure that a deadline is real before you go along with it.[94] [95] The best way to deal with deadline pressure is to probe at whatever deadline you are set. If they tell you that the deal must be done by Tuesday, say to them, 'Does that mean that if you get more of what you want but the deal is done by Wednesday, there won't be a deal?' If they hesitate or give you any kind of conditional response, you know that the deadline isn't real, because if they meant it the only response to that question ought to be an immediate 'yes'. Once you know they don't mean it, their negotiating credibility disappears and you can safely ignore the deadline and any other pressure tactics they try to exert. This can end up being a turning point in a negotiation.

Here's another story from my own experience:

I was once negotiating a deal for a joint venture with two creative music executives. The other negotiator tried to exert some deadline pressure to close the deal within forty-eight hours, and I was sure that it was just a stunt. 'So shall we stop now then?' I said, 'As I don't think the paperwork will be finished by then.' 'Oh, I wasn't exactly saying that, we just need to get it done quickly,' he responded. From that point on his negotiating credibility was gone, and this made me push him harder – that is the risk you run when your tough-guy tactics don't work. He ended up with a worse deal than had been available to him before he set the deadline.

Time pressure is one of those tactics which may be genuine. There may indeed be a deadline for the other party. If so, this kind of testing of the deadline will tease that out. If, in response to you probing the deadline, they absolutely insist that unless the deadline is met there will be no deal, you can react accordingly. Test the best position you feel you can reach within the time constraint against an alternative – your bottom line, your best alternative to this agreement, your worst alternative to this agreement, or the risk of the worst thing that could happen if this deal gets done. If the best position you can reach still sounds okay when measured against any of these other possibilities, you may choose to proceed as though the deadline is genuine and close the deal.

9. Divide and conquer

I'm sure this will be a familiar scenario to you if you negotiate in teams. You have set out your proposal to the other team. They don't like what they hear and suddenly you find that they have gone round the back door to another member of your team in order to try and undermine that proposal by finding someone who will be more accommodating. Maybe you have experienced an approach like this from the other party yourself. Someone sidles up to you and says, 'Look, I can't believe the position that your finance director, Harry, is adopting in relation to the upfront payment. I'm sure you can see that it's a bit unreasonable. If only it could be reduced by 10 per cent I think we would be in business …' It's very tempting at this juncture to say something encouraging like 'Well, let me see what I can do, I'll have a word with Harry', or 'Well, off the record, I do see your point …' Once this kind of response is made the negotiating credibility of the whole team is undermined. The other party may well be explicit to both of you about the gap they have uncovered on your team, and will seek to use it to divide you and come up with a better outcome for themselves. 'How can you continue to argue for this outcome when you and Harry have completely different views?' they may say archly, knowing that you and Harry are now going to have to have an uncomfortable conversation.

The best way to deal with this kind of tactic is firstly to make sure that your own team is properly prepared and buys into the collective position. This takes time but is a very good way of ensuring that the other team can't pick anybody off. The second precaution you can take is to make sure that only one party on your side is mandated to offer concessions. Explain that to the other team, too. That way you all speak with one voice, and when someone sidles up to you and tries to create a gap between your position and Harry's, you can say to them, 'Sorry, but Harry was just describing our joint view.' If there is no way around the proposal you have put forward as a team, the other party will just have to work with that offer rather than seeking to go round it by using divide and conquer tactics. As ever, you can just name their bad behaviour, too: 'What effect do you think it has on our team when you go round the back like this?' Or 'We're just not comfortable with you negotiating with everybody individually at once. Wouldn't it be very confusing if we did it to you, too?'

Here's a good example from HR executive Cary:

I sat down to negotiate a contract extension with the apparel union that represented our employees at the distribution centre and our manufacturing facility. I was on the management team, which consisted of an attorney, myself and the CFO. When we started the negotiation, the union went to my boss and stated that they could not trust me and that I should not be involved in the process.

This was a 'bypass strategy' on their part, because I was the one who handled all the grievance negotiations, administrated the contract and I was quite tough. My boss told them that I was not going to be removed from the team and that they had to deal with me. The negotiation continued and we were able to reach agreement on a contract that suited us.

Perfect.

---

10. 'Take it or leave it'

Take it or leave it is another very common pressure tactic beloved of tough guys. 'That's my final offer, take it or leave it.' The tactic is designed to panic you into giving in, fearing that if you leave it the deal will go away. Once again, a good response is to probe away at the ultimatum to see whether it is real. For example, you can say, 'So are you saying that if there was £1 of difference between your current position and the final outcome you wouldn't want to do the deal?' Or, 'Are you saying that even if we could expand the pie for both of us you wouldn't be interested?' If the threat is real, the answer ought to be 'yes'. It should not surprise you to hear, though, that very often if you pose an extreme question like this you will get a hesitant or conditional answer: 'Well, I'm not saying that, I'm just saying that we need the main terms agreed in our favour ...' (or some such variation). As soon as you receive that signal you know that there is still room for negotiation and the ultimatum is not as real as it sounds.

As with deadline pressure, it's at moments like this that it is extremely powerful to have considered alternatives to a negotiated outcome in your preparation phase. What would be the best alternative to not doing a deal with this partner? What would be your Plan B? If the 'take it or leave it' offer is worse than your Plan B, you ought to be considering your Plan B instead, and having that alternative will help you feel much stronger about resisting any 'take it or leave it' ultimatum. Or you could compare this proposal to your worst alternative if you don't get the deal (again, created at the preparation stage) – is the take it or leave it offer worse than your worst alternative or not? If it is, you can definitely afford to 'leave it'. Or, as we discussed when we looked at preparation, you could compare the take it or leave it offer to the risk of the worst thing that could happen to you if you *did* do this deal. Which would you prefer – that risk and the take it or leave it offer, or walking away? This kind of exercise will help minimise any feelings of desperation to accept.

11. 'What's your bottom line?'

This tactic is a favourite of pressure salesmen. They seek to short-circuit the negotiation by getting you to disclose your bottom line, with the intention that the negotiation will then travel straight to that point. If you are in a car sales room with an unscrupulous dealer, he or she will ask you this with a view to finding the most you are prepared to spend. They will then show you models at or around or maybe just above that price rather than cheaper models which are within your bottom line. A good tactic here is to walk through the question: 'It's not a question of what my bottom line is, show me some VWs.' You could also lie about your bottom line but sooner or later lies in negotiations tend to come back and cause a problem, because if the dealer realises you gave a false bottom line it affects your negotiating credibility going forward.

You could also say, 'I'll tell you my bottom line if you tell me yours,' which may sound 'fair', but this is pretty risky since you have no idea if the dealer will be honest in their response. Or you could just say, 'I don't work with a bottom line but I do have a best alternative to doing a deal with you.' If you are asked what that is, you may take a view as to whether or not you want to disclose that best alternative. If you have a very good alternative – better than they might think – it may be good to reveal that to the dealer at some point: 'Just so you know I have been into the dealership up the road and they have some excellent VWs within my price range, so if we really can't work out a deal my plan is to go up there and buy a car.' If you are not so confident about your next best alternative, keep it to yourself.

12. 'Improve your offer'

Sometimes you can make an offer and instead of responding with a proposal of their own the other negotiator simple asks you to improve your bid. 'That's not good enough,' they might say. 'We need a higher advance and royalty rate than that.' It may be tempting to feel obliged to respond to this with an improved offer, but in fact this is just a tough-guy tactic, designed to make you improve your proposal still further, without the other party needing to make any concessions of their own. This presents you with a conundrum, as if you make further improvements for them in your proposal you have no idea whether or not these are going to prove acceptable. What is to stop the other negotiator repeating that you need to improve your offer still further? At that point you will have completely wasted any further concessions you made.

If somebody makes a vague, non-specific demand that you improve your bid, the best way to deal with this is to make them be specific. A good answer would be: 'What would it take to close the deal then?' Don't make any further offers until they have told you that. Once they have told you at least you have some benchmark against which to evaluate what you want to do next. Maybe you want to improve your offer; maybe you want to propose movement on both sides. Either way, at least you know where you stand. In telling you what you need to do in order to close they may also make some further concessions themselves, taking them closer to your initial bid.

The following is a good illustration from negotiator and organisation consultant John Royce on the benefits of not responding to vague demands to improve your offer:

A senior executive in a major airline was determined to improve customer experience, to gain some competitive advantage over rivals. She wanted to give the business to a trusted supplier. We agreed all the basic ingredients and a programme of work, over a four-month period, was planned. When it came to discussing money, I was asked to attend a meeting with the three-person procurement committee. Without any pleasantries or 'climate setting' on their behalf, I was asked to give an overall project fee. I put my opening position on the table. The response was 'It's far too much'. I said that I was open to some negotiation, if they would tell me what they were prepared to pay. 'We don't negotiate that way' was their response. I said that I was not prepared to reduce my price, until I knew what the gap was between us. They still refused to say anything.

Thus, we had a stalemate situation. As far as I was concerned, the meeting was over and I got up from my seat. I thought they would ask me to sit down again but they did not. So I had no choice but to leave. I was relying on the relationship I had with the senior executive, who I hoped would put pressure on the procurement team to negotiate the deal. To my surprise, I received a phone call two days later, from the procurement chairperson, to say that they had accepted my price. I think it was their embarrassment, at trying to play games with me, together with the support from the executive, which carried the day.

13. 'Don't you trust me?'

This is a common pressure tactic used by tough guys. It seeks to make you feel uncomfortable about not taking the statements or information put forward by the other negotiator at face value. Your knee-jerk response might be 'Of course I trust you' since otherwise you are implying that the other side is being dishonest with you. Of course, once you give that response you are boxing yourself in, as the tough guy intended, because you are making it harder for yourself to disagree with data put forward by the other person as being true.

If people say to you 'Don't you trust me?' it should raise your suspicions. Honest people don't need to ask questions like this, they just behave honestly. For the same reason I always get an uncomfortable feeling when someone starts a sentence by saying 'To be honest with you ...' Why did they need to say that in relation to this particular matter? Are they saying that they weren't being honest when they made previous statements to me which they did not preface in this way? The best way to deal with issues like this is to make them irrelevant. 'It's not a question of trust, but we do need independent verification of this data, as any business person would …'

14. The positional commitment

Sometimes tough guys will deliberately lock themselves into a position so as to make it harder for you to negotiate them away from it. For example, they will tell you: 'Our board has only authorised me to agree to a 5 per cent price increase.' They believe that painting themselves into a corner will put pressure on you to agree to what they want because they have effectively cut off their own line of retreat. Once more – make explicit their bad behaviour. 'It would be very easy for me to get a resolution from our board demanding a 25 per cent price increase. Would it be helpful to both our interests if I did that?' Or 'What would you do if you were in my shoes? If I came to you with a similar *fait accompli* how would you respond?' Or you can just call their bluff. 'I can't match that position – shall we stop now?' If it's a pressure tactic the answer to that question is unlikely to be 'yes'. It may, of course, be a genuine position, but if the other party is being genuine it ought to be possible to get them off a positional discussion and on to a discussion about needs. For example, if they say, 'Our members have voted for a minimum pay rise of 5 per cent given the current threat to their jobs,' your response might be 'Okay, actually that sounds to me like you need a 5 per cent increase because you believe that jobs may be under threat. I can't agree to 5 per cent, but shall we explore other ways of giving your members the reassurance on jobs that they seek?'

15. 'I can get better somewhere else'

This is an irritating tactic, no question. The other party let it be known that they have other offers on the table and invite you to improve your proposal or risk losing out to the other offers. Often you have no way of knowing whether or not these offers are genuine. Tough guys are quite capable of inventing proposals in order to try and pressure you into agreeing what they want. Or it may be that these are genuine proposals but you don't know the terms, and in fact the terms you are offering are already better in some respects than what is proposed in these other offers. Or it might be that these other proposals contain a different deal structure which makes it impossible to compare them against your offer. For example, maybe you are proposing to purchase a company and someone else has offered your target a joint venture instead. Or it could be that these other proposals are indeed better than yours in some material way, because someone else with different strategic priorities simply values this deal differently from the way you do.

The existence of so many variables means that you are much better off not being distracted by the possibility of what someone else may have offered, and just sticking to what you think this deal is worth to you. A good way of disarming people who try this gambit is by saying, 'So, you feel you have some choices then.' There is no comeback to a comment like that other than a rather lame 'yes'. If you show that you are not interested in these other offers you may find that they mysteriously fall by the wayside and cease to be an issue in your own negotiation, because they were never genuinely competitive bids. If they are genuine proposals and they are genuinely better than yours, that is no reason of itself for you to agree to improve your own proposal beyond the level to which you would have been happy to go regardless of any competitive bids.

16. Budget busters

Budget busters exert a rather insidious kind of pressure. They try to win you over by saying that they would be very happy to agree to your terms, only there is some impossible circumstance which prevents them doing so. Maybe it's the end of their budget year, or there are financial rules or regulations which unfortunately prevent them agreeing to what you want. Or maybe the most they can afford is 10 per cent below what you have in mind. This kind of response is often not genuine at all; it's just a way of making you feel almost sorry for them and therefore agreeing to a worse deal than you would otherwise have done. Budget busters are everywhere. You might come across them at a furniture showroom: 'I'm sorry, sir, I would love to meet you on price but unfortunately the most we are allowed to offer is 10 per cent off the price you see on the sofa.' Or you might come across them in the finance department of a big company: 'We would love to support your request for an additional bonus related to sales success, only unfortunately the current sales plan does not allow for discretionary bonuses of this kind.'

Once again, you need to flush out whether or not this limitation is real. Ask the sales assistant if he has ever sold a sofa with a discount of more than 10 per cent to anybody. Or if he would be prepared to grant a bigger discount if he was up against his month end and he had yet to meet his sales quota for the month. Or if he would be prepared to agree to a bigger discount if the deal was structured in a different way. You may well receive a response which indicates that there is more room for manoeuvre than had been indicated. In fact, any response except a straight and immediate 'No, there's nothing else I can do' would indicate that there is room for further negotiation. If they do confirm there is nothing else they can do, you can take a view on what you want to do knowing at least that the limitation may be genuine. However, the chances are that you will establish that the limitation on their budget is bogus, in which case you will have made them drop the tactic, as there is no point continuing with it once you have demonstrated that you know what's going on, and once they have demonstrated that the limitation is not real.

17. Reneging after the deal is done

This can be a real problem. You think a deal is done, you commit yourself to it, you expend resources and effort and then the other negotiator seeks to avoid or renegotiate an agreed obligation. They may rely on the fact that you are in too deep to withdraw. Or that you will not wish to provoke or pursue a costly legal row in order to enforce your rights. This kind of behaviour is highly manipulative and needs to be addressed. That doesn't mean getting outraged or losing your temper or retaliating in kind. It just means making their behaviour the issue.

Here's a good story from Rob Hersov, a London-based investor and entrepreneur, illustrating the point:

My sales and marketing company had carried out a series of successful, agreed activities for a client's product range. The client then disputed the invoices by email and refused to pay, wishing to back us into a corner where our only recourse was either to move from the previously agreed fee-based model to a commission model, or to exercise a legal remedy.

I wrote back to him saying I was surprised by his email that morning, and wanted to send a swift response.

I told him it was not my company's style to dispute terms with clients legally and I certainly don't sue clients or customers. I have never needed to.

I reminded him that we had worked tirelessly with him over the course of four months to create and deliver a total of three successful events for his product which had yielded introductions and clients and that we now expected payment for our work.

I reminded him that he shared a number of networks with me. What effect did he think it would have on our relationship and my attitude to him within our mutual networking groups if he reneged in this way? How would he feel if someone did this to him? Was it his policy not to pay for work that had been delivered? I thanked him for his kind offer to continue to work with us on a commission-only basis, but reminded him that we only work on a retainer basis as had been made very clear from the beginning. I invited him to settle the outstanding invoices.

The client backed off immediately.

Through a combination of making the client's behaviour the issue, insisting the client put himself in Rob's shoes, and shaming the client into accepting their own standards, Rob was able to neutralise this form of tough-guy behaviour.

18. 'Just give me a rough estimate'

Another tough-guy tactic is to invite you to give a 'rough estimate' of what you want. The other side asks you in a 'matey' way to just give an estimate, saying they will not hold you to it. Sometimes what is intended by this is exactly the opposite. The other negotiator does want to hold you to that estimate and asks you to make that back-of-the-envelope estimate at an early stage of the negotiation before you have had a chance to evaluate properly what you want to bid. Their hope is that by putting this pressure on you, you will feel obliged to make a hasty proposal which is in fact worse for you than what you might have bid had you had enough time to think about it. If you think better of your hasty proposal later in the negotiation they hope you may feel guilty about shifting your position, so that you remain stuck with your initial 'rough estimate'. Or, if you do decide to try and change your position, they will look suitably aggrieved and say that they have been relying on your initial proposal in working out their figures (even though they accepted at the time that it was just a rough estimate).

There is a pretty simple response here which is not to make rough estimates. If someone asks you to make a proposal before you are ready to do so, the best thing to say to them is that you need more time: 'I wouldn't want to give you an unreliable figure.

Let me do a bit more work with my colleagues so that we can come up with a figure in which you can have confidence.' This will prevent this pressure tactic from being applied and ensure that you do not put yourself at risk by making a 'rough estimate'.

19. Liar, liar

If someone tells you a lie in a negotiation, it's best to stop the negotiation and make their behaviour the issue. Lying is a fundamental obstacle to any negotiation being completed in a satisfactory way since you need to be able to believe that the other person means what they say. Without that there is no trust and without trust it is difficult to get deals done, because you will always be preoccupied with looking for reassurance against a failure by the other negotiator to comply. So, if you catch someone lying, it's better to address that than pretending to ignore it. You don't have to be confrontational about it. You can use some 'disclosing': 'I'm disappointed to find that statement wasn't true after all.' Or you can check for consensus: 'I thought we had all agreed that we would be transparent and open in this agreement.'

Nobody likes being caught out when they have been untruthful but lying can be quite addictive, and if you allow a lie by the other person to go unchallenged they will repeat that lie and maybe think of some more. Furthermore, lies become institutionalised if unchallenged so that, by default, they become an accepted version of the truth. The other person will be relying on that so that in due course they can refer back to the validity of the lie as though it had become an accepted truth simply through lack of challenge. It will then become harder for you to dismantle the lie because the indignant response may be: 'Well, if it was untrue, then why didn't you say so at the time?'

Ambiguous Tough-Guy Behaviour

In equal twentieth position we have three tactics which may be 'tough-guy' behaviour or, in fact, genuine responses.

20. 'You're being unfair'

This is something you hear a lot of in negotiations. 'I'm making a very fair proposal here' or 'I just don't think you are being fair about that'. Sometimes this is used as just another tough-guy tactic. People use it to try and seize the moral high ground in a negotiation and make the other negotiator feel guilty about maintaining a particular approach or position. Often, though, people genuinely feel that the other party is not being fair on them. 'Fairness' is one of those 'social norms' or shared beliefs we tend to have about how people should behave. In negotiating terms this norm may translate into a number of fairness principles. Here are a few research-based examples:

- Everyone should get equal benefits and make equal contributions in the final agreement.
- Everyone's benefits should be proportional to their contributions.
- Everyone should make equal concessions.
- The balance of achievement of each side's aspirations should be equal at each stage of the negotiation.[96] [97]
- Concessions, once made, should not be withdrawn.

Norms like this can be very helpful in curtailing conflict by providing conceptual guidelines to the appropriate outcomes. Certainly where a single fairness principle can be applied, each party may be inclined to agree that it is both correct and brings about an inevitable solution. Research indicates that people react more positively when they perceive they are treated more fairly in this way.[98]

However, it is not difficult to see how problems can arise. Why? Because arguments about fairness in negotiation are virtually unwinnable. What happens if we disagree about which fairness norm to apply or how to interpret a norm that ought to apply? What happens if I think that my concessions have been greater than yours but you don't agree – research suggests that parties frequently view the other's concessions as smaller than their own[99] [100] – and that in practice negotiators are more concerned about fairness to themselves than fairness to the other negotiator.[101] [102]

What happens if different fairness norms point in different directions (e.g. the equal concessions and the equal outcomes rule)? In addition, everyone always thinks they are being fair in a negotiation – it doesn't matter how unpleasant they are being to the other side.

Here's a story from my own experience:

I once undertook a renegotiation of a recording agreement with the manager of a well-known boy band. The band had enjoyed some success and they wanted to renegotiate the agreement. We received a letter containing some thirty-five points that the band apparently wished to renegotiate in their favour. There were no points suggested that would have improved the deal for the record company. The letter was accompanied by a note from the manager effectively saying, 'Look forward to hearing from you. I think all of our proposals are very fair.' Needless to say, his list of demands didn't strike us that way when we were reading it …

Furthermore, there are no objective criteria for determining who is being 'fair' in an agreement. In practical terms 'fairness' is not objective; it is a very subjective issue because we all have different perceptions of what is fair. There may be some legal extremes on which we can all agree (for example, that certain contractual provisions should be outlawed as being unfair under consumer legislation), but on a day-to-day basis there is no such unanimity of views and there is no external arbiter we can refer to who can tell us which of us is being fair or unfair. This means that when someone accuses us of being unfair, we often feel quite indignant about it, because, based on our own standards of behaviour, there is nothing wrong with what we are doing. This tendency is only compounded by our tendency to see any negotiation solely or mainly through the prism of our own rights and entitlements, rather than the other party's point of view. The manager of the boy band in the example I gave above would have been baffled and annoyed if I had accused him of being unfair. The risk in calling someone 'unfair', or saying that you are being 'fair' and therefore implying that they are not, is that it sparks off an arid debate about fairness which is not resolvable but then dogs the whole negotiation.

For all these reasons, if someone accuses you of being unfair in a negotiation, or says that they are being 'very fair', the best approach is to get them off the subject altogether. This applies whether they are using 'fairness' disingenuously to try to pretend they have 'right' on their side, or because they genuinely feel they have a grievance about fairness. A good response would be something like: 'It's not a question of who is being fair, it's a question of meeting both our needs ... what I need is x.' The issue of who needs what is far less controversial than who is being 'fair', since nobody can criticise you for saying what you need. Or you can try and persuade the other party that fairness does not apply in this instance – 'It's not a question of whether our concessions are equal to yours, it's just a question of whether they are enough for you to agree to ...'

21. 'You're being unreasonable'

This is a similar tactic to using 'fairness' as an argument. Someone seeks to justify their approach by saying that it is very 'reasonable', and implies that you are therefore being unreasonable and ought to give in. Arguments about 'reasonableness' fall into the same category as those about 'fairness'. They may be advanced by unscrupulous tough guys or they may be genuinely held grievances. The consequence is the same either way, because 'reasonableness' also turns out to be something of a subjective concept in a negotiation.

It is true that 'reasonableness' can have an objective meaning in some contexts – for example, some legal statutes are worded in such a way that the court must decide on whether somebody or something has been 'reasonable' in order to affix liability. However, in these circumstances there is an objective arbiter of what is reasonable – normally a judge or a tribunal. Even then, look how variable the concept of reasonableness can be. A legal case can go through four layers of hierarchical judgement in the UK with judges at each layer applying the same test of reasonableness and coming up with a different decision on the same set of facts. However, on a day-to-day basis in a negotiation, arguments about reasonableness are impossible to win because we all have different standards of what is 'reasonable', and there is no objective standard we can defer to in order to sort it out for us.

Being accused of being 'unreasonable' also has a similar effect on us as when we are accused of being 'unfair'. It is irritating, because we may well be acting reasonably as far as our own standards of behaviour are concerned, and therefore we take umbrage. The negotiation then descends into an unwinnable debate about who is being reasonable. Once again, the best way to address this is by taking the conversation away from this kind of standard. 'What do you mean by reasonable?' might be a good question to ask. They may find that difficult to answer – they will either have to refer to some code or regulations (which are objective and therefore do provide a common reference point), or they may have to accept that any description of reasonableness is rather flawed and one-sided. Then you can move on to a more productive avenue for discussion.

22. 'I disagree on principle'

This is a cousin of positioning based on 'fairness' or 'reasonableness'. The implication is that the other negotiator is a principled negotiator and you are not. Negotiations based on 'principle' are difficult to resolve without one party giving in, which is why tough guys sometimes adopt this tactic, in order to try to 'shame' the other side into conceding. However, once again this tactic is based on the flawed assumption that there is some objective way of measuring 'principle'. One man's 'principle' is another man's flag of convenience. There is no objective standard of which principles are important and which are less important. They may be standing for one principle and you may be standing for another. Which of you is right?

Try to get the other person off 'principle' negotiations. 'Are you saying that my principle is less important than yours? How would you feel if I said that you were unprincipled? Let's find another way of describing our differences.' Once more, 'principle' is employed by people who are genuine as well as those who seek to apply pressure but the outcome should be the same – try to move the debate on to a different axis. Available research indicates that when principle is genuinely advanced to back up a demand by one party there is often no fall-back position – there is no gap in which to negotiate between one side's 'demand' and their 'limit' in the negotiation since both are framed by the principle.[103] [104] Research has also shown that genuine principles tend to be deeply felt which makes it difficult for people to rethink them so as to craft compromise agreements.[105] [106]

So, that is not an exhaustive survey of tough-guy tactics, but I hope it has given you some options so that you never again get stuck when confronted with a tough guy. I need not add that you should be selective about using tough-guy tactics yourself. So, if you read through any of these pressure tactics and think, 'Oh yes, I'd like to try that one,' then think again, and carefully. They may help you get what you want in the short term – especially in the later stages of the negotiation. However, as a rule tough guys tend to come across as users. This can irritate the other side and make them dig in.[107] [108] At the very least, use of tough-guy tactics can sour the climate, and make the deal harder to do or implement. Moreover, if you come across a sophisticated negotiator he or she will spot what you are doing straightaway. They may even respond with some of the tactics for dealing with tough guys listed above. At that point your tough-guy tactic will not have worked and you may end up feeling and looking a bit silly.

On this basis I will usually resist the temptation to use tough-guy tactics even if I have the opportunity to do so. For example, I am careful about using deadline pressure. If someone senses that you are setting a deadline because you need something, they may be tempted to test your deadline or try to get more out of you in order that your own deadline is met – so the deadline gets used against you.

Here's another illustration from my own experience:

I was once negotiating a contract for the acquisition of an independent record company which had a very promising artist signed to it. She had not broken yet, but was beginning to show momentum in the United States as a result of the use of one of her recordings on a sample by another artist. We successfully negotiated with the vendor, and then at the last minute he had second thoughts, feeling he was letting a prize go, because the longer the deal discussions went on the more valuable her contract looked. On the planned day of signature our chairman was giving a presentation at our annual sales conference. He was determined to present this artist. He kept texting me to ask if the deal was done yet as he was waiting to go on stage. I was still negotiating with the vendor and his lawyer. Though we were close to completion I was loath to set a deadline, and tell them that the deal had to be done this very day in case it was used against us. In the end we did get the deal agreed that day – so I used the deadline for myself rather than to put pressure on the seller. Signature did, however, occur later than the designated time for the chairman's speech. I rang him later with the news, expecting a telling-off for having missed his deadline. Instead I heard his cheerful voice saying, 'Don't worry, I announced the deal anyway. I knew you would get it done …

I am also wary of using some of these other tactics. Sure, you can threaten the other negotiator, but they will resent it, and they may call your bluff. If so, you had better be very prepared to implement your threat otherwise you risk looking a little foolish. You may get away with lying in the short term, but when you are found out the consequences can be severe.[109] Negotiators are likely to retaliate when they have been lied to and lying has been judged to be the most unethical of all negotiating strategies. It gives a dog a bad name, which is hard to shake off.[110] Yes, you can spout on about other proposals you have received. If that is not true you may get found out. In many business sectors today people are (increasingly) networked in ways you may not know and may be able to talk to each other and check the validity of what you are saying. Even if you do have other offers I would be wary about flaunting the fact to the other negotiator in order to put pressure on them. Think of negotiation as like being at a party. If you wanted someone else to take an interest in you and spend time with you during the evening you might not choose to spend too much time telling them about all the other amazing people at the party who you could be spending time with instead.

To conclude: be wary of using tough-guy behaviour yourself and stand up to tough guys when you need to, in order either to tip them into more constructive behaviour or to leave you alone.

Here's one good personal story to finish with:

A former chairman was actually a fantastic person, but given to temper outbursts. Early on in our relationship he rang me up to inquire about how we were getting on signing a contract. He didn't like my answer and felt I was taking too long to get the deal done. Immediately he began shouting and swearing down the phone. I was amazed and then annoyed and plunged right in and we had a good old slanging match. I remember I was at the Roehampton Club in London at the time, on a training course – a very genteel members' club with a colonial feel. The use of mobiles was strictly forbidden and I'm sure the sort of shouted language which assailed the members' ears was also forbidden. Certainly I was conscious of harrumphing and the twitching of newspapers from older gentlemen in the lounge around me.

The phone call terminated with a final mutual volley of ill temper and I then had pause to think. Immediately, some doubts started to surface. I couldn't see any way back for our relationship. My wife was newly pregnant with our first child. I began to imagine how I would tell her that I had just lost my job after a shouting match with the chairman. I didn't have long to think about it. My wife rang me about five minutes later to tell me that she was on her way to hospital with stomach pains – three months prematurely. Now I had plenty to think about. I was just setting off for the hospital when, two minutes after that, the phone rang again and I heard the chairman's PA give me a cheery 'Just putting you through ...' I braced myself for the worst. There was a pause. The chairman came on the line and said '... I just wanted to apologise. I am given to these outbursts from time to time but I shouldn't have done that and I'm sorry...' We got on brilliantly from then on and we never had another row, though I witnessed him shouting at many other people.

So, even if it seems a bit frightening sometimes, stand up to tough guys. It will generally be worth it.

20

CHANGING YOUR BEHAVIOUR

Before we close these chapters on behaviour take a look at the profile chart you did for yourself on the closemydeal website. Look at the overall balance of the profile. Which behaviour do you favour? 'I' behaviour, 'you' behaviour, 'we' behaviour or 'parting'? Now look at each sub-segment within the four overall segments. Is there one or more of those that you favour? When you use 'you' behaviour do you employ loads of exploring and listening behaviour, but rarely disclose feelings or information, or never focus on common ground? As we have seen, effective negotiators need to be able to display different types of behaviour in different situations and with different people. It is not uncommon to have one or more favourite behaviours. However, we frequently rely on our favourites too often. Remember that you always have a choice and, next time when you think you might be about to get stuck, try one of the other behaviours instead.

Finally, you can now look at all three of your profiles together. Does that reinforce any of these messages? It may be that if you almost always use 'I' behaviour your 'process' profile was dominated by the bidding and bargaining segments and your 'attitude' profile had a lot of 'using' in it. If 'you' behaviour dominated your behaviour profile it may be that your 'process' profile was led by a focus on 'exploring' and that your 'attitude' profile had a large 'losing' segment.

Is there any behaviour that you would like to display less of – or more?

I Can't Change My Behaviour

When it becomes apparent to them that they rely too much on one form of behaviour, some people say that they can't ever imagine modelling some of the behaviours which they practise infrequently. This comes up a lot. People can understand conceptually that different behaviours suit different occasions and stages and people, but they struggle to vary their own behaviour accordingly. Partly this is routed in the same internal messaging which governs the attitudes we bring to a negotiation. We develop our own patterns of behaviour in response to this messaging and we behave by default accordingly.

So individuals *can* behave differently if they alter the internal programming which tells them that they 'ought' to think or behave in a particular way. You don't have to do this all in one go. As we saw when talking about changing your attitude to a negotiation, you can give yourself a gradual self-talk over time which can make a difference. You can also use 'anchors' derived from successfully recapturing moments when you or others have behaved in the way you desire to emulate now.

You can also practise in low-risk situations. Get your feet wet before jumping in. If you find you tend to be dissociated and you want to practise being more associated because you are negotiating with someone who is very energised and animated, try it out first in a shop in an area you don't normally visit. Have a conversation and try to engage with the person behind the counter. There is no risk. If it doesn't work, you can buy your bar of chocolate, leave the shop and you don't have to go back there again. If it does work, that is a small step in the right direction to showing yourself that you can be associated in the moment if you want. The worst thing that can happen is that it doesn't work on that occasion and that you end up with a bar of chocolate.

The other approach you can take in this situation is to make sure that you have alongside you in a negotiation someone who complements your behavioural skill set. Maybe you are not so strong at a particular behaviour but they are, and maybe you can support them in areas where they have gaps.

Everybody is naturally good at some parts of the negotiating behavioural spectrum but normally a bit less effective at others – as this story from my own experience illustrates:

I once dealt with an executive who was a brilliant trader – terrific at the bargaining phase of the negotiation, and a natural and quick-thinking haggler. However, this type of person is not always so good at planning or thinking things through right to the end. That's one thing I do a lot of as I am fanatical about preparation. During one episode we were negotiating together in Paris for a deal for DVD rights with a French media owner. The person on the other side was very cool-headed and careful, and it was important we came across that way as well. My colleague got himself offside by making an offer on the royalty rate without thinking about it, and I could see that his remark was going to take us down a route towards a royalty rate well in excess of what we had planned in advance. So, I dug him out of that by taking both parties through a reasoned calculation which particularly appealed to the other side. When I had finished she remarked to my colleague, 'You are lucky Clive is with you today.' Afterwards he was grateful but said with a grin, 'Clive, you always make me feel stupid.' Not a great endorsement in a way, but, as I said to him, 'It's just an indicator of our respective strengths. Mine in preparation, yours in thinking on your feet ...'

We've now looked at the three core links in the effective negotiation chain – attitude, process and behaviour – and you have a practical framework you can use. If you have been to the app website and gone through all the statements in the questionnaire, you also have a profile of your own tendencies in relation to each of these areas. We can now move on to discuss some questions about that framework which are asked frequently and repeatedly at seminars and coaching sessions I run.

21

FREQUENTLY ASKED
QUESTIONS

Here are some of those questions which come up frequently whenever the subject of negotiation is presented or discussed.

1. Does this approach work for everyone?

It should follow from what we have talked about in this book that this framework of managing attitude, process and behaviour can work with anybody you negotiate with, *as long as you make the right choices along the way*. If something goes wrong, did you pick the right tools for the right job? Did you bring the right state of mind to the negotiating table? Were you a 'fuser'? How was their state of mind – maybe they talked collaboratively but were they destructive 'users' in disguise? Did you explore the motivations on all sides? Did you identify those motivations correctly? Did you try to address those underlying motivations in the way you put the deal together? Did you select coinage that meant something to the other negotiator and deploy it when it could command the highest value? Did you manage the stages of the negotiation in the right order? Were they all included? Did you bid too early or too late? Did you correctly identify the personality types you are dealing with? Did you work with those types and traits or against them? Did you select the right behaviour for the right occasion and for the right stage of the negotiation? Did you model your chosen behaviour(s) effectively?

Effective negotiation is about making the best *choices* from your framework as you go along. It can potentially work with everyone, but if something goes wrong it's not necessarily the framework itself that is the problem, it's just that one element of it may not have been applied effectively. It's a bit like a golf swing. Top professionals develop their swing over a long period of time and rely on it to carry them around any golf course. They modify elements of their swing to suit individual holes that need a cut or a draw, but they trust that swing. The swing is made up of many moving parts. If part of the swing doesn't function as well as it should, the professional golfer goes off and works on that bit till it comes right. He doesn't just abandon his swing and start again with a completely different methodology next week.

2. Does this approach work for any deal?

In principle, yes. Inevitably, if you work in different sectors there will be different types of expertise that sit across the top of any deal. If you work as a deal maker in the petro-chemicals industry you will be applying different sector knowledge than if you work for a bank or as a theatrical agent. If you are a government employee negotiating a procurement deal you will be applying different sector expertise than if you are negotiating an industrial lease for a factory or simply negotiating at home with your partner. Nobody is suggesting that you should be flippant about any of these differences. Relevant expertise is a crucial ingredient of bargaining power.

However, at its heart every negotiation will have a process involving the seven stages. There will be two or more participants whose attitude to the negotiation will be crucial to its outcome. The participants will have different personality traits which they will display and the shrewd negotiator will need to identify those traits and select their own behaviour accordingly. The participants will all have emotional needs which underpin the organisational wants they focus on in the negotiation. Those underlying needs will drive the negotiation whether they are explicitly addressed or not. This common framework applies whether you are merging a company, raising funding, negotiating a treaty or buying a sheep.

3. Is this just the same as 'win/win' negotiating?

No, it is not. 'Win/win' is a laudable concept but it has become so overused it is now quite hackneyed. In fact, it is more than hackneyed – it is so overused that people have actually forgotten what it was intended to mean. People will frequently tell you that of course they play 'win/win' when they negotiate, as they cheerfully try to extract as much as possible from the 'other side', and ignore what the 'other side' requires from the deal.

Even when it is applied properly, 'win/win' is a much more limited concept than the framework offered in this book. 'Win/win' tends to speak to a positive attitude to *positional* compromise. It encourages people to focus on the surface elements of the deal and arrive at compromises based on a tit-for-tat settlement of their organisational wants: 'I will give you this price in return for this delivery date.' A positive 'fusing' attitude towards both parties is certainly one of the elements that successful negotiators exhibit, but, as we have seen, they tend to look beyond the surface wants on which many people expend so much energy and focus on the underlying *psychological motivations* of both parties in order to craft more creative and profound outcomes. 'Win/win' also does not speak to the process of the negotiation – as we have discussed, managing that *process* and its seven stages is the second of the key elements of effective negotiating. Nor does 'win/win' tell us anything about the range of *behaviours* required by the successful negotiator. The framework discussed here focuses extensively on behaviour as the third crucial element of the three attributes of the effective negotiation chain – not just being flexible about your own behaviour but also understanding the personality of the other negotiator and matching your behaviour to the way in which they interpret the world for maximum persuasive impact. So, don't think of this framework as an exercise in 'win/win'. 'Win/win' only enables you to paint in black and white. This framework gives you the opportunity to paint your deals in colour.

4. Are men better at negotiating than women?

Absolutely not. Research shows that male and female brains function in exactly the same way – with maybe a slight tendency in males towards greater aggression. Nothing too remarkable in that given the way humans have evolved from the earliest times, with men generally hunting and protecting the group from attack by animals or rival tribes. Effective negotiators do not necessarily need the aggressive capability of a hunter – even less so in the age of collaborative negotiating – so women start off with the same potential as men for being good at negotiating. I have seen plenty of effective negotiators of both sexes and a lot of ineffective negotiating behaviour, too. It's just a question of whether that person applies a framework such as the one in this book and, if so, how effectively they make choices within that framework.

Yet research on individual differences suggests general deficiencies of women as negotiators.[111] Unlike men, women are apparently less likely to initiate negotiations, be less positively disposed towards negotiation, be less confident and more likely to set lower goals. Apparently women also demand and expect to receive less in compensation than men, feel less entitled, and place less value on pay than other aspects of work.

Research has also observed that women are often less satisfied with their negotiation performances and feel lower self-efficacy about their bargaining abilities. In fact, research consistently compares women negatively to men, who typically approach negotiations with an offensive and competitive attitude. One study quantified the extent to which women are less likely to initiate negotiations. In their sample of 227 working adults, men indicated they had initiated negotiations two to four times as recently as women.[112] In addition, 51.9 per cent of men negotiated job offers, whereas only 12.5 per cent of women did. It is therefore unsurprising, based on this study, that women receive, on average, starting salaries so much lower than their male equivalents. Other research has concluded that women are more inclined to make lower first offers and lower counter offers than men.[113] *The Psychology of Negotiations in the 21st Century Workplace* by Goldman and Shapiro contains more details of this and other research into the area.[114]

What accounts for this apparent differential? It has been noted that differentials in successful negotiations for men and women were much reduced or eradicated when women were told they were 'asking' rather than 'negotiating'.[115] They apparently found 'asking' much less intimidating. The differences were also marginalised when, for the purpose of the experiment, women were told they were in a position of power, or when they were asked to negotiate for a third party rather than themselves.[116] Women also fared better when they were goaded by references to their less effective stereotyping into negotiating against that stereotype.[117]

This suggests that what *can* make a difference is the state of mind *or attitude* with which a man or a woman enters into a negotiation, since that is one of the choices you make as a negotiator. If women are freed up from any attitudinal baggage associated with their sex, they negotiate just as effectively as men. I have come across women who feel inhibited as negotiators and at a disadvantage when they come up against men. If you feel inhibited and at a disadvantage as a negotiator (whatever the reason), you will make it harder for yourself to be successful. If you feel you are going to lose then losing is what will happen. So, this may in part be a problem to do with making sure you are not carrying faulty internal messages into a negotiation, rather than anything to do with what sex you are. This is backed up by academics who point out that society generally expects women to be 'nice'. Thus, when they act in a stereotypically male manner, there could be a backlash against them. Anticipation of this may cause women to negotiate less ambitiously or not to initiate negotiations at all.[118] Furthermore, this stereotyping may in turn correspond to the endorsement of masculine stereotypes of successful negotiators. This creates a dysfunctional belief or attitude which lowers female negotiating performance.[119] Environmental cues signal to women that men should be claiming more resources than them. Thus, even if a woman feels entitled, she may stop herself from acting in a 'typical' masculine way. There is no reason why women who hold these attitudes cannot change them – if necessary using some of the techniques outlined in this book.

Men can have unhelpful attitudes too, of course. If they disrespect the person on the other side, that may be translated into negative behaviours such as being dismissive, patronising, overfamiliar or just rude. These behaviours are associated with 'users' and some men bring that attitude to bear when they negotiate against a woman. Studies have examined the effect of female stereotyping suggesting women are more gullible and impressionable than male negotiators in order to show that women are more vulnerable to negative behaviour from male negotiators and to negative outcomes when negotiating with them.[120] Indeed, this kind of behaviour is often the trigger for the negative attitudes about their own negotiating ability held by some women. The response for women should be the same though – make sure your own attitude is strong enough to deal with this kind of behaviour.

Whoever has the stronger state of mind in the room, their state will prevail in a negotiation according to coacher's coach James Stokes. So, if you are up against a man who thinks less of you for being a woman then make sure you think enough of yourself to overcome that. Great preparation can do that because it gives you the confidence that you can put up with anything that is thrown at you in the negotiation – including sexist attitudes.

Abby H sent me a heartfelt summary of what she feels she sometimes has to put up with – and how to deal with it:

I was presenting to a room full of men in their fifties – a rebranding and marketing strategy to gain more of a sophisticated audience for a client – when one of the salesmen stood up, his body shaking with fury. He called me a little girl who had no right to be there. I didn't know anything and never would. He picked apart my booklet and threw it on the ground.

I was ready for this; he had been hostile to me since day one. I had created tabs on each section, just in case I would be confronted. I needed those damn tabs so I wouldn't lose my thought process and the bold Post-it tabs peeking out of my binder kept me on track. (I stole this trick from a lawyer I hired in court. While the defendant's lawyer threw a tantrum, I watched him calmly review his notes with tabs.)

The older salesman declared that the e-newsletter idea that I was implementing was spam, and the reputation of the entire company would go down in flames if I wasn't stopped. I simply listened to his tirade, waited a few beats and then continued as if nothing had happened.

Abby continues:

Is it right for a woman to be hugged after a meeting? That happens too often. I've learned to sidestep any weird lean-ins and I put out my hand and shake their hand as I back quickly out of the room. Sometimes I use my laptop as a barrier; I hold it up to my chin as I say my thank-yous and head for the door. It also works to ask where the ladies' room is; it makes men feel uncomfortable enough to step back, and I have a safe exit strategy.

I feel uncomfortable reading that example for a number of reasons. Firstly, I know that lots of men are happy to treat female negotiators equally. Secondly, I know – and the research backs it up – that unfortunately many men aren't: they wouldn't go up and hug a male presenter they had never met before at a marketing conference, but they might assume it's okay if it's a woman. Thirdly, it's a shame that this kind of behaviour causes women to have to think defensively about their exit strategy from a business meeting. Ultimately, though, I see a woman who is able to adopt a strong enough attitude so that none of this stops her from being effective and delivering the outcomes she wants. That is something we can all do equally, regardless of our sex.

This is not to say that there are not some real barriers for women in business which act as a genuine impediment to their ability to negotiate. There are some countries where religious custom and practice make meaningful participation in business extremely difficult for women. There are also many countries where prevailing attitudes make it harder for women to compete equally with men. In countries such as the US, although women make up almost 50 per cent of the labour force and graduate from college in greater numbers than men, women are still not anywhere near parity in senior positions in corporations, professional service partnerships and large-scale international organisations. For example, US women account for only 3 per cent of Fortune 500 CEOs and 15.2 per cent of Fortune 500 board seats, according to 'US Women in Business'. So, even in societies which are moving towards greater gender equality women still have much ground to make up because, historically, the boundaries of organisational life were set in periods when men enjoyed much greater control and success.

What we can say though is that, as far as outcomes in negotiation are concerned, some of the problem can be attributed to the attitudes which women (and men) bring to negotiations with each other. Some men may be less inclined to change their unhelpful and stereotypical attitudes, but women have every incentive to do so and can. That may not change the world, but it can make them more effective at negotiating, regardless of their situation.

One further point. Some studies indicate that, insofar as there are stereotypes, women are better equipped than men to negotiate in the interconnected and interdependent world in which we now live.[121] A study that asked a group of managers to list eight characteristics of effective leaders showed that the males' list included aggressiveness, confidence and objectivity in the top five. These are compatible with the competitive style of negotiation. Female managers, on the other hand, listed appreciation, recognising strengths, fairness and accessibility as the most important characteristics. These qualities are compatible with a partnering style of negotiation and 'fusing'. Two large-scale reviews have since showed that women are more cooperative and seen as more patient and empathetic and better listeners. Women are also considered less likely than men to lie in negotiations – more important than ever in a collaborative world.[122] Maybe women negotiators are about to come into their own. Certainly if they believe that themselves, even that alone will be enough to help them get more of what they want.

It follows from all this that, in principle, there is no intrinsic difference between the capability of negotiators regardless of other differences between them such as age, creed, class, educational background or ethnicity. One of the things I always liked about the music business is that, unlike some other sectors, it recognises all-comers and all backgrounds and makes no judgements about that. I like that about the practice of negotiation, too – top negotiators come in all shapes and sizes.

5. Is it better negotiating face to face or via phone or email?

I always prefer negotiating face to face. Going back to our analogy of negotiation as an exercise in being a detective, you are much more likely to be able to spot clues face to face than in a written document or on the phone. You get to experience what the other negotiator is saying directly, you can hear more easily what they are doing with their voice, you can see what they are doing with their body. The same is true for them. Intimacy is often easier to establish face to face. It's easier to build rapport, easier to talk about emotional matters. There is a problem, though, which is that modern technology is making face-to-face negotiation less and less common. This is inevitable when you consider the trends on use of mobiles and the internet. Mobile data traffic in 2011 grew 2.3-fold according to Cisco's Visual Networking Index. This was the fourth year in a row it had doubled worldwide. Tablet usage is growing fast, too. By 2016 mobile-connected tablets are expected to generate as much traffic as the entire global mobile network did in 2012. In 1993 there were ten million internet users. By 2011 that figure had reached 2.45 billion. Access still varies by country and region, but in developed countries such as the USA, Japan, France and the UK, internet users number over 80 per cent of the population. China has 500 million internet users.

In this context the trend is for electronic communication to replace a lot of face-to-face negotiation. This is a problem for several reasons. Firstly, email cuts down the amount of data you have – you only have the written words, and there is limited opportunity for the kind of feedback you get face to face which helps clarify what the other party is thinking.[123] A lot of the subtleties of face-to-face communication are therefore lost in an email and it's harder to work out or match the traits of your negotiating partner. Emails are easier to misconstrue than face-to-face communication because you only have the written word to work with, and a lot of the positive effect and the context of informal conversational interaction is lost. Emails are often written for brevity rather than to thoroughly explore issues. This tends to reduce levels of trust.[124] I have also noticed that email encourages the adoption of positions; email is by definition 'black and white' – it's much easier to adopt a position in an email rather than exploring something as intangible as people's psychological needs from the deal. As we saw earlier, positional negotiations are characterised by argument and emotional entanglement in a way that needs-based negotiations normally avoid, so this is also potentially an issue with negotiations conducted by email.

Moreover, people are often fiercer about defending their positions in an email than they would ever be face to face. It's as though when they send an email the other negotiator isn't really present for them, and so they say things which are far harsher and more strident than they would ever say if the person was sitting in front of them.[125] [126] Email is also fertile ground for miscommunication where the writer is communicating in a language which is not his or her first language. Even the best linguists often understand more spoken language than they can speak, and speak more fluently than they can write in a second language. Email negotiation also allows for more pauses than face-to-face negotiation which can encourage people to ruminate and confirm their worst suspicions of the dealmaker. So for all these reasons email can create emotional tensions quite easily. There has also been some research to suggest that negotiating online makes it easier to avoid 'leakage' of your true position and gives deceivers more time to plan their moves, and therefore makes it easier for people to behave dishonestly.[127]

Here's a good example from private equity specialist Adam Somerfeld of the disadvantages of email negotiation:

I bought a domain name for £600 and did some minor search engine optimisation in order to generate traffic. Out of the blue I received an email offer for it from an educational company in China. I received a first offer of £22,000. This company meant nothing to me so I decided to play hardball. I told them we had an offer from Microsoft into the late five figures even though it wasn't strictly true. This immediately caused them to add another £10,000 to the price. Another fifty to sixty emails followed and I knew that the longer the negotiation went on, the more likely the company were to meet my demands, out of pure frustration.

I kept making demands and setting deadlines by which I would sell the domain name to another bidder. Every time I did so they added another couple of thousand pounds to the price. In the end I set one final deadline at which point I had the only conversation of the entire negotiation, with their CFO. I eventually sold the domain name for £47,000. Had the negotiation taken place face to face I would not have behaved in such a cavalier manner, but as it was on email and they sounded like they had money I just went for it.

A good result for Adam, but of course it could just as easily have been someone else doing this to him. When you negotiate solely via email or electronic means you increase the chances of the other negotiator feeling entitled to behave in an impersonal way and like a 'user'.

What can you do about this? Here are ten tips:

- Phone negotiation is a bit better than electronic communication, because at least you have the sound and tone of the voice to work with – though research has supported the view that negotiation by telephone is less effective at building rapport than negotiation which is face to face.[128] Video conferencing is better still because you have a visual representation of the other party, albeit sometimes still a jerky and imperfect one.

- Prepare – it's even more important than normal when negotiating electronically, in order to compensate for the other disadvantages. Just because emails can be written quickly that doesn't mean that they should be. More haste, less speed.

- If you are having to negotiate by email try and have a video conference or a phone call first, or even just send some biographical information or photos of yourself to humanise the contact if you don't know the other person.[129]

- When communicating via email, make a conscious effort to include the kind of negotiating behaviours you would use if you were negotiating face to face – especially 'you' behaviours such as asking lots of questions, summarising back what the other side is saying to you, focusing on common ground and disclosing judiciously.

- You may not be able to actively listen electronically but you can use a rudimentary form of discourse analysis to look at the language of the emails you are receiving and try to work out from that what's really important to the other negotiator, and what behavioural 'patterns' they display – e.g. do they use a lot of audio visual, aural or sensing/kinetic language? If so, mirror that back to them.

- Inoculate yourself against the other dealmaker getting the wrong impression by pre-empting any misinterpretation on their part. Use expressions such as 'Correct me if I'm wrong' or 'I may not have understood this properly, but …' to disarm them and prevent them diving off at the deep end if they are irritated by what you say electronically.

- Imagine the other person is in the room when you write your email and that you are speaking to him or her – that might discourage you from using aggressive, patronising or sarcastic language in your email that you would never use face to face. Even if you think your criticism is measured, check it again. Email contains an automatic 'loud' setting because it's in indelible writing, so it's likely to be received at a far higher intensity of volume than you intend.

- Imagine that you are on the receiving end of the email you plan to send. How would you react? If you would be outraged or insulted, don't send the email in that form.

- Don't get stuck on 'positional' negotiating – concentrating just on the 'content' of the deal. Email encourages this focus on positions in relation to issues such as 'price' and 'quantity', but, as we know, effective negotiating is more about 'why' people want the things that they say they want.

- In the same vein, keep an eagle-eye open for opportunities to 'expand the pie' and create options when bargaining, as electronic communication tends to narrow issues down to what is perceived to be essential to one party rather than what could be desirable to both parties.

These tips will help you amid the common pitfalls of negotiating electronically, but face to face is always better – electronic communication methods are a crutch we should try to put aside when negotiating …

'I'VE CALLED YOU HERE TO DISCUSS THE
IMPORTANCE OF TALKING FACE-TO-FACE'

6. Is negotiating different in other countries?

Now that *is* a good question. So good that it deserves a chapter all of its own. The next one, in fact.

22

NEGOTIATING IN DIFFERENT COUNTRIES

As a professional negotiator, a question I am frequently asked and that often comes up at seminars and with clients is how important it is to understand and work with local cultural norms when negotiating internationally. It's not surprising that this issue crops up a lot. As we saw in Chapter 2, technology is bringing the world closer together all the time, so people need to be able to make deals with inhabitants of many other countries. Equally, as we noted in that chapter, a realignment of the world economy is taking place at a dizzying pace. Traditionally strong economies in the developed world such as continental Europe and the USA are stagnating, while the so-called developing countries are experiencing rapid growth – the economies of China, India, Brazil, Indonesia, South Korea, Argentina, Turkey, Taiwan and Nigeria are all growing at far faster rates. We need to be able to trade successfully with these emerging economies if we are to benefit from their momentum.

There are many generalisations about typical negotiating tactics and cultures among different nationalities. For our purpose let's take as a working definition of 'culture' an old definition put forward by Kroeber and Kluckhohn,[130] namely as 'a shared social blueprint for life – the constellation of values, assumptions, beliefs and behavioural norms that define a group of people'. It's important that if we hold these beliefs they are accurate, given the natural tendency of inhabitants of one country (as an 'in group') to hold more favourable views of their own group than of an outside group (such as foreigners).[131] Here are a few common assumptions about the local business culture in a number of countries. These generalisations have been taken from a variety of legitimate sources providing well-meaning advice on doing business abroad – in some cases they have been written by locals themselves. Many are taken from the excellent 'Culture Smart' series of books on living and working in the countries concerned. These generalisations are listed only so that we can debate them, not because they are all necessarily true all the time. In fact, as we shall see, the best approach is to understand and be prepared for these norms, but also to recognise their limitations.

I have covered India, Brazil, Russia and China below (all BRICS members) together with Japan, Mexico (which some already consider worthy of BRICS membership) and Saudi Arabia (so that the Middle East is represented). For each country I have listed some generalisations about doing business there and then provided (a) some advice to the extent that these assumptions are true (and based on the framework of negotiating set out in this book), and (b) also some advice reminding you to be open as to whether some of the relevant generalisations about negotiating in that country *are* true. Where appropriate, I have added some insights from applicable research on the subject of cross-cultural negotiations and I've also taken input from global expert on multicultural issues, David Solomon.

We start, however, with some commonly held generalisations about Britain, because it may be a good way (at least for British readers) of showing why it is sensible to have an open mind about some of these preconceptions:

- The British are a mercantile people. As they live on an island, trading with the rest of the world is a routine part of commercial and industrial daily life, and it always has been.

- The British believe that 'manners maketh man' and politeness is expected in business, too. Quiet courtesy will always be positively noted. Show some reticence and deference and remember to say 'please' and 'thank you'.

- The British tend to compartmentalise their lives and have a strong sense of privacy and of personal space. This is reinforced by the saying 'never mix business and pleasure' so there is a reluctance to get too close in business.

- Many people still use traditional forms of address (e.g. Mr or Mrs, or Dr or even Esquire). Even in email many British people are reluctant to use colloquialisms like 'hi' and may start an email 'Dear Peter', as though they were writing a letter.

- The British favour self-effacement and understatement so they don't necessarily like to be 'sold' something and they won't give you a hard sell either. This tendency towards self-effacement can make them seem reserved. Such reserve and their sense of historical tradition make them sceptical of new gimmicks and sometimes quite stubborn about embracing change. Clinging to their historical tradition vigorously and being reserved can make them come across as being superior to foreigners.

- The expression 'there is a time and a place for everything' suggests a need for order – the British are world champions at queuing.

- Tolerance, fair play and a desire for compromise are notable qualities of the British character, along with a strong sense of justice – increasingly directed at individual rights and self-interests rather than (or as well as) the more traditional sense of collective duty to others.

Addressing these assumptions

A lot of the generalisations above are 'norms' about an archetypal British person. Norms are like averages. On average you might meet more people who fit this kind of description in Britain than in other countries. But this does not mean that all British people are like this. Quite the reverse. However, let's start with some observations which take these generalisations at face value and gives some negotiating advice to the extent that they are true, and then move on to address some caveats.

In relation to 'attitude', if the British generally have an outlook which emphasises 'fairness', compromise and making sure that nobody can accuse them of something that 'isn't cricket', it may be that, generally, this translates into a 'fuser' *attitude*, which makes them prepared to accommodate the interests of both parties.

If the British generally like an organised approach to life, they ought to respond positively to organising the negotiation *process* into explicit stages. In terms of climate, the British sense of reserve may make the adoption of a 'cool' climate more comfortable for them. That same sense of holding back their emotions may, however, make it harder to have a discussion around underlying needs as the Brits may find it uncomfortable to disclose this information or to quiz the other party about their underlying motivation. So, you will have to be extra observant to work out their motivations. Their sense of what is 'proper' may make the Brits unlikely to adopt aggressive bidding or bargaining positions.

In relation to use of *behaviour*, you would expect the British sense of private space and reserve generally to incline them against sociable 'we' behaviours. Their sense of 'understatement' might make inspiring others through visualisation an unlikely choice of behaviour. You would expect them to listen politely, but their self-imposed boundaries might make them wary of active listening by way of reflecting back emotions, or of confiding or disclosing emotions (all examples of 'you' behaviour).

Equally, their sense of decorum might preclude reliance on excitable behaviours such as testing and probing the other negotiator's position or use of pressures in a negotiation. In terms of some of the variations we looked at when examining different patterns that reveal people's personality, you might expect Brits to lead with the head rather than the heart, to prefer harmony to confrontation, to prefer linear, ordered processes rather than lots of choices, and to be patient rather than in a rush (cricket matches do, after all, often last five days). You would also expect them to be more concerned with conforming rather than being too individualistic and to be more dissociated (slightly distant) in conversation rather than passionately associated. You would also expect them to be engaged by thinking that links them to the 'past' rather than concentrating on future thinking. You might not expect too much tough-guy behaviour ('it isn't cricket'), but you might find Brits working to genuinely held standards such as 'fairness' and 'reasonableness' which are difficult for everyone to agree on because they are in fact subjective.

Yes, but ...

So far so good, these generalisations are a good start and it's useful to be able to negotiate with these norms in mind. However, remember they will not apply all the time. Here are some caveats:

- There are upwards of sixty million inhabitants in the UK. They are all lumped together in the generalisations above, but of course the UK includes English, Scots, Welsh and Northern Irish inhabitants who are often very different from each other. This is not to mention regional variations between, for example, inhabitants of the South East and Cornwall, the North East and the Midlands.
- To what extent can we really generalise about the 'British' character? I'm sure that some of those characteristics

reminded you of some people you know in some ways. I'm sure you also know many British people who exhibit different characteristics – who are highly emotional, or impatient, or who can be quite aggressive and demonstrative, who are fascinated by technology and the future rather than focused on the past in the way they think about things, who are very comfortable dealing with other people's emotions or who are highly individualistic. Some British people are not overly concerned with manners or forms – in any event which 'manners' are we talking about? Manners can become outmoded over time. It is a long time since I received a letter addressing me as 'Esquire'; when I write an email I rarely say 'Dear Mr or Mrs' yet I still consider myself polite.

- The kind of cultural diversity experienced by Britain in any event may be evening out the effect of perceived generalisations about national characteristics. If there is a typically British 'character' it is inevitably being modified by exposure of different generations to individuals who originate from so many other different cultures, and this will continue to happen. There are over six million people in Britain who are of Pakistani, Indian, Black Caribbean, Black African, Bangladeshi, Chinese or other Asian origin. Almost a third of Londoners are not white, and there are reputedly 300 different languages spoken in London according to the Office for National Statistics. Over thirty million people a year visit the UK from overseas – this also has the effect of levelling out distinctively 'British' characteristics. The British also travel – up to seven million travel abroad every year. They are exposed to different countries and nationalities and those other nationalities are increasingly exposed to British travellers.

All this can even out over time what might previously have been seen as uniquely national characteristics.

It will be useful to bear in mind the kind of generalisations specified above when you negotiate in Britain – be prepared for them by all means. There are some cultural and religious conventions which it is very important to take into account, as we shall see when we repeat this exercise with respect to other countries in the pages that follow. However, ultimately you are negotiating with the individual, not the social norms. As we saw earlier, individuals have many different kinds of personality regardless of where they come from. One of the great knacks as a negotiator is to be able to select the right behaviour for the right person. These kinds of choices may have less to do with national stereotypes. They are to do with making a careful assessment of the individual in front of you.

Let's now look at negotiating in some other countries using the same method as we have used for Britain.

India

Here are some informed generalisations about doing business in India:

- Indian society is very hierarchical at multiple levels. Within a company the CEO and anyone with a senior title will automatically be given respect because of their position. Indians generally place a high importance on pleasing those in authority. Only the most senior member of the team may end up speaking at a meeting.
- This hierarchical formality means that meetings are often used largely to pass on information, affirm one's position of authority or communicate views from the top. Formal meetings are not normally used for creative purposes such as to brainstorm, generate ideas or correct weaknesses.

- The prevalence of hierarchy means it may well be that the key decision maker is not in the room when you negotiate. However, avoid the temptation to sidestep others in the hierarchy to deal with this – respect gatekeepers in the hierarchy even if they only seem to be slowing down your progress.
- People may be noticeably sensitive to mistakes being revealed or pointed out or to being held to account for errors.
- These characteristics mean that conflict is avoided. Differences of opinion are not made clear. Indians don't usually like saying no directly for fear of offence/ disappointment so it's important to listen carefully to their replies to your questions to assess their level of commitment. If you have to raise an issue of conflict be discreet about it and deal with it in private.
- There is also hierarchy among castes, family and community. From the original caste distinctions between Brahmins (priests), Kshatriyas (rulers), Vaishyas (merchants and farmers), Shudras (artisans and servants), myriad numbers of other castes and sub-castes have developed. Caste-consciousness persists despite legislative change, educational reform and the attempts by many Indians to mask their caste identity by changing their name. These distinctions are matched by class distinctions of Forward (higher castes), Backward (middle and lower castes) and Dalit for 'untouchables', though these boundaries are being blurred by a fast-growing, prosperous middle class.
- Indians have a generally relaxed view of time and deadlines, so learn to be patient. The hierarchical structure also means that deals can take a long time to progress.
- Contracts are regarded as 'fluid' documents to be changed as business develops. Business people rely on the relationship, not the piece of paper, so may be surprised if you hold them to strict fulfilment.

- Corruption could be an issue when dealing with India's huge bureaucracies. Cooperation from officials is required to deal with much red tape. Some estimate the cost of annual bribes in India at US$20 trillion.
- Finger-pointing is rude and whistling, winking or singing may be mistaken for sexual come-ons.
- Meetings can begin with a handshake; however Indians themselves often use namaste. This is where the palms of the hand are brought together at chest level with a slight bow of the head. Using the namaste shows you understand and respect Indian culture.
- Indians respect people who value and take an interest in family. They will allow family to take priority over work, whenever necessary. So, it's worth trying to find out about their family and engage with them on such personal matters.
- Indians tend to be well disposed in business to those they know and trust. So, it is important to develop personal relationships with potential business partners/investors. They may invite you to their homes to develop a personal rapport with you.

To add to these assumptions, here is some research on Indian versus US negotiators.[132] Because Indian culture is organised into distinct social groups based on language, caste, religion and region, Indians learn that many, if not most, social interactions are embedded in networks and that network members will monitor and sanction anybody who deviates from the norms for that group. Indian culture therefore supports numerous and overlapping guarantees of behaviour. This makes India a 'tight culture' whereas the United States is a 'loose culture'. In loose cultures people routinely trust on faith and therefore negotiators will extend relatively high interpersonal trust to their counterparts. However, in the tight Indian culture, people depend on institutional guarantees of behaviour in compliance with accepted norms arising from the networks they are used to. Where such guarantees are absent from negotiations, the negotiators will extend relatively low interpersonal trust to their counterparts. The research supported this conclusion with Indian negotiators showing lower trust than US negotiators.

The study also posited (and found it be true that) Indians asked fewer questions than US negotiators. The reason for this was that engaging in reciprocal Q and A requires trust, since you have to believe that counterparts will not take advantage but will instead use shared information in a mutually beneficial way.

Addressing these assumptions

These generalisations are a good starting point. Some of them will be of genuine value – especially those concerning religious or genuine cultural differentials. The caste system is deeply embedded in Indian history and culture and it would be sensible to be aware of its subtleties when you operate there. Using the namaste greeting may well earn appreciation for the respect it shows for the local form of greeting. If you were minded to sing, whistle or wink during an Indian business meeting it's as well to know that those activities could be considered inappropriate. Corruption may well be present in many countries with a large bureaucracy that is not well paid; it's as well to be aware of its presence.

If these generalisations are true, you might also expect some of the following to apply generally when negotiating in India:

In relation to *attitude*, if it is true that Indians dislike conflict there is at least the potential for 'fuser' outcomes which suit everybody. From the point of view of bargaining power it would be very useful to have 'network power' on your side since that would imply you have a way of accessing the hierarchies which are said to dominate. You could also expect a lot of use of referral bargaining power from local negotiators – where they say they have to get approval from others higher up in the hierarchy who are not present.

In relation to *process* you would expect a very hierarchical society to appreciate the kind of organised stages that a well-oiled, ideal negotiation should follow, though getting to closure may take some time. In relation to 'needs', you might expect those at the top of the hierarchy to have 'respect' or esteem needs and those lower down to have reassurance needs around not being blamed for things and not getting into trouble if things go wrong. If India has a 'tight' culture in which trust has to be earned then you could expect the climate of negotiations to be quite 'cool', especially at the beginning.

With regard to *behaviours*, you would expect that a business culture which has a relaxed attitude to timing will appreciate the opportunity for frequent breaks in the negotiation, both short and long. Equally, you would expect this kind of culture not to be so preoccupied with the behaviours which characterise bidding and bargaining which are often fast moving. However, a culture in which there is a tendency towards a lack of trust may not be one in which there is much disclosing – especially if there is something of an aversion to the risk of being exposed for making mistakes. If there is a reluctance to engage in Q and A which springs from this lack of trust, this will act as a limit on exploring behaviour, too. Furthermore 'pressure' tactics and other 'I' behaviours or tough-guy approaches characteristic of pushing your own agenda might also be out of place in a culture which does not enjoy conflict. In other words, there may not be much negotiation behaviour to work with. This, indeed, was what the research paper referred to above (Gunia, 2010) found. Looking at the kind of personality types we encountered earlier in examining behaviours, you might expect to see many people who prefer to avoid decisions rather than making them, who like to follow a linear process rather than an ad hoc or creative one, who rely on group approval rather than an individual approach.

Yes, but ...

- Remember these are only 'norms' – just averages. Are there no Indians who are prepared to be creative or brainstorm in a meeting? None at all out of a population of 700 million? Of course there are. Are there no Indians who embrace conflict? They would be a very unusual and blessed nation indeed if that was the case.

- Equally, a number of these supposed characteristics could apply to any number of different countries; they are certainly not unique to India. I don't know of any culture in which people like admitting mistakes. Nor have I yet encountered a culture where family was unimportant – it forms a central position in most human societies.

- If personal relationships in business are important in India, that is also the case in most other countries. As the world becomes more and more of a global marketplace you would expect people to value personal relationships even more as a criterion by which they decide whether or not to deal with business people from other faraway countries. Very few business people are comfortable doing deals with people they don't trust – it doesn't just apply in India.

- At the same time, insofar as these distinctions are valid, you would expect a number of them to be slowly breaking down. There are huge ethnic Indian populations in the UK, Singapore and many other countries. There has also been a reverse diaspora. These Indians returning home bring with them a sophisticated understanding of the cultures of the countries in which they used to live. As they become reintegrated into India and progress, you would expect that understanding to affect not only their own attitudes and behaviours but also the attitudes and behaviours of other Indians who might previously have had a more 'localised' approach. Bear these caveats in mind when you are negotiating in India and don't just assume that the person in front of you will reflect all the 'normal' presumptions.

Russia

- There is a highly ambivalent attitude to the 'law and regulations' – Russians like to do things their own way. This is the product of years of enforced obedience combined with the chaos following the sweeping away of communism. For this reason if you are going to sign a contract keep it simple and have it signed in English and Russian to maximise your chances of enforcement if required. Those same historical rigours associated with communism, its chaotic decline and the periods of suppression which preceded it often make Russians seem rather pessimistic in outlook.

- Personal networks are extremely important – the concept of 'Blat' exists, referring to the practice of 'I'll help you if you help me'. This practice grew up in the Soviet era so that the system of state distribution was complemented by the gaining of 'insider' access to goods and services traded through personal contacts.

- Business relationships are therefore frequently based on whether the proposed partners feel they would get along and can trust each other.

- There is a tendency towards punishment at work. This means there is a strong incentive to obey and be disciplined, but also an unwillingness to take initiatives or be creative for fear of making mistakes.

- The history of the Communist Party means that there remains a strong commitment to hierarchy – many employees generally need to be told what to do. Bosses often do not delegate.
- These factors combine to make decision making slow as people may be afraid of getting things wrong and decisions have to go through the hierarchy. There is accordingly a relaxed attitude to timekeeping and punctuality.
- Russians often don't return calls or follow up what they said they would do. Since personal relationships are considered important this is just their way of saying 'no' to somebody without being explicit about it.
- Don't rush into negotiations – allow time for hospitality first.
- Since Russians rely on personal relationships don't change your negotiating team in mid-stream.
- Russians tend to agree on general principles first and look at the big picture of the project before negotiating details.
- Corruption is present. According to INDEM, the Russian Foundation of 'Information Science for Democracy', Russian citizens pay at least US$2.8 billion a year in bribes – partly as a consequence of low salaries among civil servants and public officials.
- Face-saving is important to Russians so be very selective about picking your battles.
- When negotiating, Russians are given to theatrical behaviour with lots of use of the word 'nyet', raised voices or long, tense silences. But keep going: it's all part of the show.
- Russians are tough negotiators. Their main aim may be to obtain concessions so there could be a long process of grinding you down. Giving in too early may be seen as a sign of weakness so try to hang tough. Generally speaking, Russians go for 'maximum initial demand with minimal concessions'.

- Pitches or presentations should be kept simple and you should try to be clear and keep it short when explaining your objectives.

Addressing these assumptions

Working with these assumptions you could expect to experience a fairly rough time negotiating in Russia.

In relation to *attitude* you may expect to encounter lots of 'users' just trying to get the best for themselves and take advantage of you. These are negotiators who would seek to use every ounce of bargaining power against you – including referral power from their preference for hierarchy, and size and weight (think of the periodic tough negotiations with Ukraine over gas supplies perhaps?). It follows that you would need to marshal all your own bargaining power to match them, while recognising that use of standards such as 'rules and regulations' might not cut much ice. You would also expect to see use of a wide variety of tough-guy tactics, including threats, aggression, take it or leave it, and deadline pressures. So you would have to be able to stand up to these tactics through naming the tactic in order to get it dropped, or through asking them if they would like you to behave the same way, or through other tough-guy responses we talked about such as the use of silence or testing ultimatums like deadlines and take it or leave it. If bribery is common and doesn't fit with your business standards you might have to find creative ways of framing accommodations so that your standards are not compromised – skill at framing the issue might be essential.

In terms of the *process* you could expect to see minimal exploring and a fairly 'hostile' climate set. There might be lots of aggressive bidding and bargaining – it would certainly be important to ask for what you want and sound like you mean it. It would also be important to lead with your conditions not your concessions when bargaining, and to keep big concessions back for the end of the deal. 'Goodwill' concessions would probably be a waste of time and would be perceived as weakness. If hierarchies are strong you might expect to see lots of respect needs (at a higher level in organisations) and lots of reassurance needs (lower down the scale). During the bidding and bargaining stages it might be good to take lots of breaks since this would enable you to dispel some of the pressures against you and would also enable you to take advantage of the fact that Russians are not committed to timekeeping.

In relation to *behaviours*, based on the above you would expect to see lots of 'I' behaviour (especially stating expectations and use of pressures). You might experience negotiators who look for 'mismatches', or differences (rather than similarities), who negotiate from the heart rather than the head, who are pessimistic rather than optimistic, and who focus on the big picture rather than the details – you would need to work with these characteristics rather than against them.

Yes, but …

- Some of these 'norms' are not unique to Russia. We have already spoken about the generality of personal relationships being important everywhere. Apparently presentations should be simple and straightforward and you should be concise when presenting your objectives? I can't think of many countries where that would be a bad idea.

- Then again, we are not applying all these generalisations to all Russians. Out of a population of 140 million there will be many Russians who appreciate the benefits of working in genuine partnership. There will also be many who are optimists, who prefer to negotiate rationally rather than passionately, and who have no use for tough-guy tactics. There will be some Russian companies which are unhierarchical and have a flat organisational structure

– for example, SMEs or companies run by entrepreneurs.
Many Russians work for multinational companies – I have
worked with employees at Google Russia, and it seemed
to me that they shared many common characteristics
with other Google employees in other countries. That part
of their identity was important to them as well as being
Russian.

Once again, the best conclusion is to be prepared to encounter the
above social norms when you are negotiating in Russia, but to treat
each situation on its merits and each person as an individual before
you negotiate solely based on generalised assumptions.

Brazil

- Hierarchy is a big part of Brazilian business culture. Brazilians
  are used to defining social status, age and position when
  dealing with each other and differences in social class,
  education and family status are important. These attributes
  are equally important in their judgements of foreigners.
- Equally, hierarchy prevails in the structure of companies and
  management styles. Important decisions are usually made by
  senior staff and implemented by the rest. The seating plan at
  meetings is often hierarchical.
- Brazilians are fashion-conscious and like to adopt European
  styles. There is a presumption that caring about your appearance corresponds to caring about your business. Business
  dress is smart. Teeth and nails should be clean and polished.
- Brazilians do business through personal connections. So,
  anticipate some socialising before meetings over a cafezinho,
  or 'little coffee'. Equally, be prepared to stay on afterwards
  and take time over your goodbyes – it's part of the relationship
  building as is the exchange of business cards. Brazilians

assess who they want to do business with based on the character and attitudes of their potential partners. For this reason business entertainment is considered part of business – including lunches and dinners, though often not much business is actually discussed over the meal.

- Brazilians look straight into the eyes of the other person when speaking. Although that may feel uncomfortable, don't avert your gaze otherwise you give the impression you have something to hide.

- Meetings may not run in a formal, linear fashion. It is quite common for Brazilians to interrupt, for the flow not to follow the agenda, and for those involved to answer phone calls during the meeting.

- Brazilians analyse subjects and projects in depth so don't expect meetings or negotiations to be undertaken at speed.

- Presentations should be expressive. Style can be just as important as substance.

- The importance of personal connections means it's not a good idea to change your negotiating team in the middle of the deal.

- Brazilians often avoid direct confrontation in favour of less direct ways of showing disagreement.

- A contract normally gets signed some time after the deal is done and is not the last word in the negotiation. A contract can be altered as matters progress and deadlines and other commitments may change. There is a Brazilian expression, 'For friends everything, for enemies the law', which indicates both the importance of relationships and the lesser importance of formal agreements.

- Brazilians are not Hispanics and will not like being referred to as 'Latins' or addressed in Spanish. They are Americanos from South America (so don't use the word America simply to designate the USA).

- Emotions are often expressed rather than withheld.

Addressing these assumptions

Taking some of these social norms at face value, the following could apply. In relation to *attitude*, you might expect that Brazilians would be open to 'fusing' outcomes if they value relationships, since good relationships are often characterised by a tendency to reciprocate relational benefits. Referral bargaining power might be present in many negotiations if the hierarchical structure means that the key decision maker is not at the table. If Brazilians like to analyse situations, the extra bargaining power which comes with having information and expertise on your side would be important. If they are focused on relationships, you would expect that having an existing relationship with your negotiating partner would also be an important source of bargaining power.

In terms of *process* it sounds like climate is important and you might expect the climate of choice to be a warm one which encourages sociability (coffee drinking and meals). We have already observed in relation to Russia and India that if the business culture is very hierarchical then respect needs may be associated with paying deference to an individual's status in that hierarchy. If Brazilians are not noted for confrontational behaviour, the widespread use of tough-guy tactics would not be expected. Equally, you might avoid use of potentially provocative behaviours like testing and probing the other side's position with tricky 'why' questions which ask them to justify what they want.

If emotions are not normally withheld, you would expect the more emotional *behaviours* to be in evidence and to be useful – visualising positive outcomes, focusing on common ground, disclosure of feelings. If they like to analyse, use of proposals with reasons might be an effective behaviour. Despite this, in relation to some of the personality variations we looked at above, you might expect Brazilians generally to lead with their hearts, not their heads, and you might expect them to display associated, involved behaviour rather than dissociated, distant behaviour. You would expect them to be susceptible to visual cues given the focus on style, appearance and expressive presentations, and the habit of 'eyeing people up'. The slightly ad hoc way that meetings can be conducted might indicate that many Brazilians favour a non-linear approach in their patterns of thinking. In terms of personality 'traits' you might expect to encounter many Brazilians who are high on the scales for 'extroversion', 'openness' and 'agreeableness'. This would encourage 'sociable' behaviours such as 'sharing problems' and 'sharing solutions'.

Yes, but …

- Once again, bear in mind that some of these generalisations apply widely. We have already noted the importance of relationship building in Russia and India. It is common for countries where relationships are paramount to attach more importance to whether people are getting along than to the niceties of contracts – we have already observed that in relation to India, and we will see it's the same in China and Saudi Arabia. There cannot be many negotiating cultures in which it is sensible to change your team in the middle of the negotiation unless things are going badly with the other party – the same point has already been made with regard to negotiating in Russia.

- Furthermore, if these generalisations reflect the 'average', it's important to bear in mind that many Brazilians do not fit this average at all. There will be many Brazilians you meet who are shy, or unemotional, and do not focus on the importance of visual cues. Think about who has more in common – (i) a prosperous member of the Brazilian upper class based in São Paulo and a rural Brazilian living in the countryside, or (ii) a twenty-year-old Brazilian living in Rio and a twenty-year-old man living in London who are both obsessed with football and going to the 2014 World Cup in Brazil? It is not just nationality that binds people together or separates them. Equally, will a Brazilian with achievement needs negotiate the same way as a Brazilian who has belonging needs, or a Brazilian with strong ethical drivers? Looking at traits, will a logical and disciplined 'conscientious' Brazilian negotiate the same way as a Brazilian who scores high on the 'agreeableness' scale? Such traits, to the extent that they themselves are valid, do not fit neatly within national boundaries.

Japan

- There is a whole ritual associated with the exchange of business cards ('meishi'). Your business card represents your 'face' and so it is an extremely personal thing. After shaking hands, pass your business card (probably with a slight bow). Show you value the card received from your host and don't just shove it in your pocket without looking at it.
- The Japanese correlate age with seniority, so do not send young managers to important meetings.
- When shown into the meeting room by your host, sit at the place indicated to you. The seat of honour and other positions in decreasing order of importance are usually predetermined.
- Appreciate the etiquette of bowing. Bowing indicates respect by avoiding eye contact. It also communicates a range of messages non-verbally, such as greetings, goodbyes, thanks, apology, acknowledgement and corporate position.
- To encourage harmony, the pattern of Japanese conversation usually allows the participants to agree. Refusals will normally be indirect, and use of the word 'no' is avoided. Instead

Japanese people may say things like 'It may be difficult' or 'Well, maybe', or they may just pause silently or not reply at all.

- At the same time the word 'yes' does not have the same unambiguous meaning of agreement as it does in, say, the UK. It may just mean 'Yes I hear you'.
- Because the Japanese value harmony, reaching consensus is very important to them, especially among their own team. This can mean that reaching agreement can take longer than expected. It can also mean that Japanese executives will prefer to collect group opinions and deliver those rather than just giving their own individual point of view.
- It's critical for Japanese not to lose face – it is shameful, and they will expect you to remain calm in negotiations as getting angry shows a lack of self-respect and you lose face, too. You also lose face if you are late for meetings.
- Use the word 'we' rather than 'I'. Japan is not an 'I' culture in the way that, for instance, the US is.
- The Japanese are not given to unrestrained body language, so don't expect much excited waving of hands, touching or loud and unpredictable outbursts.
- It is normal for there to be periods of silent thinking during meetings. Don't interrupt these periods of reflection as you will be considered disrespectful.
- Decisions are usually not made in a meeting. Meetings are for set-piece exchanges or confirmation of information and for the cordial and discreet strengthening of relations with one another. Prepare well for them.
- It may be useful to hold off concessions until the end of the deal. The timing of the concessions can be an important reflection of your sincerity.
- Japanese society is still quite patriarchal and it is often not straightforward for women to progress in business.

Addressing these assumptions

Let's take these 'norms' at face value first.

Local cultural etiquette around the process for meetings, seating plans, exchanging business cards, dress code and bowing is always to be respected unless and until your hosts indicate that it's not important to them.

In relation to *attitude*, once again you would expect that there may be plenty of opportunities for 'fusing' outcomes with all that emphasis on harmony and consensus. If age confers authority, this would be a source of bargaining power in Japan, as would the authority which comes from having an existing business relationship.

In relation to *process* you would expect an organised approach, so your business partner might appreciate it if climate setting issues like choice of venue, choice of attendees, agenda and timetable are addressed in advance. You might expect a cool negotiating climate – not unfriendly but objective and orderly. The Japanese sound like they prepare well, so you would be advised to do the same. 'Needs' may be harder to identify because there is a culture of restraint in both the mode of expression and body language, so there may be fewer cues to work from. However, the preoccupation with not losing face would suggest that 'reassurance' needs may not be far below the surface. Given the desire for harmony you might expect that bidding and bargaining are not that overt. As a young lawyer I once sent a thirty-page draft publishing agreement to a Japanese company and it came back signed with no changes and no comment – no counter-bids, no bargaining. It was actually an uncomfortable moment – I wondered if I had left something out of the document!

In relation to *behaviour*, you would expect tough-guy behaviour to be out in a country where 'face' is so important. Overt 'I' behaviours like stating expectations would also probably be inappropriate. Given the use of 'we' rather than 'I' language, you might expect to be concentrating on behaviours which either emphasise the other party (listening, exploring, focusing on common ground) or 'we' behaviours like checking for consensus (make sure you are not overfamiliar, though). When exploring, you might expect to spend more time listening than speaking or interrupting the other side. This will be the case particularly if the messages you are being given are rather indirect so as to avoid confrontation. This is supported by research on negotiations between inhabitants from countries with 'low-context communication' and 'high-context communication'.[133] Low-context communication is more explicit, with meaning clearly contained in the words or the surface of a message (in this study American participants were used as low-context communicators). High-context communication is more implicit, with subtle meaning embedded behind and around the spoken or written words. Japanese negotiators were used as examples of high-context communicators – listening carefully will therefore be very important. Since the Japanese may often seem withdrawn in negotiations you might want to mirror this with plenty of use of silence and some breaks.

In terms of some of the personality typologies we looked at above, you might expect Japanese people generally to be patient rather than impatient, negotiating with the head rather than the heart, somewhat dissociated rather than passionately associated and animated, a little introverted, quite logical and linear in their thinking, looking for 'matches' in situations rather than 'mismatches' which can cause disharmony. You might also expect them to give the appearance of being decision avoiders rather than quick or decisive decision makers.

Yes, but ...

You will be seeing the pattern by now.

- Firstly, many of the generalisations above also apply in countries other than Japan. You should always prepare – not just because the Japanese may be well prepared. It makes sense to be punctual for meetings wherever you hold them – even if you suspect the other side is going to be chaotically late. So the Japanese don't like losing face? I have yet to find anybody who does, regardless of where they come from. There may be some masochists out there with a 'losing' attitude to negotiating who enjoy being humiliated, but there can't be many. On the contrary, skilful deal making the world over is often all about knowing how to ensure that parties in a negotiation don't lose face, wherever they are from.

- Secondly, you may well not be dealing with an 'average' Japanese person who reflects these norms. There are some noisy Japanese who are quite extrovert. Manchester United is a very popular brand in Asia. It may be that some Japanese do not embrace extrovert behaviour, but I bet that when Manchester United score their Japanese fans can get just as excited about it as a season ticket holder from Salford. There are Japanese people who are impatient and there are some tough-guy Japanese who don't care about harmony or about you losing face. Who has most in common, an older Japanese businessman and a young woman trying to get on in business in Japan, or two older men, one in Tokyo and the other in Paris, who share a lifelong passion for collecting stamps? Many Japanese may have a horror of losing face, but let's not forget it was Japan that spawned the humiliating reality game show *Endurance*. This show was a trailblazer for many Western reality TV shows in which contestants are subjected to ridicule and indignities. There does not seem to have been any shortage of Japanese contestants lining up to take part.

- Finally, studies have shown that assumptions about overseas stereotypes (e.g. made by Americans about the

Japanese) are often the result of assuming that the way the Japanese supposedly behave among themselves is the same as the way they behave towards foreigners.[134] There is no guarantee that this assumption is correct, so bear that in mind, too.

China

- There is a confidence and great pride in China's success, so Westerners should be careful not to behave in a superior manner.
- The Chinese are very status-conscious so a group will enter a room in order of seniority. However, the actual negotiations may be carried out by someone other than the most senior member. The concern with status means rank dictates who does the talking and interrupting is considered rude.
- When you go to a business meeting, the first thing that happens is an exchange of business cards. When someone hands you his card read it properly and don't just ignore it and stick it in your pocket.
- The Chinese tend to use formal titles such as Mr or Professor rather than first names.
- Dress should be quite formal – suits for men and trousers, suits or skirts for women are appropriate. Women should not have bare legs and should dress modestly.
- The Chinese do not generally appreciate loud or extrovert behaviour. Punctuality is both expected and valued.
- Be prepared for the Chinese to request changes to a contract even after it is signed. Long-term relationships are more important than deals reduced to paper.
- When negotiating, a Chinese person may feel that a direct 'no' would be embarrassing to both parties. So they will try to show disagreement more indirectly such as by avoiding the

question or remaining silent, or saying that something is 'not convenient' rather than 'impossible'.

- Keep your promises – the Chinese with whom you are dealing will assume that you are powerful otherwise your organisation would not have sent you. So if you are not sure you can keep your promises, don't make them.
- Chinese people have a long attention span and they do not rush to the point quickly. Impatience is regarded as a character flaw.
- Chinese meetings are not likely to lead straight to results. They are an opportunity for people to put forward their position, which they will have decided before the meeting.
- It is common to praise people in front of their peers and to show deference to superiors. These are examples of 'giving face'. The opposite is to make someone 'lose face' by making them look small, being aggressive or explicitly criticising them. This is completely counter-productive.
- Remember to maintain eye contact with whoever you are talking to. People who avoid eye contact are often considered untrustworthy.
- The Chinese are often inscrutable until they know and trust you.
- Make sure you have adequately researched their company before doing business in China. The Chinese are renowned for their organisation and forward planning so are likely to have a fairly good understanding of your business before entering into negotiations with you.
- The Chinese are renowned for being tough negotiators. Their primary aim in negotiations is 'concessions'. Bear this in mind when formulating your own strategy.

Let's add to this picture some conclusions from recent negotiating research.[135] This considered the proposition that members of collectivist cultures such as that of China generally value group harmony more than their individual interests. On the other hand, members of individualistic cultures such as Canada place primary emphasis on their own goals and are highly concerned with individual gains. On the basis of research, the study reported that common notions about the collectivist culture of China and the individualistic culture of Canada stand true with respect to assertiveness, therefore the starting assumption that Canadians (coming from an individualistic culture) would be more assertive than the Chinese was supported.

In addition, here are some findings from an empirical study of business activities and negotiation styles between Taiwan and mainland China.[136]

The negotiation styles of the mainland Chinese businessmen were reported to be characterised by the following:

1. As the establishment of a relationship demonstrates trust and security, interpersonal relationships are given much attention.

2. The Chinese like to be methodical and systematic. Hence they are not very sensitive to the passing of time. In negotiations, their judgement of the opportune moment directly affects their deal behaviour. If they believe that the time is not right, they would rather take no action than act hastily.

3. During negotiations, the Chinese pay attention and like to gain unanimous agreement on the general principles of the relationship between both parties first before handling all other issues.

4. The study also added that, based on previous research, it had been noted that it is not uncommon for Chinese

negotiators to use a variety of potentially uncollaborative tactics to gain concessions, including creating an impasse to lower expectations, saying one thing while doing another, deliberately offering something small in exchange for something big, and gradually reducing the value of a previously made offer.

Addressing these assumptions

In terms of *attitude*, if the typical Chinese negotiator is genuinely not inclined to take a 'fusing' approach, you may have to prepare yourself to deal with a 'using' attitude to the negotiation, so you will need to maximise your own bargaining power. Make sure you have a well-thought-out 'best alternative' or Plan B in order to give you confidence in withstanding any pressure. You may not have to deal with overt tough-guy tactics, though, if Chinese culture does not encourage loss of face – since, when someone is hostile, they lose face themselves as well as their target losing face.

In terms of *process*, to the extent that the Chinese typically expect negotiations to take some time, there is no need to rush. Take time to prepare since this is what they do, too. If they are generally reticent and formal, you may have to work harder than normal to elicit the needs of those involved, but you are likely to have more time than usual to explore and do that. This formality is likely to generate a cool climate – objective and data driven rather than warm and open. You would not expect a cheeky or wacky climate or (given the concern with face) a hostile one. Listening actively will be particularly important, especially as China is another high-context culture, like Japan, where messages are conveyed obliquely. If eye contact is important as an indicator of trust, you would expect to have to maintain eye contact particularly during the exploration phase when such trust is established.

Given that negotiations are not conducted in a hurry, during the bargaining phase you might expect to experience lots of use of 'parting' behaviour – from taking breaks through to use of silence as a 'withdrawal' tactic. In relation to closing the deal it would be worth bearing in mind that, unlike in some Western cultures, signing a contract is just a snapshot of your relationship. The contract does not represent the final position that the parties intend to end up in and may be renegotiated before the ink is dry. On that basis take an incremental view of your negotiation and in the bargaining phase don't feel you have to get everything at once. Also keep some concessions back in the bargaining phase – you may need them later, after the contract is signed, when the negotiation recommences.

In terms of adapting your *behaviour* to personality types you might expect many Chinese to be patient rather than impatient, rational rather than passionate when negotiating. Given the history of Confucianism and collectivism you might expect them to be conforming rather than individualistic in the way they behave – the group comes before the individual. It sounds like they work on the big picture first, leaving the detail till later, so you may need to work with this pattern. Going back to psychological typologies it also sounds as if you are more likely to encounter introversion rather than extroversion, and people who are higher on the 'sensing' scale than the 'feeling' scale. Working with 'visual cues' may also be important in your language given the emphasis on eye-contact. This is also illustrated by the fact that the Chinese effectively use 'pictures' to represent their written letters.

Yes, but ...

As usual, these norms can be a helpful starting point, but there are some caveats:

- The research observations above might suggest that a 'using' culture prevails. However, contrary to what you might expect, the 2012 research by Chang referred to above concluded that, among other things, the Chinese are more inclined towards accommodation negotiations than the Taiwanese. The Chinese seek transactional success more urgently which results in greater willingness to be more accommodating in meeting the negotiation aims. The reasoning here goes back to the fact that China was for a long time under a one-party authoritarian system and thus they are less likely to take a leadership position and more inclined to respect orderly outcomes.

- Other social norms described above will also be notable for many exceptions. Maybe, on average, you will encounter more inscrutable negotiators in China than elsewhere, but that does not mean that all Chinese are inscrutable negotiators. Not all 1.3 billion of them. Not all the time, in all situations, in every deal. Despite the norm, there must be many Chinese who negotiate passionately and with their hearts on their sleeves. Not all Chinese will prioritise the keeping of face – either theirs or yours.

- The behaviour of Chinese citizens is also likely to be situational – they may behave differently in different situations, as all of us do. One study, for example, found that in terms of the exercise of hierarchical authority, Chinese managers tended to behave in an authoritative way when intervening as a supervisor, but in a much more egalitarian way when asked to act as a third-party peer.[137]

- Furthermore, there are some generalities here that could apply in many countries. Keep your promises – not just with the Chinese but with everybody: nobody likes it when you break a promise. It breaches trust and disrupts rapport. Look at a business card that's just been given to you rather than just shoving it in your pocket. That must be good advice wherever you go. If someone has gone to the trouble of giving you some personal details about themselves, acknowledge that and take an interest in what they have given you. If China is hierarchical in its approach to negotiating, so, too, are India, Japan and Russia.

Saudi Arabia

- Almost all businesses are family businesses and in the case of many larger businesses that family is the Al-Saud family which has some fifty thousand members.
- Generally all businesses by law need a Saudi partner who owns at least 50 per cent of the business and gets an equivalent share of the proceeds – whether they are an active partner or not.
- Businesses are very hierarchical. The top boss normally has a long chain of command and must be highly respected. The boss will be referred to as 'Ustaz', or 'master'. Also business is based on personal relationships and, since this includes the man at the top of the hierarchy, this exacerbates the time delays in getting deals done.
- Hierarchy is also widespread in Saudi bureaucracy – any transaction, from getting a work permit, to setting up a business, to importing goods requires their involvement.
- There is a prevailing culture of relationships and mutual favours which some might allege is corrupt. Nepotism is also detectable which can be seen as part of a sacred duty to look after the family.
- In order to develop personal relationships you must allow plenty of time for tea drinking and social chit-chat.
- It is polite to address Saudis by their title – e.g. Mr and then their first name. Hands are shaken at meetings but not between men and women.

- Business dress is smart. Women should wear a token head covering.
- Presentations are really just for show, so don't make them too long. They will not normally influence any negotiations or decisions. It is common for initial demands to be very high, so match this and expect to inch towards common ground from widely opposing positions. Don't worry if they throw their hands up in despair and appeal to the heavens for patience – this is all part of the routine.
- Contracts are snapshots of where you stand now and always remain negotiable. It is the relationship which counts, not the piece of paper. Honour is important to Saudis but maintaining the relationship is the best guarantee of their performance.
- As face is important, if there is a dispute try and find a third party you can blame. Don't insult a Saudi face to face. If the fault is yours an apology will be respected.
- Many Saudis have a somewhat regal bearing.
- Be prepared for a long, hard stare when you first meet, but after that Saudis tend to avoid eye contact. It is rude to point the soles of your feet at someone since they have been in touch with the unclean ground.
- The ability to compromise during negotiations is crucial as you do not want to risk being too rigid and offending them.

Here is some recent research to fill out this picture:[138]

1. The Arabic-speaking Islamic culture is more event-time oriented while the Western culture is more clock-time oriented. In Arabic-speaking Islamic culture, events schedule people; in the clock-time-oriented West people plan events.

2. The Western culture encourages decision making and determining the course of action for the future whereas the Arabic-speaking Islamic culture leaves future planning to God, with the view that it will happen if it is part of God's plan. Discussions on the future may be possible if negotiations are solely based on intentions but preparing for possible eventualities is avoided.

3. In negotiations, the outcome is directly proportional to the trust involved in the process. Western culture follows the 'quick trust' approach where one is trusted until proven to be untrustworthy. In Arabic-speaking Islamic culture speed is viewed as juxtaposed to trust which is gradually earned. Trust can be gained through informal conversations preceding the discussion of the issue itself as well as abiding by the linguistic customs and conventions that the Arabic-speaking world adheres to. Westerners may view this as time-consuming and pointless small talk but the Arab culture views such conversations as methods to gauge one's respect of protocol – which is necessary in terms of trust.

4. Western culture sees the bargaining process as something that can be sacrificed if the financial gains of bargaining are counterbalanced by the time lost in the process. Bargaining in the Arabic-speaking Islamic culture began at the core of the Islamic religion where the Prophet Muhammad bargained with God for a reduction in praying to five times a day. Bargaining is therefore viewed as a trust-building mechanism.

Addressing these assumptions

There are some cultural tips here which could be crucial. For example, it's important to know about the convention regarding the soles of the feet. It's also important to understand how men and women are expected to greet each other and what dress men and women are expected to adopt.

From an *attitudinal* point of view it may be that it is the norm for many Saudis to bring more of a competitive 'using' attitude to negotiations, at least at the beginning. The kind of tough posing described above is often associated with people serving their own outcomes. Given the hierarchical nature of the business culture, and the importance of the Saudi royal family at every level, you will clearly be able to create some extra bargaining power for yourself if you can develop some network power of your own – knowing how and who to access within that hierarchy. If you can't do that, you will need to focus on other sources of power such as expertise or niche market power.

From a *process* point of view it sounds like things can take a long time, so it would be important to manage expectations – yours – at the climate setting stage of the negotiation. 'What's the likely timetable?' would be an important question to ask yourself at the beginning of this phase. It sounds like the exploring phase can go on for some time. Good. That gives you every chance to explore needs and coinage, and build rapport. Saudis may well expect well-defined bidding and bargaining stages characterised by strong bids and counter-bids, and much haggling. So, it's no use 'cutting to the chase' or offering to 'split the difference' early on. Equally, 'reasonable' bidding intended to reduce the amount of negotiating time might be interpreted as weakness, and, paradoxically, may inhibit the building of trust. It will be good to be able to package up offers of mutual concessions when you are in the bargaining phase. Be patient in getting to closure as it seems this can take some time, and may also be a moveable feast in which negotiations continue after the contract is signed.

In relation to *behaviour* it may be that some of the more robust behaviours are called for – certainly, stating expectations and proposing with reasons, using pressures and incentives and testing and probing are all 'I' behaviours associated with effective bidding and bargaining. Assertive body language may be required to support such behaviours such as making your voice a bit more strident and standing tall to match the Saudis' regal bearing. However, this is still a society in which not losing face is important, so it would be important to self-moderate your assertive behaviour and not be patronising, dismissive, sarcastic or insulting. Frequent use of parting behaviour is likely – small or possibly much longer breaks – and it may be that this gives everyone the chance to work out a deal outside the formal and hierarchical negotiating process.

As personalities, you might expect many Saudis to be more focused on the past than the future (bearing in mind the reluctance to second-guess destiny). It will be important to bear this in mind when you are trying to build in future protections to an agreement. You could also expect Saudis to be more conforming than individually orientated, given the hierarchical nature of business dealings.

Yes, but …

- Once again, there will be exceptions to some of these useful starting points. You will encounter Saudis who do not fit this picture at all. Some may display a more cooperative 'fusing' attitude. Some will not negotiate theatrically. Some Saudis may adopt a brisk attitude to business. Many wealthy Saudis love horse racing and own horses. Would a rich owner of stables in Saudi Arabia have more in common with a young female from an unrelated Saudi family or a stable owner who breeds racehorses in the UK? It's the elements that a person regards as being critical to their own identity which need to be spotted and worked with in a negotiation – those elements may or may not include a close identification with the elements of their national stereotype.

- Once again, a number of these social norms apply to many countries as well as Saudi Arabia. It's always important to avoid negative behaviours such as sarcasm and being dismissive, wherever you are negotiating. Building trust is critical in almost any country where you care to negotiate. The ability to reach a compromise and avoid being too rigid is always crucial, regardless of the culture in which you are negotiating.

Mexico

- Mexicans value personal relationships highly. 'Hard-nosed' and 'no-nonsense' approaches therefore go against the grain.
- Status and hierarchy are always important in Mexican business and in Mexico in general. You can see this in the management style with even simple decisions often being passed back up a chain of command. Bosses are expected to lead and are automatically entitled to be shown respect by those beneath them.
- If a company you are dealing with is sending its senior executives to a meeting you should do the same. If you don't, you may give a negative impression of your commitment to the transaction. Equally, if you are a decision maker yourself and you find that your Mexican counterparts are not sending along senior executives, it may be they are quietly sending a message that they don't want to do business with you.
- Mexicans are rarely blunt. They prefer to send subtle negative messages rather than give an outright 'no'.
- The family always comes first in Mexico, and so supporting

the family is always justified – even if it results in some nepotism.

- Mexicans may be fairly formal at the first meeting but more relaxed afterwards. However, you should dress formally for business meetings.
- There is lots of bureaucracy so you have to be patient with that, though Mexico has taken great steps to reduce the historic levels of corruption.
- Titles are important – they show either the owner's level of education or their seniority within a company. Respect these niceties.
- Mexicans are not slaves to the clock and have a less regimented view of punctuality, though they work very hard.
- Flexibility in timing should be matched by flexibility in planning and decision making, as decisions can be delayed or altered right up until the last moment.
- In keeping with this approach, meetings are rarely conducted in accordance with a strict agenda. It's quite common for the agenda to be ignored as conversation launches off in different directions. People come and go from meeting rooms, answer their mobile phones and talk among themselves. It is comparatively rare to have only one person talking at a time.
- Business entertaining is frequent in this relationship-building culture – especially lunch, which is the longest and the main meal of the day. Lunches are an opportunity to size each other up so that Mexicans can decide whether or not they want to do business with you. They are not about business details – though the big picture may come up.
- Mexicans love to talk and will not be too attentive to conventions about personal space once they get to know you.
- Mexican 'machismo' is a bit of a myth, as family comes first and women are in charge of the family – that's why one of the worst things you can do to a Mexican man is insult his mother.

- Mexicans are often exuberant – given their history of repeated economic crisis and recovery, 'living for the moment' is hardly a surprising approach.

Addressing these assumptions

From the point of view of *attitude*, you would expect Mexico to be a country in which it is possible to experience 'fusing' attitudes to negotiation to the extent that there is a natural inclination to avoid confrontation. In a hierarchical business environment you would expect that 'authority' bargaining power would be very helpful in getting deals closed – the more seniority you carry with you and your team, the better off you will be. You would also expect that 'network' power might be helpful, if it can gain you entry to the hierarchy at the right level. To the extent that this is a relationship-based business culture, the bargaining power of having an existing business relationship may well be significant. It may be good to have the power of 'numbers' in your favour as well, particularly if you are dealing with more than one person in a meeting and everyone is talking at once. Having more than one pair of eyes and ears means you can keep track of things even if proceedings in meetings might be a bit chaotic.

As far as *process* is concerned, it would be good to prepare – as always – but make sure your plan is flexible since it seems as if negotiations can shift about until the last minute. From a climate point of view, the loose attitude to timing and agenda would suggest that it's important to address expectations in relation to these two matters at the outset. Respect needs may be present if you are dealing in a hierarchical business culture – people may expect you to acknowledge their status. As far as bidding is concerned, given the Mexican reluctance to embrace a hard-nosed approach, extreme bidding is probably to be avoided. You may also have to be patient in waiting for the right moment to bid rather than rushing in with an offer. In the bargaining phase it would be good to keep a number of concessions back, in the expectation that the deal will keep shifting until the last minute. Being able to expand the pie with new options may well appeal to a population that seems to be tolerant of ambiguity in the deal-making process. Closing the deal may take some time if a relaxed attitude to time is the 'norm', so be prepared for that and have some incentives available to close with, or a good 'vision' that will capture the imagination of such a lively people and inspire them to close the deal with you.

In relation to *behaviours*, it would seem that tough-guy tactics are out, in spite of Mexico's reputation as the home of machismo. You would think from the above that 'you' behaviours will generally get you further than 'I' behaviours. Plenty of exploring, asking questions and listening would be the order of the day with people who love to talk. 'We' behaviour is likely to have a part to play – especially as the Mexicans are sociable and like to conduct business around social occasions like lunch, so focusing on what 'we' can achieve may be helpful and will not be considered forward.

'Parting' behaviour may be less impactful for the same reason – sitting there in silence or taking lots of breaks will run counter to the Mexican desire for engagement. In relation to the personality traits and types which we looked at earlier, you might expect to find that Mexicans focus on the present rather than the past or the future (given that history holds some unwelcome memories and the future is uncertain). Given their resilience to past economic crises you might expect to meet optimists rather than pessimists. You would expect these voluble people to be associated rather than dissociated, and more extrovert rather than introvert. The way meetings and agendas are conducted suggests that their overall approach may be non-linear rather than linear. Given the focus on family and hierarchy, you might expect to meet Mexicans who are more focused on 'others' than 'self'.

Yes, but ...

As ever, there are a few caveats to bear in mind:

- You may well meet more Mexicans per square foot who are extroverts than the average inhabitants you meet from other countries, but there are plenty of Mexicans who are introverts, I am sure. Many Mexicans may enjoy negotiating in partnership, as you would expect from a business culture apparently rooted in relationship building, but you will meet some Mexicans who are 'users', too. Some Mexicans will have a liberal approach to timing and agendas, maybe more than in other countries, but there will, equally, be Mexicans you encounter who are sticklers for punctuality and sticking to the agenda. Whether Mexican machismo is a myth or not, you will find plenty of Mexicans who are happy to play tough-guy tactics with you.

- Many of these generalisations, if true, apply to other nationalities as well. We have encountered a commitment to hierarchy in looking at Japan, Russia, Saudi Arabia and China. It is certainly not just a Mexican thing. We have also encountered an emphasis on relationship building in India, Brazil and Saudi Arabia – so this is not confined to Mexico either. We have also seen that apparently Japanese and Chinese people don't like to say 'no', so this trait is also not restricted to Mexico. Business socialisation over lunch is not unique to Mexico either.

Here's another story from telecoms executive Elisabetta, which illustrates the point:

Another thing that I have experienced so many times is a misunderstanding about lunch. For Germans or Britons or some Americans lunch seems to be a waste of time. For negotiating with people from France, Italy or Spain, however, lunch is sometimes key. I once had a colleague saying to me: 'But why are we doing lunch with them, when does the meeting start?' To which I had to reply: 'Mmm, you might have not realised, but lunch is the meeting!'

- Moreover, there will, once again, be other roles that Mexicans play (apart from being inhabitants of their own country) which may dictate behaviour outside these norms. A Mexican doctor negotiating with a patient or a Mexican boss negotiating with an underling may negotiate differently from a Mexican businessman negotiating with a potential customer from overseas.

Social Norms and International Storms

When you survey these social norms you can see why international negotiations so often go wrong – either diplomatically or at a business level. Let's take a country like the USA as an example to illustrate some of the difficulties.

In the first place, it's easy for countries with different social norms to be baffled by each other at the negotiating table:

- In the US there is a social norm of meritocracy with fluid hierarchies and boundary-less organisations. You can often see this in the way meetings are conducted, with contributions coming from every department and every level of the organisation. This contrasts with social norms for hierarchy in China, India, Brazil, Russia and Japan.

- Americans do not feel the need particularly to know or deeply trust the people they do business with. They rely on contracts to enforce business dealings. As we have seen, in other countries like Mexico, India, Russia and Saudi Arabia the relationship is far more important than the contract, so establishing trust is critical. All that small talk which may seem interminable to an American is actually a vital part of the business process in other cultures.

- The US tends to have a 'just do it' attitude as a social norm which makes them adept at reinventing themselves and adapting to change. This contrasts with the more cautious approach to change taken in, for example, China or Japan.

- The US is an 'I'-focused nation – it's okay to want to do well as an individual and to stand out. It's okay to self-promote and to make the most of yourself. Those who have ever experienced a 'hard sell' from a practised US salesperson will be nodding as they read this. This is different from collectivist cultures like China or 'we' cultures like Japan, or the social norm of self-effacement which applies in the UK.

- American communication styles tend to be direct and emphatic – 'Just give it to me straight'. Good ideas are 'immense' or 'awesome'. Bad ideas are 'dumb-assed' or they 'suck'. The bargaining style is equally direct and highly competitive. That is not the case in Brazil or India or other countries where communication can be less direct and overt bidding and bargaining are not so prevalent.

- The US has a social norm which encapsulates a 'can do' attitude and a sense of positive optimism at all times. Contrast this with the slightly pessimistic social norm we noted in Russia – a different country with a different history.

So, the first thing that can routinely go wrong in negotiations with other countries is that people do not respect or appreciate the social norms that may apply elsewhere. US negotiators may well be familiar with this criticism but it also applies when foreign companies are active in the US. Consider the unfortunate example of vacuum cleaner manufacturer, Electrolux, attempting to negotiate for the hearts and minds of US consumers, and misunderstanding the lexicon of US 'straight talking'. Their successful European campaign slogan 'Nothing sucks like an Electrolux' didn't go down so well in the US. Equally, many will remember the example of Puma who decided to create a special limited edition trainer to mark the 40th anniversary of the United Arab Emirates. It reproduced the colours of the UAE flag on the shoe. The trainer therefore sent out a rather insulting message about the UAE flag, associating it with a part of the body regarded culturally as dirty. (You may have noticed on the TV news that when there is a flashpoint some angry Muslims tread on the flags of nations they hate, because their feet are regarded as the most unclean part of the body.) The trainer was quickly withdrawn, accompanied by a public apology from Puma.

The other thing that goes wrong, though, is more subtle than this. It is that even if negotiators do understand social norms in other countries, they don't look beyond that in order to customise the negotiation to the particular individual they are dealing with. This applies to all of us, and certainly not just citizens of the US. It is important to understand and respect local cultural and religious beliefs – breaking customs concerning dress and touching, for example, can set a very poor climate. By all means be aware of behavioural norms when you do business in other countries. Generalisations about local custom and practice in negotiation can be a good starting point. You should always include them in your preparation (yes, it's not just the Chinese who believe in preparing!).

However, don't be driven by generalisations about the inhabitants of the country in which you are operating. They may be unreliable when assessing the particular individual and the specific negotiation you are dealing with.

Remember, whether you are involved in international negotiations for climate change, trade treaties or individual business-to-business negotiations, *ultimately you are negotiating with the person not the culture* ...

23

AND FINALLY...

So, now you have some of the secrets of negotiation at your fingertips. The successful management of negotiation attitude, process and behaviour can help you get more of what you want, whatever kind of deal you are doing, whether it's professional or domestic, and whoever you are dealing with.

By being conscious of these requirements you should automatically make more effective *choices* than those who don't have these skills or insights. You will have understood the purpose, process and pay-off from good negotiating. And you will be equipped for deal making the modern way, in a connected, interdependent world. In short, you will be better at getting people to say 'Yes'.

This is not just a theoretical advantage – it is a practical necessity in a world where we negotiate incessantly and where research shows that we lose large amounts of money by doing it badly.

Here's a quick summary of some of the key insights:

Attitude

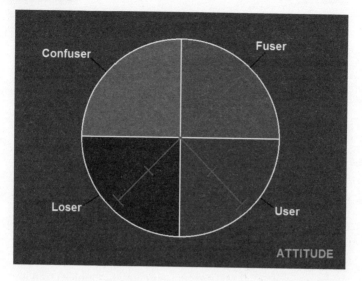

- Be a fuser – working in partnership to put the agendas of both parties together
- Don't be a user – it's old-fashioned and it doesn't work. If you beat people over the head all day, you will end up with a headache too.
- Don't be a loser – there is no glory in losing your shirt
- Don't be a confuser – distorted first impressions can often lead your attitude astray
- Marshal your bargaining power – you often have more aces than you think

Process

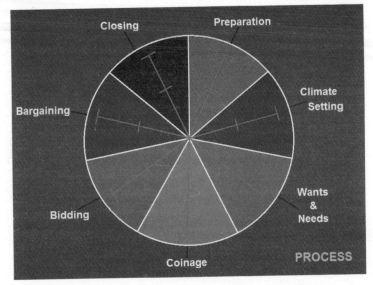

- Preparation – put in the spadework before you start
- Climate – take your weather with you to create the atmosphere of your choice
- Exploring needs – why do people need what they say that they want? This question often unblocks the most stubborn negotiating logjams
- Coinage – those loose coppers you have in your pocket may look like gold sovereigns to the other negotiator. Trade them for what you need in return
- Bidding – ask for what you want, sound like you mean it, but make sure that you have a reason that makes sense to the other negotiator
- Bargaining – keep the deal alive by reframing the issue, expanding the pie, or creating options together. Offer concessions in a disciplined way
- Close – move to closure briskly when the opportunity arises; if you wait too long you will drop the ball.

Behaviour

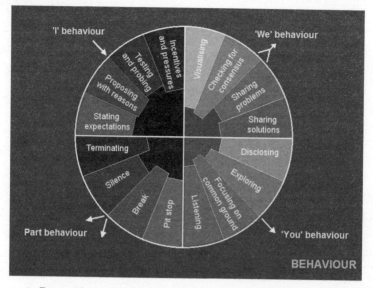

- Remember you always have a choice. Don't be a cracked record that sounds the same every time. Above is a chart showing the preferences of someone who over emphasises 'I' behavour
- 'I' behaviour – good for bidding and bargaining
- 'You' behaviour – good for the early stages. Make sure you listen – what goes in one ear should stay there
- 'We' behaviour – good for bargaining and closing – but don't suggest you jump into bed together too early in the process
- 'Parting' behaviour – take a break when you feel under pressure. Calm down then carry on
- Stand up to tough guys – nobody has the right to treat you like a doormat
- Use the right behaviour for the right person. You can be chalk and cheese, fish and fowl. If the other negotiator feels you both speak the same language you are more likely to persuade them.

With that last point in mind, as you have read through this book, you will have seen a selection of cartoons by award-winning cartoonist KJ Lamb to illustrate some of the key learnings. Why? Well, cartoons often tell a short story in a picture and a few succinct words, and we have talked before about the power of stories to help people remember insights they have learned. Cartoons can also appeal to many different kinds of learner. As we discussed above, some people may interpret the world through auditory cues and for them, the caption in a cartoon may be helpful. Others carry a very visual imprint of the world with them and so are particularly impacted by pictures. Cartoons should work for them, too. Finally, some people interpret the world through their senses. For them something that makes them smile or laugh may make the difference in helping them to learn. So, enjoy this last cartoon, which reminds us that whatever the odds, whatever the situation, there is always a way to close a deal.

Good luck with your future negotiations, and may all your deals happen ...

'WAIT — I'VE THOUGHT OF A WAY OF EXPANDING THE PIE FOR BOTH OF US...'

BIBLIOGRAPHY

Adair, W.L. and Brett, J.M. (2005). The negotiation dance: time, culture, and behavioral sequences in negotiation. *Organization Science*, 16, 33-51

Adair, W.L. Taylor, M.S. and Tinsley, C.H. (2008). Starting out on the right foot. Negotiation schemas when cultures collide. *Negotiation and Conflict Management Research*, 2, 138-163

Allred, K.G., Mallozzi, J.S., Matsui F., and Raia, C.P. (1997). The influence of anger and compassion on negotiation performance. *Organizational Behaviour and Human Decision Processes*, 70, 175-87

Alon, I. and Brett, J.M. (2007). Perceptions of time and their impact on negotiations in the Arabic-speaking Islamic world. *Negotiation Journal*, 23, 55-73

Amanatullah, E.T., Morris, M.W., and Curhan, J.R. (2008). Negotiators who give too much: unmitigated communion, relational anxieties, and economic costs in distributive and integrative bargaining. *Journal of Personality and Social Psychology*, 95, 723–738

Babcock, L., Gelfand, M., Small, D., Stayn, H. (2006). Social psychology and economics., (pp. 239-259). Mahwah, NJ, US: Lawrence Erlbaum Associates Publishers

Bazerman, M.H. (1983). Negotiator Judgment: A Critical Look at the Rationality Assumption, *American Behavioral Scientist*, 27, 211-228,

Bazerman M.H., Magliozzi T. and Neale M.A. (1985). The acquisition of an integrative response in a competitive market. *Organizational Behaviour and Human Decision Processes* 34, 294–313

Bazerman, M.H. and Carroll, J.S. (1987). Negotiator cognition. *Research in Organisational Behaviour*, 9, 247-88

Bazerman, M.H., Curhan, J.R., Moore, D.A. and Valley, K.L. (2000). Negotiation. *Annual Review of Psychology*, 51, 279–314

Ben-Yoav, O., and Pruitt, D.G. (1984). Accountability to constituents; a two edged sword. *Organisational Behaviour and Human Performance*, 34, 283-295

Birdwhistell, R. L., (1974). The language of the body: the natural environment of words. In A. Silverstein, (ed.), *Human communication: theoretical explorations* (203-220), Lawrence, Hillsdale, NJ

Bottom, W.P., Holloway, J., Miller, G.J., Mislin, A. and Whitford, A. (2006). Building a pathway to cooperation: negotiation and social exchange between principal and agent. *Administrative Science Quarterly*, 51: 29-58

Bowles, H. R., Babcock, L. and McGinn, K. L. 2005. Constraints and triggers: situational mechanics of gender in negotiation. *Journal of Personality and Social Psychology*, 89, 951–965

Brown, R. and Abrams D. (1986). The effects of intergroup similarity and goal interdependence on intergroup attitudes and tasks performance. *Journal of Experimental Social Psychology*, 22, 78-92

Burton, J.W. (1984). *Global Conflict: The domestic sources of international crisis.* Brighton. Wheatsheaf.

Carnevale, P.J.D. (1991). Cognition and affect in co-operation and conflict. Presented at the Fourth Annual Meeting of the International Association Conflict Management, Ernest Sillem Hoeve, Den Dolder, The Netherlands

Carnevale, P. (2008). Positive effect and decision frame in negotiation. *Group Decisions and Negotiation*, 17, 51-63

Carnevale, P.J.D. and Isen, A.M. (1986). The influence of positive affect and visual access on the discovery of integrative solutions in bilateral negotiation. *Organizational Behaviour and Human Decision Processes*, 37, 1–13

Carrell, M.R., Shank, M. and Berbero, J.L. (2009). Fairness norms in negotiation: a study of American and European perspectives. *Dispute Resolution Journal*, 64, 1, 54-60

Cattell, R.B. and Cattell, H.E.P. (1995). Personality and the New Fifth Edition of the 16PF. *Educational and Psychological Measurement*, 55, 6, 926-937

Ching, L.C. (2012). An empirical study of business activities and negotiation styles between Taiwan and mainland China. *African Journal of Business Management*, 6, 5328-5337

Cialdini, R.B. (2007). *Influence, the Psychology of Persuasion.* New York, HarperBusiness

Clark, M.S. and Mills, J. (1979). Interpersonal attraction in exchange and communal relationships. *Journal of Personality and Social Psychology*, 37, 12-24

Colquitt, J.A., Greenberg, J., and Scott, B.A. (2005). *Organizational Justice: Where Do We Stand? Handbook of Organizational Justice*, 589-619, Mahwah, New Jersey, Lawrence Erlbaum Associates Publishers

Cotter, M.J. and Henley, J.A. (2009). Subservient seller syndrome: Outcomes in zero-game negotiations examining the influence of the seller and buyer role/label. *Marketing Management Journal*, 19, 2, 38-51

Curhan, J.R., Neale, M.A. and Ross, L. (2004). Dynamic valuation: preference changes in the context of face-to-face negotiation. *Journal of Experimental Social Psychology* 40, 142–151

Curran, L. (1995). Notes on Non Verbal Communication, unpublished manuscript.

Dawes, R.M. (1998). Behavioral decision making and judgment. In *Handbook of Social Psychology 4th ed,* (ed.) Gilbert, D.T., Fiske, S.T. and Lindzey, G., 497–548. New York: McGraw-Hill.

De Dreu, C.K.W., Weingart, L.R., & Kwon, S. (2000). Influence of social motives on integrative negotiation: A meta-analytic review and test of two theories. *Journal of Personality and Social Psychology*, 78, 889–905.

Dewulf, A., Gray, B., Putnam, L., Lewicki, R., Aarts, N., Bouwen, R. and van Woerkum, C. (2009). Disentangling approaches to framing in conflict and negotiation research: a meta-parardigmatic perspective. *Human Relations*, 62, 155-193

Diamond, S. (2010). *Getting More: How to Negotiate to Succeed in Work and Life*, Penguin Group

Doebeli, M. and Hauert, C. (2005). Models of cooperation based on the Prisoner's Dilemma and the Snowdrift game. Ecology Letters, 8, 748-766

Drolet, A.L. and Morris, M.W. (2000). Rapport in conflict resolution: accounting for how face-to-face contact fosters mutual cooperation in mixed-motive conflicts. *Journal of Experimental Social Psychology* 36, 26-50

Dupont, C. and Faure, G.O. (1991). The negotiation process. In Kremenyuk, V. A. (ed), *International Negotiation: Analysis, Approaches, Issues*, 40-57, San Francisco; Jossey-Bass

Ekman, P. (2009). 'Lie catching and micro expressions' *The Philosophy of Deception.* (ed) Clancy Martin, Oxford University Press

Elfenbein, H.A., Der Foo, M., White, J., Tan, H.H. and Aik, V.C. (2007). Reading your counterpart: the benefit of emotion recognition accuracy for effectiveness in negotiation. *Journal of Nonverbal Behaviour*, 31, 205–223

Fiske, S.T., and Taylor, S.E. (1991). *Social Cognition* (2nd ed.). New York, NY, England: McGraw-Hill Book Company

Flyn, F.J. and Wiltermuth, S.S. (2010). Who's with me? False consensus, brokerage, and ethical decision making in organisations. *Academy of Management Journal*, 53, 5, 1074-1089

Furnham, A. and Petrides, K.V. and Tsaousis, I. and Pappas, K. and Garrod, D (2005) A cross-cultural investigation into the relationships between personality traits and work values. *Journal of Psychology* , 139, 1, 5-32

Galinsky, A.D., Maddux, W.W., Gilin, D. and White, J.B. (2008). Why it pays to get inside the head of your opponent: the differential effects of perspective taking and empathy in negotiations. *Psychological Science*, 19, 378-384

Galinsky, A.D., and Mussweiler, T. (2001). First offers as anchors: The role of perspective-taking and negotiator focus. *Journal of Personality and Social Psychology*, 81, 657–669.

Goldman, B.M. and Shapiro, D.L. (2012). The psychology of negotiations in the 21st century workplace: new challenges and new solutions. Routledge Academic.

Gollwitzer, P.M. and Sheeran, P. (2006). Implementation intentions and goal achievement: a meta-analysis of effects and processes. *Advances in Experimental Social Psychology*, 38, 69-119

Gunia, B.C., Brett, J.M., Nandkeolyar, A.K. and Kamdar, D. (2011). Paying a price: culture, trust and negotiation consequences. *Journal of Applied Psychology*, Vol. 96, 4, 774-789

Halevy, N. (2008). Team Negotiation: Social, epistemic, economic, and psychological consequences of subgroup conflict. *Personality and Social Psychology Bulletin*, 34, 12, 1687-1702

Hamner, W.C. (1974). Effects of bargaining strategy and pressure to reach agreement in a stalemated negotiation. *Journal of Personality and Social Psychology*, 30, 458-67

Harinck, F. and De Dreu, C.K.W. (2011). When does taking a break help in negotiations? The influence of breaks and social motivation on negotiation processes and outcomes. *Negotiation and Conflict Management Research*, 4, 33-46

Holaday, L.C. (2002). Stage development theory: a natural framework for understanding the mediation process. *Negotiation Journal*, 191-210

Hollander-Blumoff, R., and Tyler, T.R. (2008). Procedural justice in negotiation: procedural fairness, outcome acceptance and integrative potential. *Law & Social Inquiry*, 33, 2, 473-500

Jacobs, C.D. and Heracleous, L.T. (2005). Answers for questions to come: reflective dialogue as an enabler of strategic innovation. *Journal of Organizational Change Management*, 18, 4, 338-352

Johnson, D.W. (1971). The effects of warmth of interaction, accuracy of understanding, and the proposal of compromises on the listener's behaviour. *Journal of Counselling Psychology*, 18, 207-216

Kahneman, D. (2011). *Thinking, fast and slow*, Farrar, Straus and Giroux, New York

Khai, S.S. and Cooper, R.B. (2003). Exploring the core concepts of media richness theory. The impact of cue multiplicity and feedback immediacy on decision quality. *Journal of Management Information Systems*, 20, 263-299

Knight, S. (1995). *NLP at Work: the Difference that Makes a Difference in Business*, Nicholas Brealey Publishing.

Kolb, D.M. (2009). Too bad for women, or does it have to be? Gender and negotiation research over the last 25 years. *Negotiation Journal*, 25, 515-531

Kray, L.J. and Haselhuhn, M.P. (2012). Male pragmatism in negotiators' ethical reasoning. *Journal of Experimental Social Psychology*, 48, 1124-1131

Kray, L.J., Locke, C.C. and Haselhuhn, M.P. (2010). In the words of Larry Summers; gender stereotypes and implicit beliefs in negotiations. In Stanton, A.A., Day, M. and Welpe, I. (eds), *Neuroeconomics and the Firm*, 101-115, Northampton, MA; Edward Elgar Publishing

Kray, L. J., Thompson, L. and Galinsky, A. (2001) Battle of the sexes: gender stereotype confirmation and reactance in negotiations. *Journal of Personality and Social Psychology*, 80, 6, 942-958

Kroeber, A.L., and Kluckhohn, C. (1952). *Culture: A critical review of concepts and definitions*. Harvard University Peabody Museum of American Archeology and Ethnology Papers 47

Kuula, M. and Stam, A. (2008). A win-win method for multi-party negotiation support. *International Transactions in Operational Research*, 15, 717-737

Kwon, S. and Weingart, L.R. (2004). Unilateral concessions from the other party: concession behavior, attributions, and negotiation judgments. *Journal of Applied Psychology*, 89, 2, 263–278

Lewicki, R.J., Saunders, D.M., and Barry, B. (2010). Essentials of Negotiation. Boston, MA, McGraw-Hill

Lindskold, S. and Han, G. (1988). GRIT as a foundation for integrative bargaining. *Personality and Social Psychology*, 14, 335-345

Ma, Z. and Jaeger, A.M. (2010). A comparative study of the influence of assertiveness on negotiation outcomes in Canada and China. *Cross Cultural Management: An International Journal*, 4, 333-346

Macrae, C.N. and Bodenhaus, G.V. (2001). Social cognition: categorical person perception. *British Journal of Psychology*, 92, 239-255

McGillicuddy, N.B., Pruitt, D.G., Syna, H. (1984). Perceptions of firmness and strength in negotiation. *Personality and Social Psychology Bulletin*, 10, 402-409

Mehrabian, A. and Ferris, S.R. (1967). Inferences of attitudes from nonverbal communication in two channels. *Journal of Consulting Psychology*, 31, 248-252

Merryman, A. (2010). Organisational mutiny; employee experiences in leader oustings. Paper presented at 23rd International Association of Conflict Management Conference, Boston

Miles, E. (2010). Gender differences in distributive negotiation: when in the negotiation processes do differences occur? *European Journal of Social Psychology*, 40, 1200, 1211

Moore, D.A. (2004). The unexpected benefits of final deadlines in negotiation. *Journal of Experimental Social Psychology*, 40, 121-127

Moore, D.A. and Healy, P.J. (2008). The trouble with overconfidence. *Psychological Review*, 115, 2, 502–517

Morris, M., Nadler, J., Kurtzberg, T., and Thompson, L. (2002). Schmooze or lose; social friction and lubrication in email negotiations. *Group Dynamics; Theory, Research and Practice*, 6, 89-100

Nadler, J., Thompson, L. and Van Boven, L. (2003). Learning negotiation skills: four models of knowledge creation and transfer. *Management Science* 49, 4, 529-540

Naquin, C.E., Kurtzberg, T.R., and Belkin, L.Y. (2010). The finer points of lying online; e-mail versus pen and paper. *Journal of Applied Psychology*, 95, 387-394

Naquin, C.E. and Paulson, G.D. (2003). Online bargaining and interpersonal trust. *Journal of Applied Psychology*, 88, 113-120

Neale, M.A. and Bazerman, M.H. (1985). The effects of framing and negotiator overconfidence on bargaining beaviours and outcomes. Academy of Management Journal, 28, 1, 34-39

Neale, M.A. and Bazerman, M.H. (1991). *Cognition and Rationality in Negotiation*. New York: Free Press

Novemsky, N. and Kahneman, D. (2005). How do intentions affect loss aversion? *Journal of Marketing Research*, 42, 2, 139-140

Nyanzi, S., Pool, R. and Kinsman, J. (2012). The negotiation of sexual relationships among school pupils in south-western Uganda. *AIDS Care: Psychological and Socio-medical Aspects of AIDS/HIV*, 13:1, 83-98

Okumara, T., Brett, J.M., Tinsley, C.H. and Shapiro, D.L. (2007). Intervening in employee disputes. How and when will managers from China, Japan and the USA act differently. *Management and Organization Review*, 3, 183-204

Olekalns, M. and Smith, P.L. (2006). Loose with the truth: predicting deception in negotiation. *Journal of Business Ethics*, 76, 225–238

Petrides, K.V. and Furnham, A. (2006). The Role of Trait Emotional Intelligence in a Gender-Specific Model of Organizational Variables. *Journal of Applied Social Psychology*. 36, 2, 552–569

Pierce, R.S, Pruitt D.G.and Czaja, S.J. (1991). Complainant-respondent differences in procedural choice. Unpublished manuscript, Department of Psychology, State University of New York at Buffalo

Pietroni, D., Van Kleef, G.A., De Dreu, C.K.W. and Pagliaro, S. (2008). Emotions as strategic information: effects of others' emotional expressions on fixed-pie perception, demands, and integrative behavior in negotiation. *Journal of Experimental Social Psychology*, 44, 1444–1454

Pinkley, R.L. (2012). The effect of perception on judgments about fair compensation: implications for negotiators as price justifiers. Barry M. M. Goldman, Debra L. L. Shapiro (Eds), The Psychology of Negotiations in the 21st Century Workplace: New Challenges and New Solutions. Routledge

Podolny, J.M. (2001). Networks as the pipes and prisms of the market. *American Journal of Sociology*, 1, 33-60

Poitras, J., Bowen, R.E. and Byrne, S. (2003). Bringing horses to water? Overcoming bad relationships in the pre-negotiating stage of consensus building. *Negotiation Journal*, 19, 3, 250-263

Pruitt, D.G. (1991). Strategic choice in negotiation, in *Negotiation Theory and Practice*, eds. Breslin, J.W. and Rubin J.W. Cambridge: The Program on Negotiation at Harvard Law School

Pruitt, D.G. and Rubin, J.Z. (1986). *Social Conflict: Escalation, Stalemate and Settlement.* New York; McGraw-Hill

Pruitt, D.G. and Carnevale, P.J. (1993). *Negotiation in Social Conflict.* Open University Press, McGraw-Hill House

Raiffa H. (1982). *The Art and Science of Negotiation.* Cambridge, MA: Belknap

Ross, L. and Stillinger, C. (1991). Barriers to conflict resolution. *Negotiation Journal*, 7, 389-404

Schulz, J.W. and Pruitt, D.G. (1978). The effects of mutual concern on joint welfare. *Journal of Experimental Social Psychology*, 14, 480-491

Schweitzer, M.E., Brodt, S.E. and Croson, R.T.A. (2002). Seeing and believing: visual access and the strategic use of deception. *International Journal of Conflict Management*, 13, 258-375

Sinaceur, M. and Tiedens, L. Z. (2006). Get mad and get more than even: When and why anger expression is effective in negotiations. *Journal of Experimental Social Psychology*, 42, 314–322

Smithey, I., and Fulmer, B.B. (2004). The smart negotiator: cognitive ability and emotional intelligence in negotiation. *International Journal of Conflict Management*, 15, 3, 245-272

Sermat, V. (1967). The effect of an initial co-operative or competitive treatment upon a subject's response to conditional co-operation. *Behavioural Science*, 12, 301-313

Small, D.A., Gelfrand, M., Babcock, L. and Gettman, H. (2007). Who goes to the bargaining table? The influence of gender and framing on the initiation of negotiation. *Journal of Personality and Social Psychology*, Vol. 93, No. 4, 600–613

Tajifel, H. (1982). *Social Identity and Intergroup Relations.* Cambridge, UK: Cambridge University Press

Tajima, M. and Fraser, N.M. (2001). Logrolling procedure for multi-issue negotiation. *Group Decision and Negotiation*, 10, 217-235

Thompson, L. (1990). Negotiation behavior and outcomes: empirical evidence and theoretical issues. *Psychological Bulletin*, 108, 515-532

Thompson, L., and Hastie, R. (1990). Social perception in negotiation. *Organizational Behaviour and Human Decision Making Process*, 47, 98-123

Thompson, L. and Loewenstein, G. (1992). Egocentric interpretations of fairness and interpersonal conflict. *Organizational Behaviour and Human Decision Making Process*, 51, 176-97

Thompson, L.L. (2005). *The Mind and Heart of the Negotiator.* USA, Prentice Hall

Tietz, R. Weber, H. J. 1978, Decision behavior in multi-variable negotiations, H. Sauermann, *Contributions to Experimental Economics*, VII, 60, 87, Tübingen, J. C. B. Mohr

Touval, S. and Zartman, I.W. (1985). *International Mediation in Theory and Practice*. Boulder, CO: Westview Press

Touzard, H. (1977). La mediation et la resolution des conflicts (Mediation and the resolution of conflicts), Paris: PUF

Tversky, A. and Kahneman, D. (1992). Advances in Prospect theory: cumulative representation of uncertainty. *Journal of Risk and Uncertainty*, 5, 297-323

Ury, W.L., Brett, J.M. and Goldberg, S.B. (1988). *Getting Disputes Resolved: Designing Systems to Cut the Costs of Conflict*. San Francisco: Jossey-Bass

Ury, W. and Fisher, R. (1981). *Getting to Yes*, New York: Penguin Group

van den Hove, S. (2006). Between consensus and compromise: acknowledging the negotiation dimension in participatory approaches. *Land Use Policy*, 23, 10-17

Van Kleef, G.A. and De Dreu, C.K.W. (2002). Social value orientation and impression formation: of two competing hypotheses about information search in negotiation. *International Journal of Conflict Management*, 1, 59-77

Van Poucke, D. and Buelens, M. (2002). Predicting the outcome of a two-party negotiation: contribution of reservation price, aspiration price and opening offer. *Journal of Economic Psychology*, 23, 67-76

Velden, F.S., Beersma, B. and De Dreu, C.K.W. (2011). When competition breeds equality: Effects of appetitive versus aversive competition in negotiation. *Journal of Experimental Social Psychology*, 47, 1127-1133

Weingart, L.R., Thompson, L.L., Bazerman, M.H. and Carroll, J.S. (1990). Tactical behaviour and negotiation outcomes. *International Journal of Conflict Management*, 1, 7-31

Yousefi, S., Hipel, K.W. and Hegazy, T. (2010). Attitude-based negotiation methodology for the management of construction disputes. *Journal of Management in Engineering*, Vol. 26, No. 3, 114-122

Zartman, W.I. (2001). The timing of peace initiatives: hurting stalemates and ripe moments, *Global Review of Ethnopolitics: Formerly Global Review of Ethnopolitics*, 1:1, 8-18

Zhou, L., Burgeon, J.K., Nunamaker J.F. and Twitchell, D. (2004). Automating linguistics-based cues for detecting deception in text-based asynchronous computer-mediated communication. *Group Decision and Negotiation*, 13, 81-106

Zubeck, J.M., Peirce, R.S., McGillicuddy, N.B. and Syna, H. (1992). Disputant and mediator behaviours affecting short-term success in mediation. *Journal of Conflict Resolution*, 36, 546-572

NOTES

1. Pruitt, D.G. and Rubin, J.Z. (1986)
2. Ben-Yoav , O., and Pruitt, D.G. (1984)
3. De Dreu, C. K. W., Weingart, L. R., & Kwon, S. (2000)
4. Ury, W.L., Brett, J.M. and Goldberg, S.B. (1988)
5. Zubeck, J.M., Peirce, R.S., McGillicuddy, N.B., and Syna, H. (1992)
6. Poitras, J., Bowen, R.E. and Byrne, S. (2003)
7. Allred, K.G., Mallozzi, J.S., Matsui F., and Raia, C.P. (1997)
8. Yousefi, S., Hipel, K.W. and Hegazy, T. (2010)
9. Zubeck, J.M., Peirce, R.S., McGillicuddy, N.B., and Syna, H. (1992)
10. Poitras, J., Bowen, R.E. and Byrne, S. (2003)
11. Carnevale, P.J.D. (1991)
12. Carnevale, P. (2008)
13. Merryman, A. (2010)
14. Touval, S. and Zartman, I.W. (1985)
15. Zartman, W.I. (2001)
16. Weingart, L.R., Thompson, L.L., Bazerman, M.H. and Carroll, J.S. (1990)
17. Hollander-Blumoff, R., and Tyler, T.R. (2008)
18. Raiffa H. (1982)
19. Kuula, M. and Stam, A. (2008)
20. Fiske, S.T., and Taylor, S.E. (1991)
21. Macrae, C.N. and Bodenhaus, G.V. (2001)
22. Pruitt, D.G. and Carnevale, P.J. (1993)
23. Kahneman, D. (2011)
24. Thompson, L., and Hastie, R. (1991)
25. Cotter, M.J. and Henley, J.A. (2009)
26. Dawes, R.M. (1998)
27. Flyn, F.J. and Wiltermuth, S.S. (2010)
28. Carnevale, P.J.D. and Isen, A.M. (1986)
29. Pietroni, D. Van Kleef, G.A., De Dreu, C.K.W. and Pagliaro, S. (2008)
30. Thompson, L. (1990)
31. Pietroni, D. Van Kleef, G.A., De Dreu, C.K.W. and Pagliaro, S. (2008)
32. Thompson, L., and Hastie, R. (1991)
33. Tajima, M. and Fraser, N.M. (2001)
34. Ross, L. and Stillinger, C. (1991)
35. Curhan, J.R., Neale, M.A. and Ross, L. (2004)
36. Neale, M.A. and Bazerman, M.H. (1985)

37. Nadler, J., Thompson , L. and Van Boven, L. (2003)
38. Pierce, R.S, Pruitt D.G.andCzaja, S.J. (1991)
39. Moore, D.A. and Healy, P.J. (2008)
40. Neale, M.A. and Bazerman, M.H. (1991)
41. Bazerman, M.H., Curhan, J.R., Moore, D.A. and Valley, K.L. (2000)
42. Bazerman, M.H. and Carroll, J.S. (1987)
43. Smithey, I., and Fulmer, B.B, (2004)
44. Tversky, A. and Kahneman, D. (1992)
45. Novemsky, N. and Kahneman, D. (2005)
46. Bazerman, M.H. (1983)
47. Gollwitzer, P.M. and Sheeran, P. (2006)
48. Velden F.S., Beersma, B. and De Dreu, C.K.W., (2011)
49. Cialdini, R.B. (2007)
50. Podolny, J.M. (2001)
51. Diamond, S. (2010)
52. Thompson, L.L. (2005)
53. Ury, W. and Fisher, R. (1981)
54. Pinkley, R.L. (2012)
55. Zubeck, J.M., Peirce, R.S., McGillicuddy, N.B., and Syna, H. (1992)
56. Adair, W.L. and Brett, J.M. (2005)
57. Burton, J.W. (1984)
58. Holaday, L. C. (2002)
59. Thompson, L. (1990)
60. Van Kleef, G.A. and De Dreu, C.K.W. (2002)
61. Johnson, D.W. (1971)
62. Jacobs, C.D. and Heracleous, L.T. (2005)
63. Neale, M.A. and Bazerman, M.H. (1985)
64. Galinsky, A.D., Maddux, W.W., Gilin, D. and White, J.B. (2008)
65. Ma, Z. and Jaeger, A.M. (2010)
66. Galinsky, A.D., and Mussweiler, T. (2001)
67. Harinck, F. and De Dreu, C.K.W. (2011)
68. Schulz, J.W. and Pruitt, D.G. (1978)
69. Halevy, N. (2008)
70. Brown, R., and Abrams D. (1986)
71. Bottom, W.P., Holloway, J., Miller, G.J., Mislin, A. and Whitford, A. (2006)
72. Sermat, V. (1967)
73. Doebeli, M. and Hauert, C. (2005)
74. McGillicuddy, N.B., Pruitt, D.G., Syna, H. (1984)
75. Kwon, S. and Weingart, L.R. (2004)
76. Clark, M.S., and Mills, J. (1979)
77. Nyanzi, S.,Pool, R. and Kinsman, J. (2012)
78. Birdwhistell, R. L. (1974)
79. Mehrabian, A., and Ferris, S.R. (1967)
80. Curran, L. (1995)
81. Ekman, P. (2009)
82. Lewicki, R.J., Saunders, D.M., and Barry, B. (2010)
83. Elfenbein, H.A., Der Foo, M., White, J., Tan, H.H. and Aik, V.C. (2007)
84. Lindskold, S. and Han, G. (1988)
85. Naquin, C.E., and Paulson, G.D. (2003)
86. Pruitt, D.G. (1991)
87. Olekalns, M. and Smith, P.L. (2006)
88. Pruitt, D.G. and Rubin, J.Z. (1986)
89. Raiffa H. (1982)
90. Cattell, R.B. and Cattell, H.E.P. (1995)
91. Petrides, K.V. and Furnham, A. (2006)
92. Furnham, A and Petrides, KV and Tsaousis, I and Pappas, K and Garrod, D (2005)

93. Knight, S. (1995)
94. Hamner, W.C. (1974)
95. Moore, D.A. (2004)
96. Tietz, R. Weber, H. J. (1978)
97. Van Poucke, D. and Buelens, M. (2002)
98. Colquitt, J.A., Greenberg, J., and Scott, B.A. (2005)
99. Ross, L. and Stillinger, C. (1991)
100. Kwon, S. and Weingart, L.R. (2004)
101. Thompson, L. and Loewenstein, G. (1992)
102. Carrell, M.R., Shank, M. and Berbero, J.L. (2009)
103. Dupont, C. and Faure, G.O. (1991)
104. Dewulf, A., Gray, B., Putnam, L., Lewicki, R., Aarts, N. Bouwen, R. and van Woerkum, C. (2009)
105. Touzard, H. (1977)
106. van den Hove, S. (2006)
107. Zubeck, J.M., Peirce, R.S., McGillicuddy, N.B., and Syna, H. (1992)
108. Sinaceur, M., and Tiedens, L. Z. (2006)
109. Schweitzer, M.E., Brodt, S.E. and Croson, R.T.A. (2002)
110. Lewicki, R.J., Saunders, D.M., and Barry, B. (2010)
111. Kolb, D.M. (2009)
112. Babcock, L., Gelfand, M., Small, D., Stayn, H. (2006)
113. Miles, E. (2010)
114. Goldman, B.M. and Shapiro, D.L. (2012)
115. Small, D.A., Gelfrand, M., Babcock, L. and Gettman, H. (2007)
116. Bowles, H. R., L. Babcock, and K. L. McGinn. 2005
117. Kray, L. J., Thompson, L. and Galinsky, A. (2001)
118. Amanatullah, E. T., Morris, M. W., and Curhan, J. R. (2008)
119. Kray, L.J., Locke, C.C. and Haselhuhn, M.P. (2010)
120. Kray, L.J. and Haselhuhn, M.P. (2012)
121. Lewicki, R.J., Saunders, D.M., and Barry, B. (2010)
122. Schweitzer, M.E., Brodt, S.E. and Croson, R.T.A. (2002)
123. Khai, S.S. and Cooper, R.B (2003)
124. Naquin, C.E., and Paulson, G.D. (2003).
125. Naquin, C.E., Kurtzberg, T.R., and Belkin, L.Y. (2010)
126. Goldman, B.M. and Shapiro, D.L. (2012).
127. Zhou, L., Burgeon, J.K., Nunamaker J.F., and Twitchell, D. (2004)
128. Drolet, A.L. and Morris, M.W. (2000)
129. Morris, M., Nadler, J., Kurtzberg, T., and Thompson, L. (2002)
130. Kroeber, A.L., and Kluckhohn, C. (1952)
131. Tajifel, H. (1982)
132. Gunia, B.C., Brett, J.M., Nandkeolyar, A.K. and Kamdar, D. (2011)
133. Adair, W.L. and Brett, J.M. (2005)
134. Adair, W.L. Taylor, M.S. and Tinsley, C.H. (2008)
135. Ma, Z. and Jaeger, A.M. (2010)
136. Ching, L.C. (2012).
137. Okumara, T., Brett, J.M., Tinsley, C.H., and Shapiro, D.L. (2007)
138. Alon, I. and Brett, J.M. (2007)

INDEX